successful
organic gardening

successful
organic gardening

second edition

David R. Murray

Kangaroo Press

SUCCESSFUL ORGANIC GARDENING
This Second Edition published 2006
First published in Australia in 2000 by Kangaroo Press
An imprint of Simon & Schuster (Australia) Pty Limited
Suite 2, Lower Ground Floor
14–16 Suakin Street
Pymble NSW 2073

A CBS Company
Sydney New York London Toronto

Visit our website at www.simonsaysaustralia.com

Cataloguing-in-Publication data:

   Murray, David R. (David Ronald), 1943- .
   Successful organic gardening.

   2nd ed.
   Bibliography.
   Includes index.
   ISBN 0 7318 1267 0.

   1. Organic gardening. I.Title.

   635.0484

*The information on medicinal uses of herbs contained in this book is not intended to
be a substitute for medical care and advice. You are advised to consult a health-care
professional with all matters relating to your health, including matters that require
diagnosis.*

Internal design by Avril Makula
Cover design by Melissa Keogh
Cover and internal photography by David R. Murray
Typeset in 10.5 on 12.5 Berkeley Book
Printed in China through Colorcraft Ltd, Hong Kong

10 9 8 7 6 5 4 3 2 1

Foreword to first edition

This is not the first time I have written a foreword for one of David Murray's books. His earlier title *Carbon Dioxide and Plant Responses* helped clear away many of the myths about this gas and its various effects. Perhaps the most dangerous was that it would act as a fertiliser, bringing a new cornucopia to the Earth's crops, rather than bringing the disaster predicted for the greenhouse effect, and the other problems that he identified. This book, *Successful Organic Gardening*, will help a worthy cause. David has not only brought in new knowledge, but also gleaned from the wisdom of the past, reaching back at least 10 000 years. Readers who consider themselves already well-versed in organic gardening will be pleased and encouraged by these revelations. A glance at the chapter headings indicates how widespread are the fields that he covers. The first sentence in this book is thought-provoking: 'Why do we grow our plants in straight lines or monocultures?' David explains how we accumulated this 'horticultural baggage' down the ages, and suggests that we jettison some of it. There are indeed sound reasons why we should copy nature in our gardens, by mixing species, as happens in the wild. David also describes how integrated pest management developed because of the dangers of pesticide use, a lesson all farmers are slowly learning, some the hard way, as their products are banned because of pesticide levels.

David Murray is more than a theoretical scientist. He presents results from his own studies, both in the laboratory and in his home garden. Even such well-worn topics as composts come to new life. I particularly like his belief that we can copy mallee fowl and brush turkeys as models of the Earth's first makers of compost heaps. In my own region, we have used material from old nests for compost in the home garden. Carefully measuring the amounts of material involved, David cites how over a 20-year period he buried 8 tonnes of food scraps in his own garden. Think how much the waste-disposal problem would be diminished if many more people did this, improving their gardens at the same time. Every gardener can help to save the planet.

Warnings about what not to buy, and what to look out for, are included. So, too, are some useful addresses, ranging from manufacturers of worthwhile goods to volunteer groups, such as the Seed Savers' Network, and Heritage Seed Curators Australia. David has been a valued fellow member of the New South Wales Nature Conservation Council for many years, and an adviser to various conservation groups. Early in his professional life he understood that scientists must leave their ivory towers to spread their knowledge among workers in the conservation field, and to the world at large. This book will only add to David Murray's many admirers.

Foreword to this edition

David has maintained his involvement in the Nature Conservation Council of NSW, the Australian Plants Society, the Wildlife Preservation Society of Australia and the Seed Savers' Network. He has continued the struggle to conserve biodiversity in Australia, adding more ammunition for the fight with his recent title *Seeds of Concern: The Genetic Manipulation of Plants* (2003). I have brought his books to the attention of the national and state Ministers for the Environment, and also the media. Some years ago the national broadcaster, the ABC, telecast a discussion on carbon dioxide and plants without involving David. I pointed out to them that one of the world authorities on this subject lived nearby in Wollongong.

The lesson was well learned, as when they needed experts on the genetic manipulation of plants, Robyn Williams invited David to speak on *Ockham's Razor* (April 2004). The conservation movement needs more scientists of David's enthusiasm to aid the cause. His efforts are absolutely compatible with the American philosopher Henry David Thoreau's words 'in wildness is the preservation of the world'.

Vincent Serventy, AM

Contents

List of tables

Preface to first edition

All that glisters is not gold. Sometimes it is manure. For the home gardener, horse manure is like gold. It is just as scarce, and far more intrinsically valuable. However, the various sources of 'organic' material that might be added to the garden are not equally desirable. Gardeners have often been exhorted to put some very strange things onto their gardens, in the belief that soil condition will be improved, and healthier plants will result. Peculiar practices like sheet mulching with newspaper or seaweed have crept in, and become the new orthodoxy. Now is the time for a reformation. In this book, current horticultural practices are made to square up with ecological sustainability.

It is a glaring inconsistency for some organic gardeners to avoid superphosphate like the plague, while at the same time using 'organic' fertilisers or mulches based on cotton waste, woodchips, or peat. European carp will never be eradicated while it is relied on as a harvestable commodity, providing pet food and fishy fertilisers. These products all represent unacceptable environmental damage, and there are much better alternatives. Superphosphate has clean, green credentials by comparison, because it represents a useful application for a toxic substance that would otherwise pollute the atmosphere. This is sulfur dioxide, released mainly from coal and diesel combustion, and converted first to sulfuric acid. Untrammelled sulfur pollution contributes to serious respiratory illness and death. Through acid rain, it damages vegetation. In contrast, superphosphate safely conveys three plant nutrients into the soil: calcium, sulfur and phosphorus.

Can we really eliminate the use of pesticides? Some organic gardeners spray 'organic' pesticides instead of synthetics, and still wonder what went wrong. Spraying itself is the problem. It is done too often. By not killing everything that moves on our plants and tolerating biodiversity in the garden, we are going to make life easier in the long run. Truly integrated pest management depends very much on enlisting the aid of natural predators, ranging from the humble lady beetle and the graceful hoverfly, to the more obvious spiders that sometimes put their webs in inconvenient places.

Looking after predators also means putting the right combinations of plant together. We can develop compatible planting guilds by mixing herbs, vegetables and other plants. This may sound 'old hat', but very few people have ever suggested mixing plants in this way. Companion planting as commonly interpreted is based on pair-wise planting, and is riddled with error. This book will encourage you to observe companion plants in a scientific way, rather than following superstition and fairytales. This is a marvellous area for experimentation. Australia covers many degrees of latitude, and affords a great variety of climates and micro-climates. We need to adjust our ambitions to local conditions, and pay more attention to our own gardening experiences than to blanket prescriptions. By pushing the climatic limits for many plants, some of their traditional pests can be avoided altogether.

What about the breeding of new plant varieties and the glorious role of biotechnology? Here is another fairytale. The seed-saving networks have already provided many more 'new' plant varieties for the gardener than the very expensive gene technologies in the hands of multinational companies. Their focus is on the convenience of large-scale producers and herbicide users, and the inefficient production of F1 hybrids that force a captive market to return time and time again. Organic gardeners do not want once-only harvests of uniform plants, except in the case of sweet corn, which has special pollination requirements. Sequential production is much to be preferred, from plants that rejuvenate as their fruits, flowers or leaves are picked. Find out about the thousands of suitable varieties now available from the Seed Savers' Network (SSN) and Heritage Seed Curators Australia (HSCA), and join other gardeners in protecting our gardening heritage.

Gardening is meant to be a health-giving activity. Organic gardening should be the very healthiest kind of gardening possible, for us, and for the environment as a whole. This is the ideal that *Successful Organic Gardening* will help you strive for.

Preface to this edition

Since the first edition of this book was published in 2000, the Australian gardener has been deluged with books remaindered from the northern hemisphere. These are exactly the kind of book we do not need. If I see the word 'edible' in a title once more, I will scream. Producing a totally 'edible' garden is an invitation to a feast for all our garden competitors, and an encouragement to use pesticides to protect 'our' food. In my garden, the 'edible' plants are carefully mixed and camouflaged, to optimise the yield to me without the need for pesticides. The rush to plant everything in spring and summer is also not appropriate. We are more fortunate: we can plan to use the autumn, and even the winter, far more productively.

Drought is ever with us, and now that urban water restrictions are universal, exotic ornamental plants and turf grasses that guzzle water are no longer welcome. Some of our worst environmental weeds are much lauded garden plants in Europe, but they, too, need not be encouraged here. So I have expanded my comments on water efficiency, avoiding troublesome plants, and coping with weeds without using toxic herbicides. As I write, news comes that several well-known herbicides are about to be withdrawn in Europe, including dichlorprop, paraquat, and the triazine group, which includes simazine and atrazine. Triazines have been shown to be endocrine-disruptors, and were first banned in France in 2002. They have been used in Australia mainly by canola growers, because triazine-resistant canola has been available for more than 20 years. These herbicides are persistent, accumulating in run-off and ground water, causing untold damage to native fauna and flora and to human health. They have been banned for use by the home gardener, and the sooner they are banned totally in Australia the better for all of us. Worse still, the crop linked to past triazine use is worthless, since margarine made from canola oil affords the *least* protection against macular degeneration of the retina, compared to dairy foods and fish oils.

Other pesticides about to be withdrawn include malathion, triforine and resmethrin (a synthetic pyrethrin). Carbaryl will no longer be permitted for use on food plants. These withdrawals and restrictions illustrate a recurring pattern in mainstream agriculture — synthetic chemicals are released into the human food chain before their full effects have been appraised, then withdrawn with hindsight. Small wonder then, that diseases of the nervous system and cancers are so prevalent. This is the opposite approach to the precautionary principle. We should instead assume that there is no such thing as a safe agricultural chemical, then we would be right far more often than not.

In revising this book, I have provided more information on legumes, plant nutrients and plant propagation. Plant nutrition is an area I have explored as a plant physiologist, joining the Australian Society of Plant Physiologists in 1965. Most of my research concerned legumes, and more recently, the effects of elevated carbon dioxide concentrations on plants.

Saving seeds for the next crop is something every gardener used to do. I have been saving seeds in general since 1952, and those of peas especially since 1976. I joined the Seed Savers' Network in 1988, and am a foundation supporter.

Times have changed. The suburban gardener is under threat as never before as mindless urban 'consolidation' lays waste to our heritage, covering valuable garden soil with concrete and bricks, reducing our outdoor living space to a courtyard. What so-called planners don't realise is that suburbs consisting mainly of houses with quarter-acre blocks are photosynthetically far more productive than the same areas of land used just for broad-scale agriculture. Taking away the capacity to grow food locally is not a good idea. Conversely, the conversion of some 'agricultural' land into suburbs can be a blessing, as in many cases it is an impoverished wasteland of weed-infested pasture, nothing more than a 'green' desert. Suburban gardens in which trees and shrubs are planted and where some food is grown represent a decided improvement. For those who still have front and back yards, I trust the second edition of this book will continue to provide solutions and valuable advice.

Acknowledgments

For encouraging me to have my own garden from a very early age, I am grateful to my parents, Myrtle and Ron Murray. They taught me a great deal by example. During the 1970s, Myrtle was the source of splendid iris plants, some of which she bred (the Brookvale series, plus Araluen and Avalon Angel). I am also indebted to my mother and my uncle, Lloyd Woolnough, for historical information about the Miller family and fruit-growing in Tenterfield.

For gifts of seeds and plants in recent years, I am grateful to Dr Judyth McLeod, Dr Claudia Tipping, Mary Bennett, Daisy Burton, Mick Brew, Bob Butt, Liz Darley, Debbie Hebbard, Margaret Brooks, Marianne Baczynskyj, Jenny Simons, Jane Abbey, Robyn Cummings, Dennis Grimshaw and other members of the seed-saving networks, as recorded in *Growing Peas & Beans* (1999). For access to reference material and valuable discussions, I thank Dr Judyth McLeod, Dr Claudia Tipping, Dr Margaret Dwyer, Wendy Richardson, Jude and Michel Fanton, Bill Hankin, Charles Duggan, Despina Haise, Ray Brown, Graeme Richards, Andy Ryland, Robert Spooner-Hart, Mary Bennett and Barry Revill.

I am also grateful to Alec Bulford, for the gift of a copy of his book *Caring for Soil*; Dr Sally Muir, for copies of her research papers on silica; Judie Rawling, for discussions about invasive plants; Bill Hankin and Heritage Seed Curators Australia, for making possible my attendance at the 11th Australian Plant Breeding Conference in Adelaide, 1999; Jude and Michel Fanton, for inviting me to speak at several Annual Seed Savers' Conferences; Vivienne Legg, Dyson Devine and Marion (Mazza) Welham, for information on *Riptortus serripes* and preserved specimens; Masako Morishita, for descriptions of Daikon radishes; Di Cox, for suggesting casuarina needles as a substitute for horsetails in antifungal recipes; Dr Max Moulds and Dr Winston Ponder of the Australian Museum, for answering queries about invertebrates; Dr Malcolm Gill, for permission to reproduce data on leaf composition; the staff of the Waite Analytical Service for analysing pea seed samples, and Graham Clark, for information on rates of soil loss, and discussion of the National Association for Sustainable Agriculture (NASAA) guidelines.

I thank everyone who allowed me to take photographs in their gardens, especially Daisy Burton, Mick Brew, Jill Cockram, Jude and Michel Fanton, Sue McGregor, Elizabeth Rankin, Wendy Richardson and June Sassall. I also thank those who contributed photographs and gave permission for their reproduction in this book: Dr Helene Martin (pollen grains, Figure 18), and Dr Candida Briggs (*Solanum* seed, Figure 53).

For dedicated library research, and turning up the answers to seemingly simple questions, I thank my wife, Gayle Murray. Finally, I thank Vincent Serventy, for kindly writing the foreword; David Rosenberg, for suggesting the topic; and the staff of Simon & Schuster for their help in producing this book.

1.
Changing concepts of gardening

'Gardens need not be tamed down so that they
lose all naturalness. They will be far more restful
if they do not look so well groomed.'

Hilda M. Coley

Our gardening legacy: regimentation

Why do we grow our plants in straight lines or monocultures? Imposed symmetry is the most obvious principle guiding the kitchen garden or the cottage garden of recent times. Long before this, a regular, quadrangular design was fostered by the monasteries over many centuries, when gardening work was the normal accompaniment to prayer and contemplation. Each small division in such a garden contained only a single herb or vegetable.

This incredible orderliness was first brought by the Romans to Britain, along with their herbs and vegetables, following the Claudian conquest of AD 43–51. The French kitchen garden or potager is little different. The Romans were in charge there too — *omnia gallia in tres partes dives est* (all Gaul is divided into three parts), as Julius Caesar informed us. Many famous vineyards and chateaus owe their location to Caesar's strategic clearances, made to deprive the Gauls of protective cover near riverbanks and fords. Any appreciation of microclimate and its subtle effects on fruit quality is purely hindsight.

If we consider herb gardens from Tudor times onwards, with their clipped edges and complex patterns, it is clear that the level of intervention required was enormous. Most herbs refuse to stay exactly where they are put, bursting through box hedges (see Figure 1) and up through gravel paths with ease. Weeds likewise gain shelter in the hedges and then run through the gravel as well. These knot designs and their parodies created work for armies of servants. One solution is to abandon hedge plants and deliberately grow herbs in the pathway. Prostrate or low groundcover plants such as thyme and pennyroyal are

1

suitable for planting in the gaps among paving stones, preferably those with natural, irregular shapes.

In most forms of gardening, relentless imposition of pattern has persisted by inertia, with occasional resistance from writers such as William Robinson (1870, 1883), a perceptive critic of all he surveyed. Even he recommended a degree of simplification, such as the removal of large hedges, fruit trees, walls, old frames and jumble from vegetable gardens, as in his preface to *The Vegetable Garden* (Vilmorin-Andrieux, 1885). However, functional tidiness and garden hygiene are quite different concepts from excessive regimentation.

Ornate designs and patterns in the gardens and grounds might be appropriate to great houses with mounts, promenades, alleys, vistas and views, but we still find this high level of orderliness imposed even for the home garden. Look at any *Yates Garden Guide* and almost every book written on vegetable gardening. Small blocks of dwarf beans, spinach and radishes, for example, might be placed in front of tomatoes, and the monotonous row is obligatory for the cabbage or the lettuce. Paul Seitz (1996) says: 'Sow the seeds in rows. This makes caring for the plants and weeding much easier.' No, it does not. The gaps between rows are a total waste of space, especially in a small garden, and an invitation to fast-growing weeds.

Mint, parsley and chives must be kept in their own herb garden, nearest to the house. It is assumed that the cook cannot walk very far, or is so incapable of planning a meal ahead that she (or he) has to rush to the garden to grab a handful of herbs while the vegetables are actually on the stove.

Such conforming arrangements of plants may appeal to our visual sense of order. Yet, the plant community that a sustainable garden might be modelled on is never arranged in straight lines, and is rarely a monoculture.

Why should the flower garden be separate from the vegetable garden, and the herb garden separate from both? These are orthodox and unthinking conventions. Sometimes, vegetable gardens are deliberately concealed from public gaze by flower gardens (Shewell-Cooper, 1952). However, it is rare to find a horticultural writer who has ever recommended mixing vegetables with flowers and herbs. William Robinson (1883) did suggest putting some of the plants grown for flowers into the edges of a kitchen garden, as did Hilda Coley (1944) and Geoff Hamilton (1993). In a delightful chapter titled 'Copying Nature in Our Gardens', Hilda Coley described the consternation of her gardening assistant when she insisted on having her flowers 'all mixy-muddled up'.

Margaret Davis (1977) suggested modifying a flower garden by adding to it carrots, eggplant, capsicum, thyme, sage and parsley. Catharine Foster (1975) also described an 'integrated vegetable and flower garden', which really needed a lot more mixing, and less reliance on nasturtium. Paul Seitz, having described how to build a mounded herb garden, then concedes that 'raised herb beds also work well when combined with vegetables and flowers'. Of course they do! And Trevor Nottle (1996) challenges us to 'set aside the cultural baggage we carry with us about what gardens should look like, or what they should contain'.

This is more easily said than done. However, the sciences of ecology, biochemistry and evolution indicate that there are sound reasons for 'copying nature in our gardens', and mixing up the various plants that we might wish to have on our doorstep: flowers and herbs with vegetables, groundcover plants with fruit trees or vines, and legumes wherever possible, ranging from clover to *Kennedia*.

Legumes are vital to any system of organic gardening, because they provide combined nitrogen for themselves and for other plants.

They function as a 'gateway' for the circulation of nitrogen in both natural and reconstituted ecosystems. The trapping of molecular nitrogen (N_2) from the atmosphere and its conversion to ammonium ions (NH_4^+) is accomplished by the nitrogen-fixing bacteria contained in nodules on their roots (see Figure 139), then the plants that host the bacteria incorporate this form of nitrogen into amino acids and every other nitrogenous product that a plant needs. The parts of legumes that are shed, or severed, or eaten, transmit combined nitrogen to a vast array of other organisms, including ourselves. Legume seeds represent the most environmentally sound way of synthesising concentrated sources of protein for human consumption (see Chapter 18). Finally, a legume's root system left in the ground will provide nitrogen amounting to as much as one-third of the total requirement of the next non-leguminous crop.

Dilution is a sound principle too. A bed of staked tomatoes sends volatile chemical signals that say, 'Here I am!' very loudly, whereas a solitary tomato spread among supporting herbs is muted, and much more difficult for a fruit fly to find. Conversely, a tomato plant with its characteristic leaf scent will deter aphids from establishing a colony on it, and on its immediate neighbours. Some inkling of the new gardening ecology has been glimpsed in the concept of companion planting, in which many pair-wise combinations of herbs, vegetables and ornamentals are believed to be mutually beneficial. This concept is valuable, but very much in need of review (see Chapter 2).

Intensive pest mismanagement

For most of the twentieth century, gardeners have been encouraged to control pests and diseases with synthetic chemicals whose effects were never adequately predicted. Since the appearance of Rachel Carson's *Silent Spring* in the early 1960s, the realisation that many pesticides are not selective has become universal. The insecticide that acts as an acetylcholinesterase inhibitor is likely to affect any organism with a nervous system involving synaptic junctions — including *Homo sapiens*.

The persistence of pesticide residues in air and soil, and their uncontrolled bioaccumulation through diverse food chains, have brought havoc to wildlife and humankind alike. Shifting from very stable organochlorine products such as DDT, dieldrin and lindane to organophosphorus compounds, which do break down faster, has only multiplied the number of novel or xenobiotic compounds that we are exposed to, and postponed facing up to the key issues.

Whenever predators of particular insect pests are killed by a non-selective compound, the surviving pest populations expand faster than they would if the predators were still abundant. The broadcasting of non-selective or broad-spectrum pesticides has proved to be self-defeating. Such usage not only creates imbalances in favour of the pests, but at the same time elicits pesticide resistance that is amplified in subsequent generations, so that strong resistance becomes the norm. This 'survival of the fittest' can make a pesticide obsolete in just a few short years.

An example of this phenomenon is mentioned in the 1998 *Hort Report* prepared by the Horticultural Research and Development Corporation (page 14): 'Australian brassica growers are struggling to control diamond-back moth (*Plutella xylostella*) because it has developed resistance to synthetic pyrethroid and organophosphate insecticides'. Control of any particular insect pest becomes more difficult each time an insecticide on which growers have come to rely is relegated to the shelf by genetic changes in the pest itself.

The applied chemistry of organochlorines has been an unmitigated disaster. Inadequate disposal procedures for toxic by-products of pesticide manufacture are belatedly being addressed, after these toxins have contaminated landfill sites, known and unknown, or leaked from drums at temporary storage sites. In various ways they have migrated into the water table, or into sewage disposed of by ocean outfall, thus contaminating seafood (Beder, 1989, 1993). This legacy of the chemical age is not a happy one. The threat of incinerators being purpose-built to combust accumulated waste compounds has also been hanging over us for many years. Such incinerators would create pollution of air, soil and water on a grand scale, with dioxins guaranteed swifter entry into our food chains. It is far better that intractable compounds be stored until new catalytic methods for conversion to harmless products are applied exactly where they happen to be. In the Australian context, this has been demonstrated at Homebush Bay, Sydney.

The fruits and vegetables sold in our marketplaces today have sometimes been sampled and analysed for pesticide residues. Results for the Sydney Markets for the interval 1992 to 1995 have been published (Plowman, Ahmad and Bower, 1998). Incredibly, DDT is still being found — it was detected in 2.43 per cent or 38 of the 1566 samples that were analysed. The single most frequent contaminant in the organochlorine category, however, is the insecticide endosulfan, detected in 17.75 per cent of samples. The misguided rush to apply this compound to cotton has now generated endosulfan-resistant aphids, and these can be expected to spread to other areas. Regulations governing the use of endosulfan have been tightened, but as usual, the horse has already bolted. Such chemicals should be banned instead of being released, not restricted after irreversible damage is done.

In addition to insecticides there are fungicides. Collectively, fungicides are the most frequently encountered food contaminant in the Sydney Market survey. Those from the dithiocarbamate group (including mancozeb, propineb and thiram) occurred in 48.5 per cent of all samples, and the maximum recommended level was exceeded in 9.9 per cent of samples. These average figures do not give the complete picture, as many kinds of fruit and vegetables in the sampling made a negligible contribution to the tally of offending produce. The market fruits and vegetables with the highest frequency of dithiocarbamate contamination included kiwifruit, Chinese cabbage, capsicum, mangoes and strawberries, and in some of these instances, samples exceeding the maximum recommended level were in the majority.

It is not surprising that pesticide residues are being measured to the extent that they are. The 1998 *Hort Report* again has some revealing comments on the way capsicums and eggplants are grown for market: 'Currently, growers are relying on heavy insecticide applications which provide an unsatisfactory level of control' (for eggfruit caterpillar, not actually seen until the fruit is cut open). Synthetic pesticides are still used excessively by commercial vegetable growers, and when market prices are highest, withholding periods are not uniformly observed.

These observations suggest what not to buy, and instead, grow for yourself. A very clear message for the consumer here is to not buy any fruit or vegetable at the beginning or the end of its season. But the only way to be certain of avoiding the ingestion of pesticide residues is to grow food in the complete absence of pesticides. Increasing quantities of pesticide-free fruits, vegetables and herbs can be purchased. So far as certifiable standards are concerned, there are several organisations providing guidelines. These are the Biodynamic Agricultural Association of Australia (BDAAA), the Biological Farmers of Australia (BFA), the Organic Growers of

Australia, and NASAA, the National Association for Sustainable Agriculture Australia (see Useful Addresses). The various grades to indicate stages of compliance with the ideal have been simplified by NASAA to just two: 'organic', or 'in transition'. Similarly, the BDAAA have Grade A and Grade B (in transition), categories that both allow the use of the 'Demeter' brand. The least stringent appears to be the BFA, which has approved an extraordinary number of commercial products for 'organic' use.

Exactly what is entailed in the word 'organic' is discussed on page 7. To some operators, the word is just another marketing ploy, but to others, it is a serious endeavour. As most available organic produce is relatively expensive, you will score on freshness, safety and economy by growing as much as you can in your own garden. Strategically, lemons, passionfruit vines, herbs, snowpeas and green beans can find places even in a small garden, and are rewarding also in terms of expenditure saved.

Integrated pest management

The concept of integrated pest management (IPM) has evolved because of the inherent problems with synthetic pesticides. In the 1970s, synthetic pesticides and biological control agents were initially trialled together, with predators chosen that showed greater resistance to chemicals than the prey. So IPM does not mean that synthetic compounds are abandoned altogether, especially as there are some new ones that are better focused and have a narrow specificity.

The distinction between naturally occurring toxic compounds and synthetic ones is not always clear. For example, pyrethrins or pyrethroids are not necessarily 'an extract from the pyrethrum daisy' as the labels proclaim.

Although regarded by most gardeners as acceptable 'organic' insecticides, pyrethrins such as permethrin, fenvalerate or bioresmethrin are really synthetic versions of the natural pyrethrum found abundantly in flowering heads of certain members of the daisy family. The usual source is *Chrysanthemum cinerariaefolium*, now grown on a massive scale in Tasmania, and able to supply 10–15 per cent of the world demand (Biggs, 1997). Pyrethrin sprays of any kind should be used only in a dire emergency, since they can kill beneficial insects as well as pests.

IPM means that every available device is employed to control target pest organisms, and the sequence of deployment is worked out intelligently to give the best possible control with the least environmental damage. Quarantine measures, pheromone traps and releases of sterile male fruit flies all have their place. The strategic importance of quarantine cannot be too highly stressed. The Australian Quarantine and Inspection Service (AQIS) needs to become far more effective in excluding infested imports, in view of the regular procession of new pest species carelessly admitted over recent years. Remember the spiralling white fly and the papaya fly? Then there was the southern red mite (*Oligonychus ilicis*), found on azaleas, rhododendrons and camellias, and with the potential to affect coffee trees and rice plants. Now citrus canker has been found in Emerald, Queensland. It is farcical that AQIS should be required to oversee the certification of organic producers and products. The recent decisions of Biosecurity Australia to admit bananas from the Philippines and apples from New Zealand as imports, have fortunately been reversed. Once admitted to Australia, diseases brought with these imports would have spread unhindered. The fact that New Zealand cannot get rid of fireblight underscores how devastating this disease would be for our apple producers. Quarantine is absolutely essential as a frontline defence against plant pests and diseases.

Quarantine is a measure that should be applied whatever the scale of the operation. Every gardener should keep a watchful eye on incoming plants and seeds, and all imported gardening materials. Make sure that newly acquired plants and materials do not have the potential to ruin your whole gardening operation.

Valuable 'passive' biological control measures include removing weeds or susceptible flowering plants that harbour pests out of season, the use of deterrent plants, growing plants that provide nectar for adult predators such as hoverflies (see Figure 5) or wasps, and allowing spiders to place their webs in the tops of plants. Spiders are very important, as their webs are the original 'sticky traps'. In the absence of pesticides, many native species frequent our gardens (Clyne, 1996). In my own garden, at least 30 different spiders can be recognised, many of them brilliantly camouflaged.

Spider webs are much more selective than commonly realised. Research has shown that beneficial insects form only a minor proportion of their total prey (Jesiolowski, 1995). My observations suggest that various orb-weavers (see Figure 6) rarely trap honey bees in the summer, but golden orb-weaver females become large enough for their webs to trap the aged or injured worker honeybees as the autumn advances. At this stage, the bees that are too weak to escape are those that have already lived long and productive lives.

With appropriate caution, red-back spiders (*Latrodectus hasselti*) among pots can be useful, too. I have seen grasshoppers and cockroaches trapped by their strong webbing, and tolerated them among my pots ever since. I can take this slight risk, because my children are now adults. The red-back is actually very timid, and can even be handled without aggression. There is debate about whether this species is

really Australian, because it was not described until the late nineteenth century. Their closest relatives are from New Zealand and the United States (Child, 1977). Net-casting spiders also capture American cockroaches (see Figure 4).

Some carefully researched predator species can now be employed in a very specific fashion. The quest for useful predators has been going on quietly for more than 100 years. An excellent general account of progress in this area was published by the Brooklyn Botanic Gardens in 1960, then reprinted regularly at least until 1974 (Westcott and Nelson, 1974). From these sources, we learn that the use of hoverflies or lady beetles (ladybirds) to control aphids was first recommended in Britain early in the nineteenth century. One of those who suggested this measure was Erasmus Darwin, grandfather of Charles Darwin. The larval stages of both these beneficial insects are voracious in their consumption of aphids. Hoverflies do hover, and their elongated abdomen is banded, often yellow and black. They are nothing like carrion flies or blowflies, which is what many people picture as a 'fly'. Adult hoverflies (see Figure 5) and lady beetles need nectar, and some lady beetles eat powdery mildew fungus on peas and other plants (see Chapter 16).

Prime examples of successful biological control include the release of two kinds of predatory mite against the two-spotted mite (*Tetranychus urticae*), and the longstanding use of a small wasp that is parasitic on the eggs of the green vegetable bug (*Nezara viridula*). These examples also illustrate the need for ongoing research to find new predators, or the most effective strains of well-recognised ones. It took from 1933 to the mid-1950s to identify the most effective strains of *Trissolcus basalis*, the wasp that now controls the green vegetable bug. Moreover, the second predatory mite controlling two-spotted mite, *Phytoseiulus persimilis*, is a recent release (see Table 1).

The choice of plants to support predators can be extremely important. The flowers of borage support a wasp (*Copidosoma koehleri*) that is parasitic on potato moth, but borage does not support the potato moth itself (Moody, 2004). Various other plants — buckwheat, coriander, phacelia and broad bean — all feed the potato moth adults as well as the parasitic wasp, so planting borage provides a better way to minimise damage to potato plants from potato moth larvae. Sweet alice (*Alyssum maritimum* syn. *Lobularia maritima*) provides nectar for a native wasp (*Trichogramma carverae*) that is parasitic on light brown apple moth, but does not provide nectar to the light brown apple moth itself (*Epiphas postvittana*). This is a native species that frequents grapes as well as apples. Having white flowers is crucial (see Figure 102), as this wasp is not attracted by sweet alice flowers coloured in the range pink–purple.

Turning to soil micro-organisms for help has also been rewarding. Since the 1970s the toxic proteins produced by *Bacillus thuringiensis* have been increasingly utilised to control leaf-eating caterpillars. Preparations of whole bacteria such as Dipel provide the simplest application, while encapsulated forms now produced by Cyanamid last three times longer following application. It has been one aim of plant breeders to genetically modify selected plants so that they can produce 'Bt' proteins among the wide array of proteins normally manufactured in leaves (Gatehouse, 1991). Various strains of this soil bacterium produce toxins with different degrees of specificity for caterpillars of both *Coleoptera* (beetles and weevils) and *Lepidoptera* (butterflies and moths). However, the cultivation of Bt-transformed cotton and maize has been controversial, because these plants were engineered to express only a single protein, rather than a number that should be closer to 40 (see Chapter 17).

The examples just described have involved institutional resources and expenditure from both the public and private sectors, but the benefits should be as readily available to home gardeners as they are to market gardeners, orchardists or larger scale growers. The principles underlying the relationships of the myriad other organisms that associate with the plants that we want to grow are now understood more clearly than ever before.

Organic gardening

What exactly is meant by 'organic' gardening? Is this adjective really necessary? Many plant scientists regard this terminology as redundant, because 'organic' automatically conveys the idea that compounds containing carbon are involved, as in 'organic chemistry'. Where is the plant that is not organic? However, reference is being made to the soil in which the plants are growing, rather than to plants directly.

In his essay 'Hydroponics and Organic Gardening' (in Salisbury and Ross, 1978), the eminent plant physiologist Frank Salisbury complained on the one hand that 'organic gardening seems to be founded on mysticism'. On the other hand, he praised the results: 'In practice, however, the organic gardener is certainly right ... it is difficult to go wrong by adding large amounts of organic matter to the soil'. This is where the rediscovery of organic gardening began: with an emphasis on the organic matter or humus in the soil, and the realisation that these materials need to be constantly replenished, or else the condition of the soil will deteriorate. Many people think this is a recent discovery. It may be for some, but as Michael Ableman (1993) reminds us, these methods are 'nothing new, only a continuation of something very old'.

Up until the nineteenth century, gardeners often acquired their organic materials from the

TABLE 1. PREDATORY MITES AND INSECTS AVAILABLE COMMERCIALLY

NAME[1]	PESTS CONTROLLED	SOURCE[2]
MITES		
Hypoaspis miles	Thrips, fungous gnats	D
Phytoseiulus persimilis	Two-spotted mite (*Tetranychus urticae*)	A,C
Typhlodromus occidentalis	Two-spotted mite (*Tetranychus urticae*)	D
WASPS		
Aphytis lingnanensis	Red scale	B
Aphytis melinus	Red scale, oriental scale	D
Encarsia formosa	Various white fly	D
Leptomastix dactylopii	Citrus mealy bug (*Planococcus citri*)	B
Trichogramma species	Lepidoptera including *Helicoverpa* species	B,C,E
LADY BEETLES		
Chilocorus baileyi (blue)	Armoured scale insects	B
Chilocorus circumdatus (red)	Armoured scale insects	B
Cryptolaemus montrouzieri	Various mealy bugs	B
Rhyzobius lophanthae	Armoured scale insects	B
LACEWINGS		
Mallada signata (green lacewing)	Aphids, thrips, mealy bugs, white fly, moth eggs	B

1. Note that many of these beneficial predators do not have common names.

2. As indicated by Broadley and Thomas (1995), Ryland (1998) and Crawford (2004).

A = Beneficial Bug Company; B = Bugs for Bugs; C = Bio-Protection; D = Biological Services; E, BioResources Pty Ltd (see Useful Addresses).

dung hill, from animal manures, or from peat layers or 'muck' in swamps. A typical illustration of this practice is described by squire Nicholas Blundell of Crosby Hall near Liverpool, England, who in July 1720 wrote: 'I put some good old Muck to five of my best Flower Beds in the knot and to my bed of Forrain Tulops and to one bed in the Nursery of Flowers. I set about 1500 Tulop roots and Chives in the Nursery' (Dwyer, 1978).

The United States has long had several traditions of organic growing. John Bartram is regarded as an exceptional 'organic' farmer, because early in the eighteenth century 'he showed a talent for imaginative farming that was far in advance of his time, regularly feeding his fields with a rich liquid manure, spreading rotted compost over virgin and impoverished land during winter months' (Tyler-Whittle, 1975). His yields of wheat and hay were bountiful, with wheat averaging 33 bushels per acre. John Bartram later established a nursery near Philadelphia, and the house he built there in 1730 is still standing (Weaver, 1997).

Colonel George Morgan was another enlightened farmer and horticulturist, whose practices conform to current ideals. To avoid the hessian fly, he advocated planting a resistant kind of wheat (yellow bearded, not white or red). He used lucerne, white clover and red clover in a way that would not be understood for another hundred years, and he objected to the 'orthodox' beekeeping principle of killing the bees in order to obtain the honey. Morgan's honey received high praise from Benjamin Franklin, who regarded it as the equal of the best in Narbonne, France.

The contribution of Justus von Liebig

It is now well known that just adding soluble chemical fertilisers rich in nitrogen, phosphorus or potassium is not conducive to the long-term health of the soil. An overemphasis on the use of inorganic fertilisers by mainstream agriculture in the twentieth century is often unfairly blamed on Justus von Liebig (1803–73), but if one consults a biography (Cannon, 1963) it soon becomes clear that von Liebig was truly in the vanguard of the organic movement.

Early in his career, by 1840, Liebig correctly reaffirmed that plants did not obtain their assimilated carbon from humus. This work is often misinterpreted, and many think that what he proposed was that plants did not need humus. In fact, he advocated a return of nutrients to the soil to compensate for those removed with crops. This is a sound approach. He never intended that inorganic additions to the soil should be made instead of organic, only in combination. From his newspaper articles we know he was particularly keen on the use of human wastes and animal manures, an enthusiasm that is strangely overlooked by his current critics.

Justus von Liebig had some rousing disagreements with many other leading scientists of his time, but all of this should be placed in context. He was often right, and he was not alone in being out-foxed by nitrogen fixation and legumes. The symbiotic fixation of atmospheric nitrogen by the bacteria that live inside the root nodules of legumes was not demonstrated until 15 years after his death (Davidson and Davidson, 1993). To put the record straight, it must be noted that he was a pioneer of quantitative methods for organic chemistry. He tackled difficult substances like proteins, from which he isolated the essential amino acid tyrosine. He also made many significant contributions to the demolition of 'vitalism'. According to vitalism, living cells could not synthesise organic compounds except through the agency of a vital force. Even Louis Pasteur held that a 'vital force' of yeast cells was necessary for fermentation to take place (Schlenk, 1985).

Justus von Liebig castigated the British government over its alleged use of bonemeal crushed from human skeletons mined from the battlefields of Leipzig, Waterloo and the Crimea. Early superphosphate fertiliser was made from such bonemeal treated with sulfuric acid, a procedure devised by John Bennet Lawes at Rothamsted in 1839. He also criticised the way nutrients were not recovered from sewage, but squandered and let flow out to sea. What has changed? His telling social comments are the real reason he has been given such a bad press in the English language.

Biodynamics

The revival of organic gardening is judged to begin not with Justus von Liebig, an admirable nomination, but rather with the work and teaching of Sir Albert Howard, an Englishman who worked in India in the 1920s and 1930s (see page 11), and Rudolf Steiner (1864–1925), an Austrian philosopher. Steiner's antiquated ideas and superstitions entertain a strong element of the mysticism that Frank Salisbury complained of. Since biodynamics 'seeks to stimulate and enlarge the life force in the soil and in the plants and animals it supports' (McLeod, 1994b), then Frank Salisbury is right to be concerned. What really worries scientists about Steiner's ideas is that they see the ghost of vitalism returning, long after its official exorcism by von Liebig and others. To scientists, the 'life force' is an unnecessary hypothesis. Steiner's grasp of cosmic influences owed more to astrology than rational thought and science. His plant groupings are simply a rehash from the seventeenth-century herbalist Nicholas Culpeper (see Chapter 8). Such fossilised botany, cut off from all contemporary and later insights, is the very opposite of dynamic. Dowsing with a small pendulum to see which seeds are viable and which not, and planting seeds only when the moon is waxing, or by a sign of the zodiac, betray superstition and credulity rather than a meaningful understanding of seed physiology. How could a 'waxing' moon possibly encourage water uptake by seeds? Gravitational arguments fall flat, because there is no increase in the gravitational attraction of the moon in proportion to its apparent illuminated area. The 'Moon Calendars' published in such magazines as *Better Homes and Gardens* (2004) and the *Australian Women's Weekly* (2002) indicate 'adversity' for most gardening activities most of the time. Anyone following these regimes would be hamstrung, and unable to get anything done in time.

The Moon was once an independent planet that was probably swung into an orbit around the Earth (that is, 'captured') about 3600 million years ago. Alternatively, it was re-formed from debris after the collision of a precursor planet with Earth that vaporised parts of both at a much earlier time (Mason, 2002). This alternative hypothesis has been advanced to account for a higher ratio of ^{57}Fe to ^{54}Fe in Moon rocks compared to the Earth, and to my mind it is rather fanciful. Ockham's Razor comes down in favour of the 'capture' model. However the Moon arrived, it had an essential part to play in the development of the first living cells on Earth, because the consequent tidal fluctuations provided a mechanism for mixing potential cell components and nutrients (Murray, 1997b). Life as we know it would not have evolved on Earth without the influence of the Moon.

The Moon reflects light from the Sun. But full moonlight does not convey enough red light intensity to register via the light-detecting pigment phytochrome (see Chapter 6), even for plants standing above ground (Salisbury, 1969, page 27). So how could the 'phase' of the Moon, which is the pattern of light that it reflects to a given point on Earth, have any influence on seeds covered by soil and not even able to perceive much daylight? It makes considerable sense for moonlight not to interfere in plant responses to daylength accompanying seasonal change, where flowering at the wrong times would have serious consequences for the ability of plants to reproduce and survive.

Then there is substance 500, produced by incubating cow manure in cow horns (Podolinsky, 1985). The effects of substance 500 could probably be explained in biological ways, but beneficial results are attributed to vague 'energy-raising' properties. The biodynamic 'energy field' is utter gobbledegook. Biodynamics is resoundingly unscientific, and serves as the main focus for those who want to ridicule organic methods. Even benighted hydroponic growers who think they need to add vitamins to their plants' nutrient solutions do not attract the same level of derision among professional plant physiologists.

I have concerns, too, about the BDAAA's reluctance to take the trouble to restore soil fertility properly. In their own words (from a pamphlet titled *Agriculture Standards Certification and Marketing*): 'we do not rely on regular, large applications of compost or organic matter, which are impractical to apply on large-acreage farms'. Well, there you have it — how can the biodynamic system be truly organic if its adherents today are too lazy to keep adding organic matter to the soil?

Organic gardening and human health

Sir Albert Howard devised practical solutions to farming problems in Indore by encouraging the incorporation of plant wastes and both human and animal manures into composts. These could then be used safely to restore soil fertility, instead of expensive chemical fertilisers, beyond the financial reach of individual farmers (Howard, 1943, 1945). In fact, he implemented what Justus von Liebig had been advocating, and what had become commonplace in the nineteenth century (Maiden, 1887). The Indore composting method became popular, and was given royal endorsement, being adopted for the Balmoral Castle and Windsor Castle palace gardens (Shewell-Cooper, 1952).

The efforts of Lady Eve Balfour (1975) also deserve mention. The first edition of her book *The Living Soil* appeared in 1943. She, as well as Sir Albert Howard, inspired the formation of Soil Associations, not only in the United

Kingdom but also in such far-flung places as New Zealand and Tasmania. These were commenced in the early 1940s. Much later, the Henry Doubleday Research Association established the National Centre for Organic Gardening at Ryton, Coventry.

Robert Rodale (1971) describes how his father, J.I. Rodale, was attracted to the Indore method in the late 1930s. Under the Rodale family's influence, the concept of organic gardening expanded in the United States to take in the idea of wholesomeness, especially with regard to the absence of pesticide residues. The Rodale family founded the journal *Organic Gardening*, later *Organic Gardening and Farming*, and in 1959 published the first Encyclopedia of Organic Gardening. Several authors cited in this book have published via Rodale Press.

In Australia, Keith and Irene Smith began publishing *Earth Garden* in 1972, closely followed by Megg Miller with *Grass Roots* in 1973. Both journals are still being published. Bill Mollison and David Holmgren coined the term 'permaculture' in 1978 (see McLeod, 1994b). Attempts to codify permaculture as a 'new' system with its own curriculum have drawn much criticism. Giving out certificates for superficial mastery of dubious 'knowledge' in a very short time frame does not do justice to the seriousness of the issues. Permaculture puts far too much emphasis on design, and not enough into understanding the properties and requirements of plants. Nor do its founders take the threat of weeds seriously enough, as evidenced by their espousal of plants like vetiver grass (*Vetiveria zizanioides*) and their own articles (Holmgren, 1997). Furthermore, in seeking to ban annuals from the garden in favour of perennial or self-perpetuating plants, extreme permaculture devotees are adopting an untenable position. I still hear comments from permaculture 'teachers' to the effect that 'annuals need too much hard work'.

Just imagine how impoverished your garden would be without any annuals — with no summer salad vegetables, no parsley, no rocket and no basil! How would we encourage children to garden without the rapid growth responses of radishes and beans? One of the chief advantages of an annual life-cycle is that pest populations can be reduced to zero when a food plant disappears from the scene completely for a portion of the year.

This is an obvious benefit derived from growing annuals. By insisting on the proscription of annuals, some permaculture adherents have put themselves at odds with sustainability, and alienated the majority of the gardening public. Most home vegetable gardeners grow tomatoes and beans — both annuals. Legumes are needed in the garden to aid nitrogen supply. Annuals, biennials and perennials *together* are essential for successful organic gardening.

Fortunately, permaculture is not a monolith. On the positive side, some members of the permaculture movement provide valuable support for the rescue of heirloom varieties of garden plants via the Seed Savers' Network (see Useful Addresses). The theme of self-sufficiency for food production was extended by Michael Boddy, Richard Beckett and Janet Boddy (1980), and Sally Gordon (1981).

Although total self-sufficiency is an impossible goal in a suburban backyard, we should all try to be self-sufficient for something. We should aim at 'cooperative self-sufficiency', as suggested by the Southern Exposure Seed Exchange in the United States. Every nation should be self-sufficient for basic food production. Australia should be self-sufficient for vegetable seed production, but this prospect is remote, with 55 per cent of seeds for market vegetables currently imported. The herbal remedies that people flock to buy at health food shops are prepared from ingredients that are 95 per cent imported. This statistic is a 'tame and abject disgrace', as George Washington might have put it. If people ate properly, from a wide range of fresh vegetables, herbs and fruits (see Chapter 18), they would rarely need any of these supplements.

Gil and Vincie Wahlquist established the first organic vineyard in 1971. This is the Botobolar Vineyard in Mudgee, New South Wales (see Figure 8). The wine label describes exactly what is meant by organic gardening: 'The grapes used for this wine were grown without the use of pesticides, herbicides or chemical fertilisers. The vines were not irrigated. The wine represents the character of the vineyard and the year.' Mudgee is a land of wine and honey. To cap each bottle, beeswax was used instead of lead, aluminium foil or plastic.

Many people who have purchased Botobolar wines over the past 30 years have noticed an excellent diagram explaining how the vineyard ecosystem works, printed on the carton. Key elements are proper spacing of vines, leaving spiders in place, and encouraging groundcover of herbs and grasses as habitat for earthworms below ground, and quail above. Some have been motivated to adopt the same principles, and there are now enough organic winemakers to form the Organic Vignerons' Association of Australia (OVAA).

In summary, Geoff Hamilton (1993) provides a definition of organic gardening as follows: 'There is nothing mystical or magical about organic gardening. It is simply a way of working with nature rather than against it, of recycling natural materials to maintain soil fertility, and of encouraging natural methods of pest and disease control rather than relying on chemicals to do the job.'

Ecological sustainability

Ecological sustainability is the concept underpinning Agenda 21, which was devised at the UN Conference on Environment and Development (or Earth Summit) meeting held in Rio de Janeiro in June 1992.

Ideally, to be ecologically sustainable means that human support systems should continue indefinitely without further adverse impact on the environment, and in particular on the biosphere. Rehabilitation of damaged habitats should also take place.

For Australia, this means that some enormous areas, equivalent to whole European countries, should be retired from intensive food or fibre production. Our inland waterways should be cleaned up and allowed to flow properly while this is still possible, or we will have no indigenous fish left, and no riparian vegetation. On the Murray River, three-quarters of all Murray River red gums (*Eucalyptus camaldulensis*) are unhealthy, because of stress. To counteract the greed of upstream guzzlers and polluters, we need fully integrated legislation, where 'regard for the principles of ESD' is more than mere lip-service.

Consider the soil. It takes a long time to develop from parent rocks and minerals. It is an asset that requires great care. Yet, some farmers allow rates of loss of the order of 100 tonnes per hectare per year to occur and then expect the government to bail them out. This is certainly not ecologically sustainable, and fortunately only a minority of farmers has the attitude that the world at large should thank them for degrading their property while they overproduce an unsaleable commodity.

Australian soils are often impoverished in one or more plant nutrients because they have been weathered and leached for something like 200 million years. The rejuvenation of soils brought about by recent glacial redistributions of newly crushed rock fragments in many parts of the northern hemisphere did not take place to any appreciable extent in Australia. Detailed maps of mineral deficiencies have been constructed, so no matter where we live there is some information about what kind of remedial fertiliser is most probably needed to permit the growth of introduced plants, including those that we depend upon for food. In some places with a cobalt deficiency, remediation is not possible, as all attempted measures only make things worse. These areas should be evacuated and put back under native vegetation.

Apart from the limitations of the underlying geography, many gardeners buying residential properties in cities and suburbs have found that the previous topsoil was stripped off during subdivision. They have had to pour in gypsum (calcium sulfate) and compost to contend with excessive clay, while some nearby football field has prospered at their expense.

For growing food plants, inputs to the soil that are finite such as mined rock phosphate, limestone or dolomite are a major ongoing concern. The world's most accessible nitrate and phosphate deposits have already been exhausted. Limestone quarrying can often be detrimental to delicate cave systems, rare fauna and scarce fossils. Once a mineral reserve is mined and dispersed, it is gone for good. The geological and biological processes that produced it in the first place may take thousands, millions, or even hundreds of millions of years to reproduce similar deposits.

It is a great pity that wetlands have never been as highly valued as they ought to be, but the days of sacrificing peat and sphagnum moss, one of its precursors, are now numbered. Wetland habitats provide a haven for endangered species. Often the vegetation history of an area is recorded by the pollen grains preserved in the peat, and this can be deciphered by an expert palynologist —

provided the peat is left undisturbed. These indications of past climate change are assuming much greater importance as we ponder the prospects for the immediate future.

Most gardeners have long ago realised that it is not necessary to use peat at all in potting mixes or as a general soil conditioner. It causes excessive acidification (for example, as indicated by Llewellyn, Hudson and Morrison, 1981) and generally has little or no nutritional value. Superior alternatives include 'cocopeat' or 'coprapeat' derived from coconut fibre, rice husks or homemade compost. These are all renewable and readily available. Pulverised coconut fibre used in media may protect against the 'damping off' fungus *Rhizoctonia* according to a note in *Australian Horticulture* (Vol. 97, No. 6, page 32). If you really must have moss, buy some that has been grown specifically for harvest, or dry out the mosses that are already growing in the dampest part of your garden. Preparations described as 'peat' today may actually have little or no peat in them. Take 'Killarney Peat'. This brand freely admits on the label that it is a mixture of coconut fibre and sphagnum moss peat, and the proportions are not specified. Brunning's 'peat' is produced entirely from composted pinebark — so why is it called 'peat'? Other brands are obviously prepared from pinebark, but do not admit the substitution.

Consuming mineral or other resources at a faster rate than their replacement is not ecologically sustainable. However, the rates of consumption of these limited resources could be massively reduced if wastes were to be revalued and reused, and if nitrogen-fixing plants such as legumes were used more often instead of manufactured urea, ammonium or nitrate salts for nitrogenous fertiliser. About half of all synthetic nitrogenous fertiliser is wasted, and the cost of its production in terms of energy consumption and carbon dioxide evolution is unacceptable. Naturally produced urea is not being recovered from sewage, but is usually allowed to pollute our waterways, breaking down to ammonium ions and contributing to toxic algal blooms or outbreaks of water weeds. Over the whole of Australia, thousands of tonnes of urea are being wasted every year.

Taxpayers' money spent cleaning up outbreaks of blue-green algae, water hyacinth (*Eichhornia crassipes*) or alligator weed (*Alternaria philoxeroides*) in rivers would have been far better spent encouraging people to use self-composting toilets (see Savannah Environmental Pty Ltd under Useful Addresses), or recovering soluble nutrients from sewage and run-off before they cause problems. Land adjacent to sewage treatment works could be set aside as receiving wetlands, where the bacteria associated with the roots of *Phragmites australis* can convert ammonium ions to nitrate, and this can be taken up by the reeds themselves. Systems like this have been incorporated into effluent processing from zoological gardens, as at the Western Plains Zoo in Dubbo. Filtered sewage water is passed through *Phragmites* reed beds at Highgrove House, the residence of the Prince of Wales in Gloucestershire, United Kingdom. In the United States, water hyacinth is cultivated to do this same job, then harvested and processed to yield biogas (methane) as a renewable source of energy.

There is no excuse for failure to treat sewage water and storm water completely, recovering potable water and plant nutrients. Separating water from its remaining dissolved solutes and suspended particles is not difficult. The reverse-osmosis technology to do this was invented in Australia. It can be powered by photovoltaic cells and the sun, yielding water of drinkable quality that costs just a few cents per litre. At last, something constructive is happening. From October 2005 onwards, BlueScope Steel in Wollongong will receive 20 million litres per day of properly treated effluent that will allow them to forego 70 per cent of the potable water they would otherwise have drawn from the Avon Dam (Levy, 2005).

Transport and carbon dioxide emission

Australian agriculture ranks second after the energy sector in greenhouse gas production (ABC Television, *Landline*, 27 June 2004). This is an extraordinary statistic! On top of that, transportation of food is a major issue for ecological sustainability. The folly of centralised produce markets was recognised long ago by William Robinson (1883): 'To bring the vegetables grown at Chiswick to Covent Garden and cart them back to Hammersmith is a needless waste of force'. On a global scale there is a great deal of unnecessary trade in foodstuffs, such as canned tomatoes from Italy arriving in Australia and being offered at a price below that of local products, which have been carried much shorter distances. Similar instances have been described as 'dumping' by the Chair of Ausveg, Michael Badcock (ABC Television, *Landline*, 3 July 2005).

Growing more food closer to where it will be consumed could yield an enormous saving in the energy expended on transport, which translates to a significant reduction in carbon dioxide emissions from the fossil fuels consumed. It is extremely wasteful to expend more energy on transporting, processing and packaging foodstuffs than is represented by the caloric value of the food itself. This 'needless waste of force' is unsustainable. Moreover, 'balancing the carbon dioxide equation is the bottom line for ecologically sustainable development' (Murray, 1997a, 1997b). Without this balance, the annual rate of increase in global average atmospheric carbon dioxide concentration will not be abolished. Consequently, the quality of human

life in the future will certainly be ruined. The United Nations Organisation is taking this problem seriously, and helping to apply solutions in many densely populated cities (UN Development Programme, 1996).

Growing more food for ourselves becomes the new imperative — but it is really an old one. 'Dig for victory' was the motto when gardeners dug up their front lawns in order to produce a certain supply of vegetables during World War II. The apogee of the home vegetable gardener was in the early 1950s, when so much home produce was grown that it affected market prices and returns to commercial growers (*Your Garden*, April 1953, page 8). There is nothing to stop us growing more for ourselves today, except 'stiff convention' (Bubel, 1977); that is, a reluctance to be seen growing vegetables in the front garden (see Figure 121). Winning the peace is more difficult than winning the war, however, because the loss of self-sufficiency entailed in economic globalisation of food and seed supplies is not widely enough perceived as subjugation and defeat. Moreover, the World Trade Organisation aids and abets multinational corporations intent on bypassing the environmental controls of democratically elected national governments.

QUO VADIMUS?

Where do we go from here? Most previous gardening books are stuck in the rut of regimentation, with no critical appraisal of companion planting or 'organic' fertilisers, and no guidance on the key issues of ecological sustainability. To be organic gardeners today, we should:

- avoid using pesticides, even 'organic' ones
- learn to live with predators such as the praying mantis (see Figure 7), lacewings, lady beetles, hoverflies, robber flies (see Figure 175), wasps and spiders
- always include legumes in lawns, groundcovers and gardens

- seek out hardier, disease-resistant and tastier varieties of fruits, vegetables and herbs
- experiment with mixed plantings likely to be advantageous
- avoid plants that are unsuitable for the area, or could present insuperable problems
- use physical methods of weed control rather than herbicides
- return to the soil more than we take from it, and
- minimise waste.

It is pleasing that the Royal Botanic Gardens in Sydney have set a great example to other public gardens by adopting policies consistent with these guidelines since 2003.

Gardening is a health-giving activity, undertaken to some extent by almost everyone. Above all, organic gardening is healthy gardening. By returning to organic methods we can also be reassured that we are eating at least some pesticide-free food, lowering our risk of cancers and neurological diseases. Ending the indiscriminate use of broad-spectrum pesticides and herbicides will also protect our indigenous fauna, flora and micro-organisms. A healthy environment ensures healthy people, whereas an unhealthy environment guarantees ill-health.

2.
Companion planting

'The strawberry grows underneath the nettle,

And wholesome berries thrive and ripen best

Neighboured by fruit of baser quality'

William Shakespeare, *Henry V* Act 1, Scene 1

The concept

Competition and cooperation are the key ecological principles fundamental to human understanding of the ways plants live with one another, and with other organisms. These principles are not mutually exclusive, and many apparently competitive or parasitic relationships are symbiotic in a broader sense. Take cicadas, for example. Their dependence on the roots of trees to provide total nutrition during the nymphal stages is at first sight parasitic. But is it really? As spring arrives, the maturing cicada nymphs drill new tunnels through the soil, right to the surface. The ground near host trees becomes literally peppered with small but obvious holes. As a result, air is carried to much greater depths below the soil surface than usual, improving the availability of oxygen to the whole root system. This is a major benefit to these trees at a time when the potential for growth rate to increase is raised by increasing temperatures and longer days.

Are plants that are apparently competitive, jostling one another aside for space, always purely competitive? The answer is often no, and the simplest view of companion plants is that they are plants that help one another when grown together. Strictly, however, there are two sides to the concept of companion planting. First, there are those plants that seem to do well when planted together, perhaps better than either would do alone. Roses and onions fit this synergistic model, with the onions apparently keeping the roses free of black-spot fungus or aphids, while the root systems of each feed at different levels in the soil, avoiding direct competition.

Conversely, there are plants that seem to antagonise one another, such as basil and rue, or beans and fennel. In his preface to the book *Companion Plants and How to Use Them* by Helen Philbrick and Richard Gregg, the publisher Devin A. Garrity crystallised the whole concept as 'the ability of certain species of plants to help each other by their mere presence, and its opposite, plant antagonism where both do poorly'.

There is certainly something in the idea that stinging nettles (*Urtica dioica*) protect fruits, not only those that grow beneath them, like William Shakespeare's strawberries (*Fragaria vesca*), but also those that grow above them, like apples or stone fruit. Does the stinging nettle gain anything from these associations? Even if it gains nothing but space, it is doing well in a competitive world. Nettles employed as companions for fruit trees or bushes can be cut for a variety of uses, taking care to wear gloves rather than braving the stinging hairs that coat their leaves. Apart from medicinal or tonic uses (Ody, 1998), or inclusion of the young leaves in soups, one novel application of nettle leaf extract is as a green dye to camouflage young lambs, to prevent them being taken by wedge-tailed eagles (ABC Radio, *Australia All Over*, 12 September 1999).

Plants cooperate in many ways. When certain tropical trees and shrubs are mixed in plantations, the overall productivity is increased because the climate near the ground is modified to suit the shorter species, and other benefits accrue as well. In Ootacamund, India, the Australian native tree *Grevillea robusta* (silky oak) is used to lightly shade tea bushes, obtained long ago from China. In Central America, the cocoa bean tree (*Theobroma cacao*, the source of chocolate) is interplanted with a legume, Madre de Cacao (*Gliricidia sepium*). Not only does this leguminous tree contribute to the nitrogen requirements of the cocoa bean trees, but its leaves are shed completely just before flowering, providing an organic fertiliser and mulch in situ. As an added bonus, its seeds are toxic to marauding rats.

Even wheat, conventionally sown as a monoculture, yields more when interplanted with other species. In 1893 William Farrer recommended planting crimson clover (*Trifolium incarnatum*) with wheat. But the

'clever clover' concept has been around for a very long time. There is graphic evidence that clovers and climbing peas were the normal companions of cereals grown in fields in Europe for hundreds of years (see Figure 9).

We could think of many reasons why various plants might be able to assist others in a mutually beneficial way, but reciprocal antagonism is more difficult to fathom. Some instances may be based on allelopathy, which is what happens when one kind of plant inhibits many others with its root secretions. Allelopathy is the ultimate competitive weapon. The classic example is black walnut (*Juglans nigra*), which allows nothing to grow in a spreading zone around each tree. The strawberry guava, an invasive plant pest in Hawaii and on Lord Howe Island, acts in the same way. Species of *Artemisia*, including wormwood (*A. absinthium*), release allelopathic terpenoids. In the same family (see Chapter 9), sunflower is also allelopathic. The tree of heaven (*Ailanthus altissima*) has been shown to stop growth and seed germination of other plants by releasing from its roots a natural herbicide called ailanthone (Heisey, 1996). The introduced camphor laurel tree (*Cinnamomum camphora*) has a longstanding reputation for suppressing indigenous Australian plants, but whether this results from biochemical rather than just physical factors remains to be determined. At least a dozen weeds flourish in camphor laurel leaf compost.

Some plants can impede the successful growth of neighbours indirectly. Certain species are toxic to honey bees (see Table 3 on page 25). This adverse effect on pollinating insects may be why lily-of-the-valley (*Convallaria majalis*) so often appears to act as an unsuitable companion, despite having 'a delightful perfume' (Liddell, 1994). But rue (*Ruta graveolens*) has an unjustified reputation for antagonism. Rue belongs to the same family as oranges and lemons (Rutaceae). Volatile compounds from the oil glands in its leaves may deter some insects, but this should be of no consequence to basil until flowers appear. Even then, rue may not deter all pollinating insects. The opposition of rue and basil is predicated on the biodynamic 'principle' that because one is sweet and the other is bitter, they should exert a mutual antagonism. This is nonsense. In fact, rue grows amicably with many garden plants (see Figure 11).

Folklore and fable

The rue/basil myth is just the tip of the iceberg. Most of what has been written about companion planting is derivative nonsense or misguided invention. Lists have usually been reproduced without testing or checking. Some advice is not only worthless but counterproductive. Who would seriously consider planting detestable weeds like morning glory (*Ipomoea indica*, see Figure 16), camphor laurel, or castor oil plant (*Ricinus communis*, see Figure 15)? Morning glory kills other plants by covering them with its own leaves and cutting off their light. It is also poisonous. Once escaped from gardens, it does enormous damage to native vegetation. The seeds of castor bean contain one of the most potent human poisons ever described: a protein called ricin. Oblivious to these major drawbacks, and to noxious weeds legislation, some Australian writers are still recommending that we grow these plants. Not in my backyard!

Legumes are generally very helpful plants, and should be planted whenever possible so that other plants can gain from their nitrogen-fixing capability. But conventional companion-planting 'wisdom' precludes planting legumes with onions and closely related plants such as garlics, leeks and chives. This is a clear example of companion planting lore that must be challenged. The mutual antagonism that is supposed to occur is seldom witnessed. Indeed, Philbrick and Gregg (1966) approved of planting leeks with beans, stating that these 'in moderate quantity are a good combination'. I have grown onions safely with peas for more than 30 years. Paul Seitz (1996) also indicates that onions may be good neighbours for peas and beans (see Figure 12).

Because peas do not need insects to visit their flowers to bring about pollination, it does not matter if nearby onion, garlic or similar plants deter insects from visiting their flowers. With beans, this can be a positive advantage. As well as deterring pest insects, garlic, chives and summer-growing members of this group can be placed as 'guardians' to dissuade bees from visiting bean flowers when the opportunities for crosspollination need to be reduced, such as when two or more varieties of runner beans or lima beans are being grown. By the same token, care must be taken not to plant too many onion relatives close to plants that do need insects to bring about pollination, such as the cucurbits.

Carrots are almost universally presumed to be beneficial to legumes. But research conducted by the Rodale Research and Development Group found that carrots and lima beans interacted negatively when planted together — with reductions in yield of 17.4 per cent and 28 per cent respectively (page 123 of Wolf, 1977).

One combination approved of generally is the herb sweet basil with tomato. The basil is supposed to deflect the attentions of fruit fly, while the tomato keeps aphids off both. But this duo will quickly come to grief if green looper caterpillars (*Chrysodeixis eriosoma*) hatch out and eat their leaves. Do not think herbs are altogether immune from insect attack just because they often have aromatic foliage. They are not. Every plant can be eaten by something. Beans, peas, mint, pelargonium, *Osteospermum ecklonis*, nasturtium, *Iresine herbstii*, zygocactus and even blue heliotrope

(*Heliotropium europaeum*) are also attractive to the green looper, which is athletic in its mobility, and has a remarkably wide potential diet.

There is a lot more to successful organic gardening than following the lists of 'approved' companions. In many cases of alleged stimulation or improved flavour, all that has been observed is neutrality. Companion planting needs to be removed from the realm of imagination, and to embark on an experimental phase. After all, the authors of a landmark book on this topic admitted that its content was only 'an indication of what remains to be discovered' (Philbrick and Gregg, 1966). We need to adopt a common-sense approach. By looking at associations of several plant species rather than pairs, we can begin to model our gardens on cooperative natural systems, where interactions work to the mutual advantage of all the plants allowed to participate.

Plants as pest deterrents

Putting the right plants together is a vital aspect of deterrence. A good example is Nancy Bubel's suggestion of surrounding hills of cucumbers with rings of radishes, in order to repel the striped cucumber beetle. This is a modern embellishment for an ancient guild or companion system. The Iroquois Federation of North America is credited with growing cucurbits as groundcover with beans, which were allowed to climb maize plants that had been sown earlier (see Figure 13). The origin of this guild is more ancient still, going back to the peoples of Mesoamerica, who first cultivated climbing beans with maize plants as supports at least 5000 years ago. Cucumber is not an American plant, but it slots in where the American cucurbits did. Radish is not an American plant either, but its use enhances the effectiveness of the whole combination.

From what has just been advanced in support of growing members of the onion group with legumes, it will be appreciated that this should not be done extensively if cucurbits (pumpkins, squashes, zucchinis, melons, cucumbers) are to be involved as groundcover. However, many coastal areas do not favour cucurbits, as the humidity is generally too high. Powdery mildew affects the leaves, and then there is a failure at the fruit-setting stage. Do not waste time growing cucurbits if your plants are doomed to perpetual flowering and zero fruit production. Grow onions, leeks, garlics and chives instead.

Other variations of the Iroquois system include growing cobbler's peg (*Bidens pilosa*) plants as supports for the climbing beans. Cobbler's peg (also known as farmer's friend or tickweed sunflower) is one of those plants that has a root exudate that deters root-knot nematodes, and its crushed leaves deter white fly (see Chapter 9). Make sure that any support plants have a head start, and are at least 30 centimetres tall before the bean seeds are planted. Once the beans are showing, add in the cucubits and finally the radishes. Because radishes are best grown quickly to avoid excessive bitterness, sow replacements before the first approach picking size. Several sowings will be necessary to accompany the cucurbits to maturity.

This strategic assembly consists only of annuals, unless you choose to grow climbing scarlet runner beans (*Phaseolus coccineus*) instead of climbing *Phaseolus vulgaris* beans. A radical alternative approach requires the mixing of perennials with annuals. However, such a strategy contradicts earlier organic writers such as Allan Swenson (1973), whose attitude to perennials is: 'All should be grouped together in a permanent location where they will not interfere with the annual crops.' Trevor Nottle (1997) confirms that this ostracism of perennials occurred in Australian gardens, too: 'Closer to the house, on the perimeter of the intensively cultivated plots, perennial vegetables such as horseradish, rhubarb and asparagus were grown'.

This is convenience planting, not companion planting. It is time to break the mould. Perennial plants should not be placed together in the same bed just because they are perennials. In the same vein, save yourself some backbreaking work by not putting only annuals together and blitzing the terrain between seasons. What we need is medley planting by virtuoso gardeners.

Gardens should evolve over the year, and their occupants should change gradually, season by season. Each garden bed I have is different with regard to the number of perennials left in place, as annuals come and go. One bed has mostly perennials: strawberries, iris, garlic chives, yarrow and fennel, but with scope for adding in broad beans, plus volunteer *Nigella damascena* and *Bidens pilosa* that regenerate from the soil's seed bank in late winter. This guild evolved over 20 years, beginning with the iris, strawberries and *Nigella damascena*, the latter two species providing groundcover, especially in spring. It is difficult to keep weeds out of beds where perennials like iris undergo periods of slow growth during the winter. But then annuals like *Nigella* and *Bidens* compete for spare space in the spring, helping to minimise the opportunities for really troublesome weeds to become established during the warmer seasons.

Another of my beds has rhubarb, yarrow, passionfruit, iris, sweet potato, leeks and 'perpetual' spring onions (see Figure 3), while another has lavender, onions and garlic chives, with most of its space available to annuals. Tall peas, broad beans, potatoes and climbing beans are planted in these beds every year. Basils, tomatoes, cos lettuce, beetroot, tatsoi, cabbage and other vegetables are also planted individually in gaps, in different positions each year. The cos lettuce is now on automatic,

coming back from seeds deliberately scattered over the soil at the close of the season. These combinations are not prescriptive; they illustrate what is possible, and leave open many alternatives.

Similarly, with pots, annuals and perennials should be mixed to best advantage. Because basil alone is not adequate to keep white fly from settling on beans or tomatoes, pelargoniums of the right kinds can be used as well, and these plants last for many years in pots (see Chapters 5 and 10). The healthiest four-o'clock (*Mirabilis jalapa*) plants I have ever grown shared a pot with a central tomato plant. These perennials resprouted from tubers after the tomato seedling had been installed in the centre of the pot (see Figure 37) in which the four-o'clocks had been grown from seed the previous year. Nothing bothered these four-o'clocks at all, in contrast to their miserable precursors.

In growing our favourite herbs and vegetables, we should also seek to involve indigenous plants, since almost by definition these are best suited to local soils and climatic conditions. This will impact on future ideas about companion planting and 'sustainable' horticulture. For example, the long-lived leguminous climber running postman (*Kennedia rubicunda*) growing on a mesh fence (see Figure 10) provides not only a windbreak and screen, but also nitrogen to the soil and plants around it. Some indigenous trees produce edible seeds or fruits, and they can be integrated into an organic system just like introduced fruit trees (see Chapter 14). The suitability of leaves shed from native trees for compost is endorsed in Chapter 3.

The opposite of deterrence is attraction. Do not fall into the trap of establishing 'decoy' plantings in order to divert the attention of pests from the main gardens. Get rid of plants that support aphids when there are no predators. Eradicate weeds like *Solanum nigrum* when the 28-spotted lady beetle is likely to be about, so that this leaf-chewing pest does not have the opportunity to leapfrog onto your potatoes (see Figure 86). A decoy planting is an invitation to a feast. The results can be disastrous. The only decoys I employ are ageing plants of bean and tomato in autumn and winter, productive veterans left in place after harvest to entice snails and slugs out of areas about to be replanted with vulnerable seeds.

Living groundcover

Not all 'weeds' are harmful or likely to deprive cultivated plants of the nutrients that we intend them to receive from carefully prepared garden beds (see Chapters 3 and 4). Spare some of the shallow-rooted weeds with attractive flowers (see Table 2 below and Figure 36). Allow them to serve as groundcover instead of mulch in the winter and spring. They provide all the advantages of mulch, without the many disadvantages (see Chapter 7). These plants will lessen the impact of raindrops, reducing erosion from the base of stems, and allow smaller droplets of water to penetrate the soil surface rather than run straight off. Or they can intercept the harsh, drying rays of the sun, maintaining an even temperature within the soil, slowing down the direct evaporation of moisture, and preventing the development of an impenetrable surface crust. Some of them can also provide nectar to adult hoverflies in the critical late-winter, early-spring period (see page 24).

You might prefer to get rid of oxalis and scarlet pimpernel if animals are likely to poison themselves eating the leaves. But chickweed is an edible green, and this plant has been used to heal wounds or treat skin irritations for centuries (Ody, 1998). The numbers of these weeds can easily be controlled by thinning, and by trimming off flowering shoots to reduce the numbers of seeds formed.

Supporting pollinators and predators

Flowering plants did not begin to evolve as a recognised seed-bearing group until about 130 million years ago, in the Cretaceous Period. At first pollen was produced by numerous stamens, and scattered on the wind. Insects in their adult forms found pollen, and also nectar, to be useful sources of nourishment. Over time some plants adjusted by producing less pollen, which altered in its

TABLE 2. A GUILD OF ATTRACTIVE 'WEEDS' THAT CAN SERVE AS GROUNDCOVER		
COMMON NAME	**BINOMIAL**	**PLANT FAMILY**
Chickweed	*Stellaria media*	Caryophyllaceae
Scarlet pimpernel	*Anagallis arvensis*	Primulaceae
Scrambling fumitor	*Fumaria muralis*	Fumariaceae
Scrambling speedwell	*Veronica persica*	Scrophulariaceae
White clover	*Trifolium repens*	Leguminosae
Yellow or horned oxalis	*Oxalis corniculata*	Oxalidaceae

surface features from smooth to rough, giving such grains better adhesion to insect exoskeletons (see Figure 18). The flowers of some species became highly specialised as to the kind of insect or other floral visitor that could obtain the rewards of nectar or pollen on offer, and by visiting more than one flower, the insect became the willing agent of the direct transfer of pollen from the anthers of one flower to the stigma of another.

Insects also evolved in response to changes in flowering plants, even though the first insects had evolved from arthropods when land plants first developed, about 300 million years earlier. Beetles are regarded as 'primitive' pollinators, seeking flowers with numerous stamens and abundant pollen, which they eat directly. There are more than 300 000 species of beetles, and although there is a great diversity of lifestyle, many are co-adapted to visiting flowers.

European honey bees (*Apis mellifera*) are more highly evolved, with parts of the lower jaws fused to form a tube protecting the proboscis, through which nectar is taken up. Honey bees also have 'baskets' on their hind legs to receive collected pollen. Derived from ancestral wasps, honey bees first evolved in the Tertiary Period, from about 60 million years ago. The changes and counterchanges that have gone on among flowering plants and major dependent groups of insects, birds and even some mammals are described now as 'co-evolution', supporting views first advanced by Charles Darwin and John Lubbock.

Today we often find that plants grown for one particular reason are multifunctional, and even without us realising it, they may deter some pests directly, or support their predators simply by flowering. Many traditional garden plants fulfil both roles. There is an important range of predators to consider, including the green lacewing (*Mallada signata*), a number of wasps, and the lady beetles and hoverflies already mentioned.

The nutritional requirements of nectar and pollen collectors can best be provided by growing a mixture of plant species, so that a single source does not predominate. It is well known that honey bees need a variety of pollen sources so that their requirement for protein is fully met. Worker bees make 'bee bread' from pollen to feed their young. Without adequate nutrition, the numbers of bees will not increase. That is why beekeepers who utilise eucalypt flowers for the production of fine-flavoured honey provide alternative and superior pollen sources for the sake of the bees, both in advance of the peak eucalypt flowering periods, and afterwards.

Looking after honey bees has been high on the gardening agenda for a long time. The earliest evidence for deliberate keeping of bees comes from Egyptian reliefs dating from 2400 BC. Greek pottery hive fragments have been found dating from the eighth century BC (Mayor, 1995). Thomas Hyll in his 1579 composition *A Profitable Instruction of the Perfite Ordering of Bees* cites Virgil, who 'willeth bushie trees to be planted and stand right before the hives, like as the Pear Tree, the Peach tree, many kinds of Apple trees and the Ivy tree also because it giveth out much honny. And he willeth these plantes and hearbes to grow neare hande, as the Rosemary, the red and damaske rose, the white Lillie (Madonna) the violets, the Flouredeluce (Iris), Time, the hearbe Baulme (lemon balm), the Borage and Buglosse flowers and many other sweete and wholesome flowers.' Keeping bees, and observing which plants they favoured, is evidently the way ideas about plants belonging together first developed. This sixteenth-century list could still serve as a blueprint for an organic garden, except that we might delete ivy because of its potential to cause dermatitis, and to be spread as a weed into native bushland.

Many nectar-seeking insects have sensors in the proboscis that assess the composition of nectar. The production of nectar by nectaries occurs at precise stages of flower development, coinciding with pollen release, and the stigmatic surface becoming receptive to pollen. Nectar is sweet because of its high sugar content. Any of sucrose, maltose, glucose and fructose may be present, and the proportions vary with species. Total sugar concentrations between 30 and 60 per cent by weight are possible, but nectars with relatively low sugar contents (about 20 per cent) are preferred by insects. Nectar is also rich in amino acids. The relative proportions of amino acids and sugars can change during the day, and this too can influence the timing of visits by different nectar-seeking insects.

Nectar production is subject to 'feedback' control. It stops if nectar is not removed, and resumes to replace the nectar consumed by visitors. Floral structure can assist the regulation of nectar composition following secretion: for example, if the petals are fused to form a floral tube, the nectar pooled in the base of the tube is protected from concentration that might otherwise result from the evaporation of water. Flowers may open for only part of a day, closing in the hottest part of the afternoon. These measures extend the period over which the nectar remains attractive.

To maintain a nectar supply it is necessary to have some plants flowering in the garden for as much of the year as possible. This vital aspect of organic gardening requires knowledge of the time of the year that flowering begins (see Chapter 6), how long each flower can last as a source of nectar or pollen (see Figure 17), and the duration of flowering. Good gardeners often store this kind of information intuitively. I know that in my gardens sweet alice, rosemary, perennial basil and *Tradescantia virginiana* all flower for most of the year, providing food for hoverflies and honey bees over the vital winter period. In addition, the African daisy *Osteospermum ecklonis* flowers from March onwards (see

Figure 67), and the succulent *Crassula arborescens* flowers from May to August, overlapping with jonquils and then freesias.

The aim of the organic gardener should be to provide this continuity of flowers without growing plants that might be toxic to bees, or to humans (see Table 3). The inadvertent consumption of 'raving' honey has altered the course of battles and cost many soldiers their lives at different times in history, particularly in the Caucasus, in regions south or east of the Black Sea (Mayor, 1995). The plants responsible for this include *Rhododendron ponticum*, now used as rootstock for grafted varieties of rhododendron, and oleander, well known as a street shrub in suburban Australia. Avoiding the plants listed in Table 3 is a giant step towards having a bee-friendly garden, and making sure that any honey produced is not overburdened with grayanotoxins, compounds that cause optical delusions, disorientation, delirium, nausea, respiratory inhibition, unconsciousness and death.

Noting the frequency with which the family Ranunculaceae is mentioned in Table 3, the organic gardener might hesitate to embrace clematis as a companion plant, despite the encouragement of Barry Fretwell (1995). Clematis may well be 'a stunning addition to your garden', but most parts of these plants are poisonous, and a possible cause of dermatitis.

Pollen and respiratory ailments

Plants producing pollen grains that cause hayfever (allergic rhinitis) and asthma when inhaled by sensitive people should also be excluded from the garden. The surface of the eye and the nasal lining mimic the receptive stigma, and stimulate the release of glycoproteins from pollen grains. The interaction of these glycoproteins with the

TABLE 3. PLANTS BEST EXCLUDED FROM THE GARDEN BECAUSE OF THEIR TOXIC EFFECTS ON HONEY BEES (*APIS MELLIFERA*) OR HUMANS EATING AFFECTED HONEY [1, 2]

COMMON NAME	BINOMIAL	PLANT FAMILY
PLANTS TOXIC TO BEES		
Canadian buckeye	*Aesculus californica*	Sapindaceae
horse chestnut	*Aesculus hippocastanum*	Sapindaceae
karaka (NZ)	*Corynocarpus laevigatus*	Corynocarpaceae
buttercups	*Ranunculus* species	Ranunculaceae
azalea, rhododendron	*Rhododendron* species	Ericaceae
native pea	*Swainsona greyana*	Leguminosae
garden tulip[3]	*Tulipa gesneriana*	Liliaceae
PLANTS YIELDING HONEY TOXIC TO HUMANS		
monkshood[4]	*Aconitum napellus*	Ranunculaceae
snowdrop anemone	*Anemone sylvestris*	Ranunculaceae
angel's trumpet	*Brugmansia* species	Solanaceae
lily-of-the-valley	*Convallaria majalis*	Convallariaceae
tutu tree (NZ)	*Coriaria sarmentosa*	Coriariaceae
daphne	*Daphne* species	Thymelaeaceae
candle larkspur	*Delphinium elatum*	Ranunculaceae
golden rain tree	*Laburnum anagyroides*	Leguminosae
	Melianthus major	Melianthaceae
dogbane or oleander	*Nerium oleander*	Apocynaceae
azalea, rhododendron	*Rhododendron* species	Ericaceae
kalmia (USA)	*Rhododendron maximum*	Ericaceae
black locust	*Robinia pseudoacacia* (Figure 19)	Leguminosae
linden	*Tilia americana*	Tiliaceae

1. Compiled from information in McBarron (1976) and Mayor (1995).

2. Leaves or other parts of these plants may be strongly poisonous also.

3. Tulips do not produce nectar, so honey escapes the addition of tulip toxins, whereas the bees receive them in the pollen.

4. Fortunately honey bees are disadvantaged compared to bumble bees, which are co-adapted to the size and shape of this flower.

human immune system is an evolutionary accident. Not everyone is sensitive, but it is true that people in Australia and New Zealand have the highest incidence of asthma and related ailments in the world.

Sufferers are affected by some species more seriously than others. Identifying culprits is often fraught with difficulty. In the United States, wind-dispersed pollen grains from trees such as white oak (*Quercus alba*) and birch (*Betula* species) cause hayfever. So do pollen grains from ragweed (*Ambrosia psilostachya*, different from ragwort, *Senecio jacobaea*), sage bush (*Artemisia tridentata*), wormwood (*Artemisia absinthium*), Kentucky bluegrass (*Poa pratensis*), Bermuda or couch grass (*Cynodon dactylon*), stinging nettle, lamb's tongue (*Plantago lanceolata*) and dock (*Rumex crispus*).

In Australia, introduced deciduous trees and grasses produce most of the pollen that causes hayfever and asthma (Knox, 1979; Ragg, 1998). Perennial ryegrass (*Lolium perenne*) presents a major problem, because it is so widely grown. Persuading farmers to grow more appropriate alternatives is difficult, but at least the local environment can be improved by always mowing grasses as they flower. Buffalo grass (*Stenotaphrum secundatum*) has a relatively low allergenic effect.

Pollen grains from various species of *Acacia* are often wrongly blamed for respiratory problems. Acacia pollen does not travel far in the wind, as it is released in groups of 12 or 16 grains still adhering to one another. An aggregate like this (called a polyad) is transferred readily by birds and insects, and a single polyad placed on a stigma is sufficient for the seed production of a whole pod. This is typical of co-evolving systems, and is a more effective way of ensuring fertilization than shedding vast quantities of pollen on the wind. Species of *Photinia* used for hedges are also wrongly blamed for causing hayfever and asthma (Burke, 1992). Similarly, Mark Ragg's concern about the whole daisy family (Compositae) is misplaced, because most pollen in this family is transferred by birds and insects rather than being carried by the wind (see Figure 18). This family is too important to the organic gardener to be banished for no sound reason.

Contact dermatitis

Well-known culprits in this regard are the rhus tree, *Rhus succedanea*, and English ivy, *Hedera helix*. It is not so well appreciated that some Australian native plants can also cause blisters and welts in sensitive individuals. Popular cultivars of *Grevillea* (see Figure 20) are included in this group (Freeman, 2004), as are callistemons, and in my own case, *Crinum pedunculatum*. Just brushing *Crinum* leaves with bare skin as the plant prepares to flower in November results in marks like phenol burns. So be on the lookout for unexplained skin blemishes, because everyone is different. Plants that affect other people may not affect you, and vice versa.

3.
Preparing compost

'The answer lies there in the soil ...'

The Archers, BBC Radio, 1970s

The value of organic matter in the soil

The answer to many problems of plant growth does indeed lie in the soil. Inadequate preparation will be shown up by what happens later on, when it may well be too late to redeem the situation. Alternatively, careful preparation will yield healthy soil and productive plants. For the successful organic gardener, soil preparation begins with compost preparation, so that an abundant supply of uncontaminated organic material can be introduced to the soil as often as it is needed. But why is organic matter so important?

Soil is a mixture of organic and inorganic particles of various sizes that supports the growth of myriads of living organisms, all intimately involved in the welfare of plants. Active root systems extract nutrients from the soil, overcoming the constant problem of balance between the availability of water, required in great quantities by the shoots and leaves for transpiration, and oxygen, required for the roots to support their own growth and functions. Because oxygen is only slightly soluble in water, the more water held in the soil, the more slowly oxygen diffuses to the

roots. Waterlogged roots receive practically no oxygen, and if this situation persists unrelieved for too long, stressed plants will die.

As a soil dries out, the availability of oxygen improves, so root activity increases again. Plants are most productive during this drying-out part of the soil hydration cycle, since the deepest roots can still be in contact with water, although it has retreated from the soil surface. But if the soil becomes too dry, the leaves will close their pores (stomata), cease photosynthesis, and the roots will not receive enough sugar from the leaves to keep growing and taking up mineral nutrients. The growth of the whole plant will be limited once again.

Management of this reciprocal compromise between the availabilities of water and oxygen is greatly assisted by the presence of organic matter in the soil, because the porosity is improved. The gas space and the water-holding capacity of the soil are both increased. Good soils drain readily, facilitating access to oxygen by the roots, and lowering the risk of waterlogging. Soils with severely depleted organic content are defective by comparison. They can hold only about one-fifth the water content of soils with an adequate organic content. When water is applied to such poor

TABLE 4. MINERAL NUTRIENTS REQUIRED BY PLANTS AND LISTED APPROXIMATELY IN ORDER OF AMOUNT NEEDED: MICRONUTRIENTS ARE THOSE FROM IRON ONWARDS[1]

NAME	ATOMIC SYMBOL	FORM[2] TAKEN UP
Nitrogen	N	NO_3^- nitrate (anion)
		NH_4^+ ammonium (cation)
Potassium	K	K^+ — a cation
Calcium	Ca	Ca^{2+} — a cation
Chlorine	Cl	Cl^{-1} — chloride anion
Magnesium	Mg	Mg^{2+} — a cation
Sulfur	S	sulfate
Phosphorus	P	soluble phosphate
Silicon	Si	silicate/silicic acid
Sodium	Na	Na^+ — a cation
Iron	Fe	Fe^{2+} — ferrous cation
Manganese	Mn	Mn^{2+} — a cation
Selenium	Se	selenate
Zinc	Zn	Zn^{2+} — a cation
Boron	B	borate
Copper	Cu	Cu^{2+} — cupric cation
Molybdenum	Mo	molybdate
Cobalt	Co	Co^{2+} — a cation
Nickel	Ni	Ni^{2+} — a cation

1. Expanded from Table 1 of D.R. Murray (1988).
2. An '-ate' ending indicates a negatively charged ion, or anion.

soils in a dry state, it tends to run off rather than penetrate.

The ability of the soil to hold cations (positively charged mineral ions) depends partly on the presence of clay minerals (aluminosilicates), and is improved considerably by an organic component called humus. This long-lasting organic fraction was originally named after the Latin word for soil. It was once believed that humus was derived from cellulose. But it was not until the late 1920s that the origin of humus was discovered (Wilkins, 1927). Humus is a breakdown product of lignin, a packing compound interspersed among cellulose fibrils in the walls of xylem vessels, which form capillaries and constitute one of the major sap-conducting tissues in land plants. This polyphenolic substance is the same material that has to be removed whenever paper is made from wood pulp, which might contain 30 per cent lignin. But the value of lignin in the garden is enduring: it aids transport in living plants, then after the death of those plants, it contributes to the ongoing ability of the soil to produce more plants. These slowly degraded organic residues improve the capacity of the soil to hold cations such as potassium and magnesium, rather than have these leach away with each shower of rain.

In addition to their structural contributions to the soil, organic materials derived from plant detritus act as slow-release sources of nutrients, for plants, animals and micro-organisms. The mineral nutrients required by plants can be listed approximately according to how much is needed (see Table 4), noting that species differ from one another in the details of such ranking, and broadly speaking, total anion uptake is balanced by total cation uptake. The division of plant nutrients into three categories has long been a feature of *Yates Garden Guides*, ever since the 1979 edition. Perhaps it is not surprising that a purveyor of synthetic fertilisers would place

N, P and K uppermost in their marketing strategy, and devote the top category of 'Major Elements' to just these three! Then follows a group of so-called 'Secondary Elements' — calcium, magnesium and sulfur — followed in turn by several trace elements or micronutrients. The number of nutrients admitted by Yates advanced by one (molybdenum) between 1940 and 1979. But the main problem with the Yates classification is that these so-called 'secondary elements' are normally present in plants at higher concentrations than phosphorus (see Table 6 on page 35).

In contrast to the Yates treatment, plant physiologists have conventionally ranked mineral nutrients into just two categories: macronutrients and micronutrients. The dividing line is arbitrary, and generally drawn at iron. Macronutrients are all of those nutrients needed in relatively large amounts, and micronutrients are those needed in much smaller quantities. Yates' 'Major Elements' and 'Secondary Elements' together comprise most of the macronutrients, with the addition of chloride, sodium and silicon (see Table 4). Chloride is often a major anion in plants — for example, it is the predominant anion in the latex of banana plants (Kallarackal and colleagues, 1990).

The significance of silicon

Yates Garden Guide used to state categorically that silicon was not an essential plant nutrient. Many prominent textbooks also neglected silicon for many years. Yates eventually drew a reluctant conclusion that 'silicon may be a nutrient for some plants' (at last, in the 41st edition, 2002). In his book published in 1930, B.V. Rossi claimed that silica was necessary for healthy roses; specifically, for the firmness of the stem and the glossiness of the leaves. He

was right. Plant anatomists provided detailed evidence for the role of silica in the 1970s, then the more enlightened physiologists followed suit (Bidwell, 1974; Salisbury and Ross, 1978). Long ago I reviewed the structural evidence that supports the view that silicon satisfies all the appropriate criteria for being considered an essential plant nutrient (Murray, 1988).

Grains of quartz sand (silica, or silicon dioxide, SiO_2) are an icon of stability. Yet some of the silicon in soil is present in solution as silicic acid. This is taken up by root cells, carried through the xylem capillaries, then deposited in cell walls as opaline silica bodies. This material has a variable water content like opal: $SiO_2.nH_2O$. The locations between cells where silica bodies form are determined with great precision as leaves or bracts develop and grow older. These silica 'phytoliths' give structural support or stiffness, and sometimes sharp edges to the leaves that produce them, as in wild oats (*Avena fatua*) and other grasses. A bristly surface is sometimes produced, too, as for the leaf of the native sandpaper fig (*Ficus coronata*). The glandular hairs on the upper surface of this leaf become so strongly silicified that the dry, dead leaf literally turns into sandpaper.

By contributing to the strength of plant cell walls, phytoliths enhance disease-resistance, inhibiting the ability of pathogenic fungi to penetrate leaf surfaces. For example, cucumber plants grow more slowly and are more susceptible to powdery mildew (*Sphaerotheca fuliginea*) in silicon-deficient potting mix (Sally Muir and others, 1999). Phytoliths also make it more difficult for a variety of herbivores to chew the leaves. This is not a foolproof defence, however, as caterpillars simply start with the youngest and softest leaves.

Because they are readily identified under the microscope, phytoliths are very useful to archaeologists. Phytoliths returned to the soil may improve the availability of silica to the next plants grown in such soil. Provision of silica is also a subject of interest to hydroponic growers, who deprived their plants of silica by dissolving 'pure' chemicals in deionised water, and switching from borosilicate glass to all-plastic nutrient preparation and circulation systems. Now they have to put it back (Morgan, 1999). The ash derived from rice husks is one possible source, for potting mixes as well as hydroponic solutions (Bulford, 1998). Organic gardeners have no such problems.

Supporting beneficial fungi

Complex polysaccharides and cellulose derived from plant cell walls provide carbon and energy sources for beneficial fungi. These fungi produce cellulase enzymes, like snails, that allow them to access the glucose units polymerised in cellulose. One group associates with the roots of plants, forming a fuzzy coating of mycorrhizae. Mycorrhizal fungi can then acquire organic nutrients directly from a host plant, while functioning as an extension of the plant's root system. Consequently, the plant is better able to acquire mineral nutrients. Usually phosphorus uptake is improved, and sometimes the uptake of zinc, manganese and copper as well. In the heath family (Ericaceae) and in some eucalypts, nitrogen uptake is also improved.

Mycorrhizal fungi manufacture and transmit growth-stimulating hormones to the shoots of the plants they are connected to. One immediate effect is to alter the shape and internal anatomy of the roots themselves. Very few plant families do not engage in mycorrhizal associations, the main one encountered by gardeners being Cruciferae (Brassicaceae), the mustard family. Another is the snapdragon family, Scrophulariaceae, which includes snapdragon itself, foxglove (*Digitalis*) and *Diascia*. Fossils show that

symbiotic associations between primitive plant roots and fungi first occurred in the Silurian Period, about 400 million years ago, so the loss of the association is fairly recent.

The same mycorrhizal fungus can sometimes link different species of plants via their roots, mediating an improved distribution of nutrients, and providing a mechanism that could explain mutually beneficial companion planting in some cases. Research is needed to explore the possible benefits of such interactions.

There are other beneficial fungi that depend on the organic matter in the soil, including *Trichoderma* species, and *Gliocladium virens*, the natural antagonists of parasitic fungi like *Fusarium*, *Pythium*, *Rhizoctonia* and the agent of onion white-rot, *Sclerotium cepivorum*. *Trichoderma* species also produce hormone-like compounds that stimulate the growth of cultivated plants such as lettuce, tomatoes and peas.

For soils or potting mixes depleted of *Trichoderma*, an inoculum pellet called 'Trichopel' has been developed in New Zealand, and is now available in Australia. Such pellets will be useful for reclaiming soils harbouring fungal disease, but the organic gardener should already find *Trichoderma* alive and well in a soil conditioned with properly prepared compost. In this regard, it is important to exclude sawdust from your compost. I know sawdust was all the rage 35 years ago (Rodale, 1971), but it has to go, for one very important reason. Composts prepared with adequate bark content have the ability to suppress pathogenic fungi, but composts prepared instead with sawdust or sphagnum peat lack this ability (Hoitink and Fahy, 1986). To maintain this suppressive capacity in your soil, properly prepared compost should be incorporated two or three times per year.

Supporting beneficial bacteria

Aerobic soil bacteria typically number 10^9 per gram (one thousand million per gram) and account for 0.1 per cent of the weight of the soil (Leeper, 1986). They are often concentrated near the roots of growing plants, where they can utilise malic acid and other organic secretions from the roots in addition to substances derived from the breakdown of the soil's particulate organic matter. The *Rhizobium* and *Bradyrhizobium* bacteria that can fix nitrogen inside nodules on legume roots depend on such carbon sources when they have to survive as free-living bacteria, awaiting opportunities to colonise the roots of legumes. Some soil bacteria contribute to plant nutrition by releasing compounds that chelate iron or other cations naturally, holding them in forms suitable for rapid uptake by plant roots. Certain strains of *Pseudomonas aeruginosa* are also able to protect plants against *Pythium* damping-off fungus through the production of these iron chelates (Ryder, Stephens and Bowen, 1994).

Beneficial soil bacteria include *Nitrosomonas* that converts ammonium ions to nitrite, and *Nitrobacter* that converts this nitrite to nitrate, the source of nitrogen most readily taken up and assimilated by cultivated plants. The bacteria gain energy from these oxygen-dependent conversions. Ammonium ions are often a nuisance to plants because they interfere with the uptake of potassium, and the sooner they are converted to nitrate the better. Yet other bacteria can oxidise elemental sulfur to sulfate, so if sulfur powder is used against certain pests and diseases (see Chapter 16), or to acidify the soil (see Chapter 4), it is eventually converted to a form that plants can utilise.

The interactions among plants and soil micro-organisms are dynamic and complex. A soil rich in organic constituents in various stages of breakdown clearly has the greatest capacity to bring about optimal nutrition and health for growing plants. This is why some writers emphasise 'feeding the soil' rather than feeding the plants.

Sources of material and basic principles

The organic material in the soil is gradually broken down by microbial activity and detritus processors such as earthworms and mites (see Figure 23), and most is ultimately released as carbon dioxide. It therefore needs to be replaced. In a natural plant community, this happens automatically. Various shed plant parts fall to the ground: leaves, flower parts, stalks, twigs, fruits, seeds and bark. This material is supplemented by the droppings of leaf-eating insects and roosting or nesting birds. Sometimes the fall of material is so abundant it looks and sounds like rain. How deeply this organic matter is carried into the soil depends upon the kind of ecosystem in which this is happening. Sometimes the 'litter' on the soil surface is mobilised as ash after the passage of a bushfire. But whenever food plants are cultivated, and removed from the scene afterwards, alternative organic materials must be deliberately added back to the soil and incorporated thoroughly.

The best organic fertilisers are those produced on site from local ingredients. Just throwing anything sold as 'organic' onto our gardens is no longer good enough. We need to analyse where everything comes from, and what it represents. On the face of it, renewable products should be favoured for use, but we still need to read the fine print, and avoid products that involve detrimental environmental consequences in their manufacture (see Chapter 4), or have adverse effects following their application.

If you do need to buy a bag of compost or potting mixture, purchase a product from a reputable nursery that adheres to standards for microbiological safety, low sodium salt content, and appropriate pH (Australian Standards for Composts, Soil Conditioners and Mulches, AS 4454, 1999; Australian Standards for Potting Mixtures AS 3743, 1996; and see Standards Australia under Useful Addresses). Read the label very carefully, and if possible, find out what the ingredients were, so that likely sources of contamination can be avoided. Also try to find out how long the product has been sitting on the shelf, slowly losing its nitrogen content. One of the recent improvements in the standards is assessment for nitrogen 'draw down' potential, rather than provision of a simple carbon/nitrogen ratio, which can be meaningless in practice. Wear a mask while opening the bag in case the mixture is dry, and contains *Legionella*. This is a slight risk for gardeners, but one easily guarded against.

Food scraps and worm farms

Where does it all come from? The preparation of many common vegetables and fruits involves the generation of significant quantities of peelings, trimmings, seeds, pods or cobs (see Table 5). The least waste comes from grapes and flat green beans (stringless). Most comes from bananas, avocados, sweet corn, borlotti

TABLE 5. THE PROPORTION OF 'GREEN WASTE' GENERATED BY NORMAL FOOD PREPARATION IN THE HOME				
FRUIT OR VEGETABLE	**MASS OF WHOLE**	**EDIBLE PORTION**	**NON-EDIBLE PORTION**	
	g	g	g	as % of total
garden peas (37 pods)	257	105	152	59
borlotti beans (10 pods)	115	59	56	49
flat green beans (7)	131	127	4	3
carrot (one)	104	83	21	20
potato (Pontiac, one)	260	213	47	18
capsicum (red, one)	300	257	43	14
eggplant (one)	499	475	24	5
onion (one)	157	136	21	13
mandarin (Imperial, one)	100	77	23	23
avocado (one)	169	101	68	40
banana (one)	164	112	52	32
grapes (Red Globe)	940	923	17	2
grapes (sultana)	483	472	11	2
sweet corn (one cob)	341	188	153	45

(shelling) beans and peas. A great deal also comes from items not included in Table 5, such as broccoli and cauliflower, where the amount of non-edible stalks and leaves varies widely according to the ministrations of the individual greengrocer, but can be about half.

Fruit and vegetable scraps can be processed completely by a combination of burial and composting. With few exceptions, most household vegetable peelings, fruit skins, spoiled fruit, bread scraps, nut shells, fruit stones, and broken, aged wine-bottle corks should be excluded from the compost heap and buried directly, to avoid attracting rodents, and in the case of citrus fruits, culturing fruit flies. The key proviso then is to wait at least two months for sufficient breakdown to occur before planting in these areas. Alternatively, choose positions near the roots of established ornamental or fruit trees, or where nothing else is going to be planted for a long time. This also isolates any incoming pesticide residues that might still be on vegetable or fruit skins, keeping them well away from productive vegetable beds, and providing them with the microbial environment that might accelerate their breakdown. I have a border garden with enough space for five such burials, which I use repeatedly. I also harvest soil for iris pots from this area.

The amount of material not sent to landfill is significant, in my own household averaging 400 kilograms per annum for a family of three or four. Over 26 years at our present residence, more than 10 tonnes (10 000 kilograms) of food scraps have been buried on site. This total excludes some green materials such as carrot tops, rhubarb leaves, sweet corn sheaths and pea pods that have been composted before being added back to garden beds and pots. These burials have contributed to soil condition over that time, and reduced the amount of methane that would otherwise have come from anaerobic breakdown under landfill. It is important not to allow methane

(CH_4) to form and escape, because it is a much more intense greenhouse gas per molecule than carbon dioxide, and globally its current rate of release is accelerating much faster than the annual rate of increase in carbon dioxide (Serventy, 1990; Gribbin and Gribbin, 1996; Murray, 1995, 1997b).

Another approach to dealing with these same materials would be to set up a worm farm, but these were little known until about 10 years ago, and appeal particularly to latent gardeners who do not have much space in their yard, or perhaps have only a balcony with a few containers instead. Worm farms consist of a stack of interlocking plastic compartments. New compartments are added, with food scraps, from the top, then covered with a piece of damp hessian. The scraps have to be cut finely. Farmed worms do not appreciate orange peel and onion or garlic skins, so these items have to be kept separate and still present a disposal problem. But garden earthworms are not so fastidious. I don't have to cut their food up for them, and everything I bury eventually disappears.

Farmed worms show excellent population control, matching egg-laying activity to the availability of food. They migrate upwards, leaving the lowest compartments for harvesting the castings. Recent improvements in design have resulted in circular stacks rather than rectangular, plus an outlet tap for surplus liquid (see Reln Plastics Pty Ltd under Useful Addresses). Worm casts can be used directly as potting mix, and are valuable for the conditioning of extremely sandy soils (Firth, 1996).

Composting

Making compost is not as difficult as the aficionados pretend. There is no need to worry about specially built compartments, herbal or microbial accelerators, or putting the layers of ingredients in the 'right' order. Nor is there any need for fancy shredders and tumblers, which consume electricity — another 'needless waste of force'. Forget the gadgets, the smelly anaerobic containers, and the straitjacket of recipes. There are no prizes for having your compost ready in 14 or 16 days either, which is the boast of many writers. Speed is not the essence. Once you have had a heap for 12 months, and you keep on making new heaps, then you will have all the compost anyone could ever need. Patience is the chief prerequisite of good compost.

I simply pile everything in a heap on the ground as contributions come to hand: fallen leaves, shed bark, cut grass in season, green prunings, most weeds and selected green vegetable waste (as listed on page 33) added into the outer coating. Shed leaves have usually had most of their nitrogen, sulfur, potassium, phosphorus and magnesium withdrawn while they were attached to the plant they came from, but pruned green leaves and stems, weeds and grass clippings provide a complete spectrum of plant mineral nutrients (see Table 4 on page 28). There is no need to worry about nitrogen. The carbon/nitrogen ratio will look after itself if green trimmings and grass are used in addition to nitrogen-depleted materials. A good time to supplement heaps with prunings is at the close of summer or the beginning of autumn. The slaters (wood lice) in a healthy compost heap can make a layer of green mulberry leaves disappear while you watch. They will even eat rhubarb leaves (see Figures 25 and 26), despite the oxalate content that makes them poisonous to humans.

The contribution of mown grass to compost is highly significant, both for its nutrient content and for its periodic temperature-raising effect, to be discussed shortly. Some gardening writers show an unreasonable bias against lawns, and their composts would be lacking accordingly. Make no mistake: grassed areas are indispensible. There should always be enough space to walk around in, and for children and dogs to play on. Lawns cushion falls, saving many a broken arm or leg. At the front of a house, grassed areas are necessary for clear vision and security. Especially on slopes, grasses bind the soil and reduce erosion by wind or water. The choice of grass species to include or exclude is important (see Chapter 2), but compared to the water-impermeable and ultraviolet-reflecting alternatives, grasses are much more desirable.

Grassed areas provide a habitat for earthworms underground at some extraordinary density — sometimes between 500 and 700 per square metre. Once upon a time, worms that made casts in lawns were killed off with potassium permanganate, lime water or 'commercial formulas' (Hurley, 1956). Such concern with the tidiness of a patch of grass seems truly incredible to us now, and was symptomatic of the level of chemical warfare that gardeners were encouraged to wage. Casts are a visible sign that all is well underground. Lawns also provide habitat for some beetles, crickets and grasshoppers, and their parasitic wasps. These include the large blue flower wasp (*Scolia soror*, see Figure 30), which lays eggs on scarab beetle larvae underground, and *Diamma bicolor,* which lays eggs on scarab beetle and mole cricket larvae (Hadlington and Johnston, 1982; Crawford, 2005). All of these insects provide food for native birds.

It is essential, too, that homes have trees and shrubs of appropriate dimensions for shade, privacy, cooling, soundproofing, buffering from the effects of wind and weather, and as an added bonus, fallen leaves. This would be the case whether we sought out those with edible fruits or nuts, or not. The range of trees to choose from is enormous, and in Australia leaf-fall is not confined to autumn, as would occur with solely deciduous trees in much of the northern hemisphere. Even from

TABLE 6. MINERAL COMPOSITION OF TYPICAL HEALTHY LEAVES (OR EQUIVALENT PARTS) OF A RANGE OF AUSTRALIAN NATIVE PLANT SPECIES,[1] BY WEIGHT[2]

MACRONUTRIENTS (PER CENT)

Species	N	Ca	K	Cl	Mg	S	P
Acacia podalyriaefolia	2.82	0.68	1.00	0.49	0.22	0.18	0.13
Acmena smithii	1.21	0.55	0.85	0.25	0.25	0.29	0.11
Amyema miquelii	1.13	1.48	2.71	0.83	0.20	0.13	0.19
Brachychiton populneum	1.65	1.53	1.41	0.05	0.27	0.20	0.14
Casuarina glauca	1.37	1.83	0.47	0.50	0.28	0.12	0.09
Philotheca myoporoides[3]	1.39	1.00	1.29	0.68	0.14	0.15	0.10
Eucalyptus mannifera	1.48	0.72	1.10	0.33	0.12	0.14	0.17
Grevillea shirlessii	0.91	0.65	0.77	0.09	0.15	0.16	0.06
Persoonia levis	0.99	0.26	0.52	0.19	0.14	0.09	0.06
Pittosporum undulatum	1.42	1.61	1.74	0.29	0.29	0.16	0.09

SILICON, SODIUM AND MICRONUTRIENTS (PPM)

Species	Si	Na	Mn	Fe	Zn	Cu
Acacia podalyriaefolia	290	240	138	75	30	9
Acmena smithii	1180	620	416	79	15	4
Amyema miquelii	320	180	865	69	67	13
Brachychiton populneum	1540	160	55	174	24	4
Casuarina glauca	850	530	494	57	21	4
Philotheca myoporoides[3]	660	800	155	70	15	3
Eucalyptus mannifera	470	90	527	60	21	5
Grevillea shirlessii	710	510	247	67	10	3
Persoonia levis	840	900	490	76	65	2
Pittosporum undulatum	630	1330	350	63	378	9

1. Ten species from the analyses in the report to the Australian Flora Foundation prepared by Malcolm Gill and Peter Moore (1996).

2. Per cent by weight can be converted to ppm (parts per million) by multiplying by 10 000.

3. Formerly *Eriostemon myoporoides*, see Paul Wilson (1998).

deciduous trees, leaf fall is staggered species by species, commencing in autumn, but not concluding until the very end of winter. Some people think 'evergreen' means an absence of leaf shedding, but nothing could be further from the truth. Leaves senesce and fall from trees all year round, as many Australian native trees have two growth seasons, when new leaves are formed on extending shoots. So there is often an extra peak of leaf loss in spring.

Shed leaves from both native and introduced tree species can and should be composted, because this helps to circulate nutrients from deep within the soil. Some gardeners avoid composting eucalyptus leaves because there is a view they might be toxic. Others are reluctant to compost the leaves of native plants because they are supposed to lack nutrients compared to the leaves of northern hemisphere imports, and in the recent past, they used to be burnt! This is yet more nonsense. Our indigenous detritus consumers and soil micro-organisms are already well adapted to the leaves of native plants, and to coping with fluctuations in the composition of their food supply.

A comprehensive report on leaf composition commissioned by the Australian Flora Foundation has shown exactly how typical leaves of native plants compare to one another (see Table 6 on page 35), and to those of introduced cultivated plants. High manganese content is one difference that stands out in comparison to European figures. Compost prepared from these leaves might therefore contribute excessive manganese, particularly in soils that are too acid. However, the chemistry of manganese is more complex than that of magnesium or iron (Leeper and Uren, 1993), and in practice, this manganese accumulation in leaves of native species does not appear to present a significant problem for the gardener.

Silky oak (*Grevillea robusta*) leaves break down very well on their own, or mixed with horse manure. They are shed abundantly in early spring, often still green, which means they retain higher contents of nitrogen, potassium, magnesium, phosphorus and sulfur than when the leaves have died and turned brown before shedding. Batches of these leaves kept for about one year provide ideal mulch for the root zones around fruit trees (see Figure 78). Flame trees (*Brachychiton acerifolium*) also shed their leaves just before flowering in October to November, sometimes completely. These are thin leaves (see Figure 24), little changed in 50 million years according to the fossil record, and they break down more rapidly than *Grevillea* leaves. I would expect flame tree leaves to resemble the kurrajong (see Table 6 on page 35), so they would not have a high manganese content, and could be richer in silica than many of the other native species that have been analysed.

Flower parts, especially the showy stamens, fall from eucalypts and acacias in vast quantities throughout spring. All of this material may be had by sweeping and raking. Thin bark peels from growing eucalypts from midsummer onwards. When damp, it breaks up easily by hand. Use some for mulching around ornamental or fruit trees, but mince the rest with the mower when the lawn is mown, and add it pre-mixed with grass clippings to the compost heap. Throughout spring and summer, higher ambient temperatures contribute to acceleration in breakdown rates, and this is the most productive stage of the year for compost formation.

Add crushed egg shells, snail shells and cicada cases (see Figure 32) to the heap, or to the garden directly. The egg and snail shells are effectively limestone, and provide a little more calcium. The chitinous cicada cases release chitosans, active against some pathogenic fungi. There is no need to add crushed rock preparations, including rock phosphate, to the compost heap. These are better employed directly in the garden bed. Never add seaweed.

It will take forever to break down, and apart from concerns about sodium content, it will certainly contribute too much iodine, which above 1 part per million is toxic to many plants. Add horse manure only if you have a reliable supply, free of sawdust or wood shavings, and after initial ageing (see Chapter 4).

By all means add human or animal hair picked up with a carpet sweeper around the house, plus any disused cobwebs from odd corners, or stray feathers. These discarded forms of protein will boost the available nitrogen. So, too, will old seeds that have been kept too long in a cupboard or drawer. Clean them out, and put them all in the compost heap. Throw in worn out coir doormats, cane baskets and bristle broom heads. Everything organic can be composted, given enough space and time, but do not put in meat scraps, fish heads, prawn shells or dead birds and animals, or you will attract carrion flies, and the disapproval of your neighbours. Yes, there are authors who boast about putting dead foxes or other 'road kill' into their heaps. This is not to be encouraged. Dead animals, especially household pets, should be buried at a proper depth in suitable parts of the garden.

The compost heap as a habitat

How often do we read that the compost heap should be placed in a sunny position? On the contrary, the heap should be positioned to avoid direct sun for as much of the day as possible, and it should be sprayed with water to keep the surface moist if the weather is hot and dry. A partial, temporary cover is sometimes useful to keep off strong winds or rain. Do not put the heap against a wooden fence though, as the palings will become part of the compost.

The heap should be rearranged with the gloved hand from time to time, loosening around any sticks or twigs to maintain aeration. When compost is needed, mine carefully from the edges into mature regions with a trowel, putting worms and other occupants back if they are accidentally removed. I use a sieve, shaking gently, so that worms are not abraded. Material that is slowest to decompose, such as sticks, stems and the bases of fishbone fern, should be covered again by material that will break down faster. But there is no need to cover the heap with soil, or turn it over frantically every few days, disrupting and killing the occupants unnecessarily. Set it up properly and then forget about it except for routine maintenance and withdrawals.

Keep the height of the heap between 70 centimetres and 1 metre, and allow the same distance across. These dimensions are less than those suggested by Sir Albert Howard (5 ft high by 5–10 ft across) because the aim should be to avoid any anaerobic breakdown leading to methane production. The surface area to volume ratio should be regulated with this in mind. When in doubt, begin another heap. The unadorned, uncovered heap, or barrow, according to length, blends naturally with a garden environment. This is more than can be said of the concrete, brick and wooden constructions for composting that are often advertised.

Why would anyone suggest putting concrete or bricks under or around their compost heap? Containment like this impedes aeration, promotes odour and restricts access to useful feeders. Relying only on fungi and bacteria, the overall process will slow down. Contact with the ground allows a variety of earthworms to move in. Both native and introduced worms are likely to be attracted. The most obvious native worm in the Illawarra region, *Didymogaster sylvaticus*, reaches a length of 8 centimetres, is as thick as a finger in diameter, and has a habit of squirting when disturbed. The compost heap is the original worm farm, and authentic compost should always receive a useful quota of worm casts during its development.

The compost heap is a special habitat, promoting biodiversity in its own way. It is the right place in the garden for springtails, slaters and millipedes, arthropods that find concealment by day and food by night. Thousands of tiny mouths will accomplish quietly what a raucous shredder might begin — a reduction in surface area to volume ratio. The waste products from detritus feeders will then be passed on to the microbial links in the chain of decay.

Leopard slugs (*Limax maximus*), which can reach a length of at least 15 centimetres, are detritus eaters and scavengers, and will soon frequent the heap at night (see Figure 28). Although an introduced species, they are spectacular, and less of a nuisance in gardens than the plainer kinds of slug. Vivid red mites (*Bryobia cristata*), large enough to be seen with the naked eye, normally frequent leaf litter and the compost heap, and they do no harm to garden plants. This species is not to be confused with the much smaller *Bryobia rubrioculus*, a pest of pome fruit, plum and almond trees.

Assorted predators, such as the centipede (*Ethmostigmus rubripes*, see Figure 29), and scarce Australian native snails such as *Thersites novae-hollandiae*, may also be found occasionally in the compost heap (see Figure 31). Take care to avoid being bitten by the centipedes. Wear gloves, and do not overreact by trying to kill them — just leave them alone. They are supposed to eat slugs. At times when the surface of the heap is brown rather than green, various moths also seek shelter, doubtless because of the camouflage provided.

So by not doing most of the things Sir Albert Howard did, we have arrived at a much closer imitation of nature. The simpler method of preparing a compost heap described here

mimics the mallee fowl or the brush turkey, Australian megapod birds whose successful egg incubation depends on getting the temperature of their heaps just right. According to research reviewed by Vincent Serventy (1966), the male mallee fowl can sense the temperature by inserting his tongue. The male birds decrease the temperature by opening up the heaps and scratching in sand, keeping them close to the optimum of 33°C. The temperature requirements of a backyard compost heap are very flexible, and not as stringent as they are for these birds. The outermost layers do not need to exceed the temperatures of the cut-grass envelopes added from time to time between spring and autumn (see below).

What about weeds?

Concern is often expressed about the possible spread of weeds from cut seed heads put into compost and later dispersed around the garden. However, there is no need to exclude weed seeds, such as those of wild oats (*Avena fatua*), small shivery grass (*Briza minor*) or African veldt grass (*Ehrharta erecta*) included with mown grass. These seeds cannot survive the elevated temperatures that occur whenever freshly cut grass is added as a top layer to the heap. This is not mere assertion, but reliable experience.

Measuring this increase with a thermometer (see Figure 27), I found that the temperature of a barrow-load of grass cut one summer evening had risen from 25°C on cutting to 40°C only four hours later. It then climbed overnight to 48°C, fluctuating in the range 48–51°C for most of the next day. The temperature then reached 53°C after 24 hours, staying in the range 54–55°C for the next 11 hours. It ranged between 53°C and 50°C for another 30 hours before descending gradually. What seeds could possibly survive three days of slow cooking like this? Any on the very top surface are likely to be covered next time the grass is cut.

More abundant garden weeds such as carrot weed (*Cotula australis*) and privet plants (*Ligustrum species*) arise from the droppings of birds that pass overhead, while others like moth vine (*Araujia hortorum*) or fleabane (*Conyza* species, see Figure 83) develop from seeds that are blown in. Weed introductions are negligible from aged compost that is produced in the way described here.

Nevertheless, there are some weeds that should not be composted without preliminary treatment. If bulbs and bulbils of onion weed (*Nothoscordum gracile*, see Figures 79 and 82), or the corms of the pink-flowered *Oxalis latifolia* are dug up, they should be squashed underfoot, not just thrown on top of the heap. The best time to attack these weeds is autumn, when they resprout after a period of dormancy. The removal of onion weed requires persistence over a period of years. I have seen presenters on television using a paintbrush to dab onion weeds with glyphosate. Should you be tempted to use this herbicide, you will find that the onion weed is resistant (see Figure 80).

If mats of the shade-tolerant, white-flowered creeper *Tradescantia albiflora* are raked up (see Figure 81), they should not be left to dry out on the ground or be put into the compost either. Fragments of this plant can survive for up to two years in leaf litter and then generate new plants. The simplest way to deal with this *Tradescantia* is to drown it. Place the runners in a bucket, weigh them down with a brick, submerge with water, then cover the bucket with a loose lid to block light. After two weeks the *Tradescantia* stems are totally dead, and the contents of the bucket minus the brick can be poured safely around any fruit tree. Squashing and drowning are two simple physical methods that can be applied generally to any problem plants likely to grow again if just thrown onto a heap.

Coffee and tea

The tea plant is *Camellia sinensis*. Australians used to be a nation of tea drinkers, and my father always tipped the used tea leaves onto mint and rhubarb. Some plants may not appreciate such treatment, and to play safe, tea leaves and teabags can certainly be composted. If you prefer chamomile or other herbal teas, the extracted leaves are a worthwhile addition to the heap. The massive flower-drop from ornamental camellias in autumn, winter and spring is also a valuable source of compostable material.

Most of the world's coffee comes from seeds of *Coffea arabica*. Even after extraction, coffee grounds are a valuable boost to compost (see Figure 22) because of their high residual contents of nitrogen (more than 1 per cent) and phosphorus (about 1 per cent). The grounds with their filter paper can be submerged in the heap. Alternatively, with the popular move to plungers, it is an easy matter to rinse these outside, throwing the suspension of grounds onto the compost heap, or directly onto the garden. Do not allow fine coffee grounds to concentrate in one place, however, as crusts may form that repel water. Keep them well mixed with the surface material in a pot or garden.

As an extra benefit, coffee grounds can act as a deterrent to cutworms, which are caterpillars that hide just under the soil surface by day, destroying seedlings by night. Australian cutworms include caterpillars of the bogong moth (*Agrotis infusa*), which migrates in large numbers in the summer (McMaugh, 1991).

To avoid tea and coffee produced with the aid of pesticides, buy organic products through Oxfam or Trade Winds Tea and Coffee Pty Ltd (see Useful Addresses). Some excellent coffees grown on the north coast of New South Wales without pesticides are also widely available.

4.
Preparing the soil

'In the sweat of your brow shall you eat bread ...'

Genesis 3:19

Planning and digging

When we purchase an existing house with its gardens, much of the hard work in deciding which plants to put where has already been done. Even so, there is always scope for revision, and for adding gardens where none existed before.

I have done this with two homes, first in Melbourne, Victoria (1971–79), then in Wollongong, New South Wales (1979 onwards). In both instances, vegetable gardens were lacking, and the 'baseline' soil had been derived from indifferent Quaternary alluvial deposits.

The long axis of a garden bed or series of terraces (see Figure 33) should be approximately north–south, and the bed should be positioned to capture enough full sunlight for the successful growth of the chosen plants. For convenience it should not be too wide, so that the centre is within arm's length of either side. It does not have to be perfectly rectangular. A bed can be lozenge-shaped, or curved on any boundary. Some can be circular. Suit yourself according to the spaces available, and if a position proves to be unsatisfactory, keep trying. The very first vegetable bed I prepared on the western boundary of my current garden was ultimately given over to agapanthus, recovered from the old chook pen, plus sundry native shrubs.

To dig over a garden bed from an established lawn, the simplest preliminary softening-up treatment is to shade the area with old carpet or boards, or flattened cartons held down by bricks for several weeks. It is not necessary to treat the area with a herbicide, or worse still, a compound like methyl bromide, as recommended by Peter Bennett (1988). Methyl bromide is a compound that is organic in name only. A recognised carcinogen, its horticultural applications have been phased out worldwide. Methyl bromide converts living soil to dead soil. No organic gardener worthy of the accolade would ever have considered using such a noxious chemical.

Before digging the proposed garden area, make sure the soil is moist enough not to raise dust with every movement. Then dig, turning every spade-full, removing all grass plants and runners, which should be gathered, chopped and composted. Even with established beds there is no escape from digging. Pretending to imitate nature by dropping organic matter on top of the ground is a superficial approach in every sense. Yes, this is 'natural' in a forest habitat, but this is the wrong context for a garden, where a much greater depth of enriched soil is required, and disturbance is necessary to obtain this depth rapidly. A 'ruderal' or rubbish-tip context is the right one for vegetables.

So-called 'no-dig' or 'instant garden' methods are more trouble than they are worth, and they are dishonest as well. I have actually read 'no-dig' instructions that begin: 'first dig over the soil that will form the base of the garden'! The serious disadvantages of not digging are legion. Sources of specific nutrients or pH-adjusting materials such as lime or ash cannot be mixed adequately, resulting in substantial sub-optimal zones for nutrient uptake, and consequent deficiencies. No-dig gardens may sometimes look good enough to photograph, but just wait until the wind blows. Because of prior soil compaction, root systems cannot extend to a proper depth, leaving plants with inadequate support once tested by the weather. Waterlogging is more likely, too. Newspaper, the bottom layer in many no-dig formulae, has already been stripped of most of its nutritive value, and contributes heavy metals such as antimony from the print. Sheet mulches like newspaper or sawdust subtract nitrogen while they break down, and assist pathogenic fungi. Straw, pinebark chips or other plant remains left on top can hide slugs and harbour diseases, and their exudates inhibit seed germination or seedling growth. Fungal spores released from mouldy mulches can trigger attacks of hayfever and asthma. Why court this litany of disasters?

The time-honoured practice of digging garden beds should not be dispensed with lightly. The advantages of digging were discovered by our Stone Age ancestors. The oldest digging implements that have been found so far include mattocks made of elk or red deer horn (c. 7500 BC), from Starr Carr in

northern England, and hoes made of flint (c. 7000 BC) from Russia (Mithen, 1998). We would not discard the wheel if someone suggested we now do without it, so why single out cultivation technology for such unwarranted revision?

Digging is splendid exercise, taken at whatever pace we are capable of, at any age. It is good for us, and good for the garden. The surface soil becomes compacted with the pelting of rain and the passage of time, but digging with a spade or a fork aerates the top layer, breaking crusts and releasing compaction. The tendency of soils to sediment vertically, forming a clay-rich lower horizon, is interrupted. Routine digging with a spade around the edges of a bed also allows us to intercept and detach the feeding roots of nearby trees or vines that would surreptitiously take away the nutrients intended for vegetables. Without digging, we might never know about clandestine root competition.

Always choose a spade or fork of appropriate size and the best available workmanship. The spade I have used since 1971 is only 1 metre long, has a small rectangular stainless steel blade, and is perfectly balanced in the haft, just above the blade. It is used a little, and often. There is no need for intermittent heroics with an oversize shovel that will leave you in the hands of a chiropractor.

Digging and cultivating also bring to the surface dormant weed seeds, providing the exposure to light that many need for their dormancy to be overcome. Allow these seeds to germinate and then dig the seedlings under. Treat them as a very short-term 'green manure' (see page 48). A trowel will often do. The depth of this second digging does not have to be as great as the initial depth, which should generally be about 60 centimetres. Do not attempt to gain this depth all at once if clay is being brought to the surface. It is much better to increase the depth of useful soil gradually, with once-only additions of gypsum and sand, followed by compost and manure over several years. A bed that is dug fairly often is much easier to dig than one that is neglected, and rarely is there any need to dig over the whole bed at once.

Animal manures

Manures, like composts, require patience. Always keep animal manure for about two months before applying it directly to the garden. Although the nitrogen content becomes less on storage, there are several reasons why manures should not be applied when absolutely fresh. First, young seedlings may find the nitrogen content excessive, and this will burn the leaves. If the seedlings happen to be legumes, their roots will not be able to form nitrogen-fixing nodules, and this will slow their growth and reduce the yield of pods later on.

Second, fresh manures will precipitate a number of problems for specific plants, such as forking of the roots in carrots and parsnips, and rotting of iris rhizomes or strawberry roots. The flavour of some plants can be altered; for instance, the leaves of rocket (*Eruca sativa*) are detrimentally affected by fresh manure (Fanton and Fanton, 1993). Third, intact weed seeds contained in the manure, such as those of onion weed (*Nothoscordum gracile*), will germinate. This fact was much better appreciated in the past, and according to Maiden (1920): 'Unless such manure is very carefully rotted, it always contains seeds of weeds, which flourish exceedingly'.

Finally, stable manures may initially contain high concentrations of drugs administered to control parasites, such as ivermectin. These drugs are also toxic to earthworms. They need time to break down, so that horse manure will not have an adverse effect on local garden worm populations. This is also the reason that fresh animal manures should not be added directly to the general compost heap. Keep them in separate heaps or containers. By putting horse manure in a loosely covered tray that is open to the ground, worms can gain entry. When the manure contains a population of healthy earthworms, it is certainly ready to be added to the garden.

It used to be possible to collect manure in the wake of passing horses, but increasing urbanisation has restricted the places where horses are now kept, and moved them farther from the centres of population. Be on the lookout for riding clubs or racetracks and stables. West of Sydney, between Luddenham and Richmond, horse manure is still readily obtainable and sold by the bag. Horse manure is worth seeking out, because the benefits of a single application last longer than one year.

Mushroom compost

Spent mushroom composts may seem attractive, but remember that the mushrooms have already removed much of the nutritive value represented by the original base medium. This used to be animal manure with some straw (Hurley, 1956), but according to *Good Fruit and Vegetables* (Vol. 9, No. 5, October 1998, page 9), the substrate now consists of 'wheat straw direct from wheat farms or stables, and cotton hulls and meal'. Volume for volume, any pure animal manure is obviously much better value.

There are other reasons to shun mushroom compost. The mushroom fungus (*Agaricus bisporus*) will out-compete more useful mycorrhizal fungi once this material is added to the soil, and may even proceed to produce new mushrooms. Furthermore, to initiate formation of the mushroom fruiting bodies, a nutrient-poor capping medium of clay-rich loam, or peat, would have been added over the substrate culture. Extra clay is probably not wanted in your garden, unless you have extremely sandy soil. Peat adds nothing to the mineral value of the compost, while representing unacceptable environmental damage in its extraction. Mushroom growers formerly used sandy loam as the capping medium, and with very little imagination they could devise an alternative medium from safe, renewable sources.

The adoption of cotton wastes for the substrate medium is disturbing, given the massive environmental damage that cotton-growing continues to cause, and the cocktail of pesticides likely to be in the waste. This is still so despite the reduction in pesticide use accompanying the adoption of genetically modified cotton varieties that express Bt-proteins. But this substitution is not surprising, given the copious amounts of 'cotton compost' now being marketed. The replacement of manure in this way will reduce the vitamin B_{12} content of the mushrooms, and is probably the reason for the increased cadmium content detected in Sydney Market mushrooms (see page 44). However, it is not necessary to give up eating mushrooms altogether. Healthy home-grown mushrooms can still be produced in the conventional way, with a compost prepared from fresh horse or cow manure plus straw, and a capping medium of soil (Hurley, 1956; de Vaus, 1976).

Applying compost and manures

The preparation of compost has been discussed in Chapter 3. When compost is ready for use, it is brown, with a soft, crumbly texture, and practically no smell. Whatever faint scent it does have should be attractive and earthy, not repulsive.

When applying composts and aged manures, aim to blend them into the soil so that the resulting mixture is as homogeneous as possible. It is a fallacy that these additions need to be placed in concentrated bands directly under the planting rows, so that the seedlings do not have to search too far afield for what they need from the soil. With a proper blending, each plant will develop a very effective root system that facilitates the uptake of nutrients, usually in cooperation with fungi and bacteria, as described earlier. The more extensive the root systems, the better the stability and long-term productivity of the plants.

Be generous with composts or aged manures. Put out a layer 5 centimetres or so deep before digging and mixing. Do not wait too long before doing this because manures will develop a hard crust if they are allowed to dry out, then they have to be coaxed back to a hydrated state. Cow manure is much worse in this respect than horse manure. Finally, rake the soil to remove any loose weeds, pebbles or large pieces of leaf or bark that might conceal small slugs. The whole garden bed should now have enough material in it to be raised well above the surrounding lawn or paths, and before planting, it should be kept reasonably moist. Surround your garden with rocks or solid edging if you prefer to, noting that there is some concern about wood treated with copper-chromium-arsenate, because of leaching. A solid border provides support for groundcover herbs spreading from the edge, or for strawberries. But wherever kikuyu grass (*Pennisetum clandestinum*) or couch grass (*Cynodon dactylon*) is abundant in the lawn, it is simpler to retain the option of chopping the runners off with the spade at the garden edge.

Providing extra phosphorus

The faeces of birds are much richer in phosphorus than the manures of most large herbivorous animals, where phosphorus content is generally about 0.3 per cent. The value of bird droppings was realised long ago by the Inca peoples, who removed guano deposited on rocks by seabirds and transported it from the coastline to the mountains and the inland valleys where food plants were grown. The Incas were expert at restoring or building up soil fertility, and in their calendar had a special month set aside for digging and manuring the soil. Digging tools such as the foot-plow (*chaquitakla*), developed and used over thousands of years in the Andes, are still used today (Ableman, 1993).

Most substantial guano deposits have long ago been mined out, not by the Incas but by fertiliser companies, in order to make superphosphate. One result of prolonged superphosphate application on pastures and in food-growing regions of Australia is high residual soil cadmium content. This is now reflected in higher than acceptable cadmium concentrations in some root vegetables and mushrooms (Plowman, Ahmad and Bower, 1998). Another unintended result has been an increase in the content of soil phosphorus unavailable to plants. The common ability of soils to immobilise added mineral nutrients in the absence of adequate organic content has not been widely appreciated until recently, but the use of superphosphate in soils with abundant organic content should not present a problem. I used to grow peas for research purposes in soil amended with measured quantities of a supplement including superphosphate and micronutrients, but since 1986 I have used a phosphorus-rich fertiliser derived from poultry manure instead. Dynamic Lifter is a dried, pelletised preparation that is very easy to handle, hygienic and reasonably priced, especially as a 35 kilogram pack. Its composition is given in Table 7.

Dynamic Lifter will help to counteract soil acidity, because a suspension in water has a pH close to 7 (see next page). In parallel to

TABLE 7. THE COMPOSITION OF DYNAMIC LIFTER (MINIMUM ANALYSIS) AS AT OCTOBER 2004 (% BY WEIGHT)[1]		
Nutrient		%
Nitrogen		3.5
Phosphorus	water soluble	0.4
	citrate soluble	1.5
	citrate insoluble	0.5
	Total P:	2.4
Potassium		1.6
Sulfur		1.0
Calcium		5.4
Iron		0.2
Manganese		0.05
Zinc		0.03

1. Dynamic Lifter is also stated to contain less than 1 mg per kg of cadmium, less than 0.2 mg per kg of mercury, and less than 20 mg per kg of lead.

concerns about administered drugs contaminating horse manure, it is rumoured that some poultry farmers use excessive quantities of antibiotics. However, the amounts left after processing are unlikely to persist for long in a well-prepared garden soil. Because Dynamic Lifter is more concentrated than fresh poultry manure, it should be used sparingly and often, rather than tipped in once or twice a year (unless you are preparing pots for legumes, when once per crop is sufficient). The manufacturer's recommendation is 100 grams per square metre before planting, then the same again at six-weekly intervals. Many people are inclined to forget about the follow-up applications, so this six-week interval becomes much longer in practice. Home gardeners are often unfairly blamed for phosphorus-rich run-off that contaminates local waterways, but it is rarely the home gardener who is at fault. Currently, it is the turf farmers who are creating major phosphorus run-off and eutrophication problems, because they apply massive layers of poultry manure as their sole fertiliser.

Very few people today keep their own poultry. If you keep caged birds like budgerigars, then the cage rinsings can be directed to composts or gardens. If you happen to live near a racing-pigeon fancier, it is worthwhile asking to purchase pigeon wastes. Alternatively, if you have enough trees in your garden, you will be able to attract birds, and rake the naturally limed areas beneath their favourite roosting or nesting positions into a valuable phosphorus-rich dressing. Make sure it is buried about 10 centimetres deep to reduce problems with weed seeds.

Adjusting pH

The pH is a conventional measure of acidity or alkalinity, with a value of 7 representing neutral. The numeral is the negative logarithm of the hydrogen ion or proton concentration. It is important to remember that each unit represents a tenfold difference in concentration, so a soil at pH 5 has a hundred times the hydrogen ion concentration of a soil at pH 7. Slightly acid soils, in the range between pH 6 and pH 7, will suit almost all common garden plants. Even if their exact optimum is outside this range, most herbs and vegetables will manage sufficiently well in this vicinity. Some of the plants that require a decidedly acid pH are listed in Table 8. Ryan (1991) stated that tomato, pepper and potato should all be grown 'below 5.6', but this general advice is incorrect. Although belonging to the same family as potato (Solanaceae), tomato, sweet pepper and eggplant should all be grown in the range pH 6 to pH 7. The

TABLE 8. GARDEN PLANTS THAT REQUIRE SOIL WITH AN ACID pH

Plant	pH range
Camellia	4.5–5.5
Erica	4.5–6.0
Gardenia	4.5–5.5
Magnolia	5.0–6.0
Fuchsia	5.5–6.5
Oriental lily	5.0–6.0
Cranberry	4.5–5.5
Blueberry	4.5–5.5
Potato	4.5–6.0
Sweet potato	4.5–5.5
Hydrangea (with blue flowers)	4.5–5.5
Iris ensata (Japanese iris)	5.5–6.0

precise optimum for tomato is pH 6 to pH 6.5 (Gould, 1983).

Although superphosphate is often blamed for making soils too acid, the acidification on solution is transient, balanced afterwards by other reactions (Kennedy, 1992). Ammonium salts are far more acidic, because the conversion of ammonium ions to nitrate by soil bacteria releases hydrogen ions, then nitrate has to be taken up and assimilated by plants in order for hydroxyl ions to partly balance this acidity. If nitrate is leached away, plants do not get the opportunity to make this adjustment, and soils can become overly acid. Irrigated fruit trees in New South Wales and Victoria subjected to annual applications of ammonium sulfate at 1.25 tonnes per hectare suffered a decline in yields as the soil pH was lowered from 7 to 5 (Leeper and Uren, 1993). Don Burke (1983) described an extreme case of ammonium sulfate abuse — a gardener who had top-dressed his lawn with nothing but ammonium sulfate for 15 years. The soil where the grass had struggled was measured at pH 3, while that in an adjacent garden receiving run-off was pH 4.

If your soil needs to be made acid to suit plants such as those listed in Table 8, there are several additives commonly used. Iron sulfate and aluminium sulfate are often recommended for shifting the colour of hydrangeas from pink to blue. Powdered sulfur is also very good, and following Stan Peck (1974), I have used this at a rate of 85 grams per square metre to correct a potting mix for oriental lilies where I had inadvertently included Dynamic Lifter. A single application of fine powder dug loosely into the top 5 centimetres of soil was sufficient to remove all signs of nutrient deficiency.

Soils usually need adjustment in the alkaline direction to correct moderate over-acidity. Applications of wood ash, rich in potassium, or lime, limestone (calcium carbonate), or dolomite, which is magnesium-calcium carbonate, are all useful for making these alterations. Ash and lime are stronger than limestone and dolomite. Apply any one of these carefully, no more than twice a year. Ash was once used more extensively in the garden than now, and to feed his roses, Rossi (1930) would avidly collect the same materials to burn that I would compost or bury. The easiest way to apply ash is as a slurry. Suspend about 400 grams (one baked-bean can full) in about 9 litres of water in a bucket. Use an open container to distribute the suspension at the base of your plants rather than a watering-can, which will block up.

It is crucial not to have a soil pH that is extremely acid (less than pH 4.5) or even moderately alkaline (above pH 8), because many nutrients are then 'locked up' and made unavailable, even though their apparent concentrations might appear to be adequate. Extremely acid soils would impose a deficiency of most nutrients, while permitting toxic

amounts of iron to be taken up. At the other extreme, an alkaline soil inhibits the uptake of most trace elements. Furthermore, an alkaline soil that becomes waterlogged loses its nitrate, not just from leaching, but also because certain soil bacteria reduce it in place of oxygen, releasing nitrogen oxides and nitrogen gas (Davidson and Davidson, 1993).

Never apply too much pH-adjusting material. The 'inorganic' view that calcium has to come from calcium salts like lime or limestone in order for plants to get enough is thoroughly mistaken. You would make the pH too high trying to provide enough calcium in this way. Calcium should come mainly from compost and manures, by virtue of the large amounts combined in plant cell walls as calcium pectate.

To check soil pH, there are inexpensive kits available that rely on the colour change of an indicator dye. The dye can be in solution, or lodged in indicator papers. These kits are sufficiently accurate for the purpose. Probes are also available.

Mineral fertilisers

For healthy plant growth there must be enough of every one of the essential nutrients (see Table 4 on page 28), but there is considerable flexibility in the make-up of the total intake of anions. To get gardens started, it is reasonable to apply inorganic formulations such as Yates' Gro-Plus and Brunning's Complete Australian Gardener Mixture, while these are still available. In the future, when sources of ingredients become scarcer, it may well be a different matter. The salts of sulfates in these mixtures represent a worthwhile use of sulfur dioxide, recovered from coal-fired electricity generation and other industrial processes as sulfuric acid. This outlet is far better than if sulfur dioxide were simply allowed to pollute the atmosphere, contributing to respiratory illness and mortality in cities, and destruction of nearby vegetation from 'acid rain'.

Do not hesitate to correct underlying soil nutrient deficiencies. If plants are not growing as fast as they should, and the early leaves turn uniformly yellow, it is likely that there is a shortage of nitrogen, sulfur (see Figure 21) or potassium. If plants show yellowing of early leaves while the veins stand out green in relief (see Figure 34), suspect a magnesium deficiency. Clovers are good indicators of magnesium deficiency, often showing a pinkish colour in the yellow zones extending inwards from the margins of each leaflet (Millikan, 1984). Once the pH has been shown to be satisfactory, apply Epsom salts (magnesium sulfate), or Hortico Trace Elements or the equivalent to cover other possibilities as well. At a recommended rate of 25 grams (a dessert-spoonful) per square metre, Hortico advises that 'one application will last for several years'. In fact, one application at this rate may be all that is ever needed. Once compost is available and applied continually, supplements of this kind may never be needed again.

Chemical supplements should always be used sparingly, as the aim is to establish a balance, rather than trigger toxicity from any excesses, or impose artificial shortages by overwhelming competition; for instance, too much zinc or manganese can impose an iron deficiency. Be especially careful when growing legumes. Ammonium sulfate or phosphate should never be used as a supplement when growing peas or beans, not just because of the acidity generated, but because nitrate derived from the ammonium ions in the soil may suppress the formation of nitrogen-fixing nodules on their roots, leaving the plants nitrogen-deficient at later stages of growth. This is exactly the same reason why fresh manures are damaging to legumes.

With the appearance of biosolids from more complete sewage treatment, and Dynamic Lifter as organic sources of nutrients rich in phosphorus, inorganic formulations are already receding in importance for the home gardener. Nevertheless, using inorganic mixtures for remediation has always been acceptable from an organic perspective. Sir Albert Howard incorporated rock phosphate into his composts. Using rock phosphate directly is no different in principle from using superphosphate, which is derived from rock phosphate by treatment with sulfuric acid. Many people who oppose its use do not realise that superphosphate is a source of calcium and sulfur, as well as phosphorus (see Glossary). Do not ignore the potential benefits of superphosphate as a slow-release source of sulfur. It is not the use of superphosphate per se that has created major problems in Australian agriculture and horticulture, but the overuse, especially in the absence of sufficient organic matter in the soil.

Preparations of ground rock or mineral-rich sands are also available. Robert Rodale (1971) described the effects of 'greensand', which was rich in iron, magnesium and potassium, and could improve soils that had too much sand, as well as soils that had too much clay. It was derived from marine deposits, and may well have been exhausted by now. The widespread use of such marls began following a geological survey involving Dr George H. Cook, the first Professor of Chemistry at Rutgers University (1854–88). The popularity of such fertilisers was enhanced by results obtained at the New Jersey Agricultural Experiment Station, which commenced under Dr Cook's guidance.

Quarry dust has been used as a mineral fertiliser from at least Roman times. Crushed granitic and other rocks have good contents of potassium, calcium, magnesium and iron. Louise Riotte (1974) recommended crushed granite as a fertiliser for grapevines. A crushed rock preparation has been promoted in Australia under the name 'Alroc'. The No. 1 mix has good contents of phosphate, as well as the abovementioned elements, but has excessive manganese, and very little sulfur. Crushed rock preparations will benefit soil, but only in the long term, in the same way as the minerals that already comprise the parent soil particles. They will be dissolved by plant roots and their attached mycorrhizae very slowly. It is commonly believed that all inorganic additions will be more rapidly available to plants than organic materials. This is not so. Do not expect immediate miraculous improvement in plant growth just from adding Alroc to the soil at 30 grams per square metre. Such preparations are most beneficial if the organic content is built up at the same time. Add some powdered sulfur, superphosphate or pure gypsum as well, to compensate for Alroc's lack of sulfate minerals.

Green manures

Growing your own 'green manure' is the cheapest method of adding extra nitrogen to the soil on the first occasion when a garden bed is planted. Because legumes host nitrogen-fixing bacteria in nodules on their roots, they have an in-built supply of assimilated nitrogen that makes them independent of the low nitrate content of an impoverished soil. The incorporation of whole legumes into the soil improves both the general organic content and the available nitrogen content, which will benefit any non-legumes that grow next.

Vetches, lupins, peas, medics or clovers can be grown for this purpose. Flowering is a convenient stage at which to interrupt growth, since most of an annual legume's nitrogen fixation has occurred by then. Chop finely, as the fragments should be sufficiently small and well mixed with the soil for breakdown of plant proteins and nucleic acids to occur uniformly and quickly. It should be possible to maximise the nitrogen available to the next plants by putting them in about three weeks after digging in the legume crop. This practice has been widely adopted for more than a century, ever since the precise function of root nodules was discovered in the late 1880s. Rossi (1930) recommended that red clover be grown as a green manure, preferably over two seasons, to rejuvenate 'tired' rose beds. Before chemical fertilisers were used routinely for sugar cane in Australia, cow peas were grown just to provide a nitrogen source for the cane crop. What a good idea.

Immature legume pods from which the peas or beans have been shelled are still rich in organic forms of nitrogen, and provided they are free of disease, they too make excellent green manure. Plants that are not legumes can also be dug in — for example, young weeds — but there is no gain in nitrogen by doing this. Some authors recommend buckwheat or herbs like yarrow, comfrey or borage as green manure crops, in the mistaken belief that they can increase the soil's content of phosphorus or other mineral nutrients. This proposition is sheer hocus-pocus, the kind that Justus von Liebig would have enjoyed debating. It is impossible for these plants to return more phosphorus to the soil than they took out while growing — unless some bird has generously splattered their leaves.

The main reason to avoid using plants other than legumes as green manure relates to the nitrogen requirement of the micro-organisms taking part in the breakdown of the newly chopped-up plant material. Some of this nitrogen is ultimately lost again to the atmosphere. When legumes are used there is plenty of nitrogen, little of which was in the soil before the legume was grown, so microbial withdrawal or 'draw down' is not a significant loss. But with non-legumes, any loss of nitrogen does matter, because it is subtracted from what was in the soil before the green manure crop was grown. So why go backwards? Forget about non-leguminous green manures.

What about seaweed?

Like comfrey, seaweed has a cult-following bordering on the fanatic. But the limitations of seaweeds were well described by gardening writers in the 1940s, and it is difficult to understand why so many 'organic' gardening gurus today are so enthralled. Apart from smelling obnoxious, seaweed can be guaranteed to deprive the soil of nitrogen during its lengthy breakdown, and to drive the pH too low. Another very good reason for leaving it on the shoreline is that its composition more closely reflects the saline medium in which it grew. Certainly, 'the ocean is the world's greatest storehouse of minerals' (Carson, 1951), but there is far too much sodium in seaweed for it to be used habitually on valuable garden beds. Although some sodium is needed by cultivated plants, this amount is small compared with the need for potassium (see Table 4 on page 28 and Table 6 on page 35). And the iodide content of a dried seaweed preparation has been measured at 1700 parts per million (Balfour, 1975).

The extra sodium from seaweed is superfluous, as there is plenty in the soil already. Sodium deficiency is not a condition likely to be encountered in Australia at all. In many inland regions, excessive removal of native vegetation has allowed the water table to rise, carrying salt into the surface soil, where it forms a visible crust. Estimates of land areas lost to salt are increasing exponentially week by week.

The coastal edge of Australia is well supplied with salt spray carried by the wind. This has the advantage of also providing soils with iodide (I^{-1}). This form of iodine contained in plant foods is essential to human health, as it is converted to hormones produced in the thyroid gland. However, the evidence that iodine is an essential nutrient for plants is inconclusive. Growth-stimulating effects of iodide up to one part per million have been reported for barley and tomato plants, but the same very low concentrations inhibit pea plants, and promote yellowing of their leaves and stipules (chlorosis).

With the occasional exception like beetroot, most herbs and vegetables are very sensitive to sodium chloride. Too much will cause stunting, chlorosis, necrosis (formation of dead patches within the leaves), leaf loss and death. In addition, most plants are also sensitive to sodium or potassium iodide at concentrations above one part per million. This is not very much. It is therefore unwise to add any sodium chloride or sodium iodide to garden soil that can be avoided. Seaweed as a source of both is eminently avoidable.

5.
Pots and containers

'You wanted to be surrounded by something
that wasn't just dust and dead leaves ...
The hot weather used to destroy any garden that you'd make ...
Of course the great thing was pots. We had pots and pots and
pots all along the edges of our verandahs.'

Lady Deborah Dring, *Plain Tales from the Raj* (Allen, 1975)

The advantages of pots

Having some plants in pots helps to make use of sunlit spaces on the tops of walls, beside paths, patios and verandahs, at the base of the rotary clothes-line, or in the shelter of trees, next to boundaries. The appearance of the garden and the approaches to the house can be made much more complex and interesting by using pots. Sometimes the more substantial cost of building a raised garden bed can be avoided. Single tomato or capsicum plants accompanied by smaller companions all suit large pots, those at least 30 centimetres in diameter and about the same depth (see Figure 37). Many dwarf or semi-vining beans that sprawl are better off in pots, so that their pods do not touch the soil. If garden space is limited, dwarf fruit trees may repay planting in pots, tubs or barrels.

Keeping varieties of the same plant separate is much easier in pots. This is what Mary Bennett wrote in response to reading this advice in my earlier book, *Growing Peas & Beans* (Murray, 1999): 'This may sound strange, but in all the years I've been seed-saving I have never thought of growing in pots. Just a simple idea like this has "transformed" me. With over 100 varieties to grow, I was really at a loss how to keep this up as I get older.'

Control of water supply and drainage are more certain in pots than in the open garden. Protection from drenching rain can be provided by putting spare pots upside-down over those containing young plants, especially overnight, when the lack of light makes no difference. Tending plants in pots is easier on the back, an important consideration with advancing age. The extra distance that snails and slugs have to cover in order to reach the leaves of plants in pots is also an advantage, giving extra time in which to intercept them.

Keeping certain plants in pots is an essential part of quarantine. For example, root-knot nematodes might affect only a single tomato plant, and this might not be apparent until the plant is pulled out at the end of the season (see Figure 38). The pot from which an infested plant came can be treated by sowing French marigold (*Tagetes patula*) or cobbler's peg (*Bidens pilosa*) — see Chapter 9. Incoming plants of any kind can be observed in relative isolation and checked before their accompanying soil or potting medium is irrevocably mixed with your own garden soil.

Many herbs are suitable for growing in pots, and for several reasons. First, special conditions can be catered for, such as plants being kept fairly dry, or at alkaline pH, or both. Herbs like salad burnet (*Sanguisorba minor*), which is found naturally on chalky soils, or narrow-leafed lavender (*Lavandula angustifolia*), from dolomitic soils, can have their soil pH moved to the correct higher range without this retarding the growth of neighbouring plants. Potentially invasive herbs like the mints can be confined. Runners going over the sides of pots are fairly obvious, and can be trimmed off to keep these plants in check. And lastly, having many smaller pots of plants such as pelargonium or basil gives greater flexibility in their disposition amongst larger pots of annual vegetables, especially dwarf beans or tomatoes, when there is a need to deter white fly (see Chapter 2). This is a far more attractive option than dangling yellow sticky traps everywhere, collecting the innocent as well as the guilty.

Camellias are acid-loving plants (see Table 8 on page 45) and their seedling stages are best moved through a series of pots. I have adapted the first medium suggested by Savell and Andrews (1982), as follows:

2 parts good garden soil
1 part compost
1 part coarse sand
1 part pulverised charcoal
1/2 part well-rotted cow manure.

Remember, though, that smaller pots may dry out faster, or heat up excessively in the sun. If they dry out unnoticed, the soil may repel water when this is next added, compounding the stress. Pots in this condition should be taken into the shade and stood in water in a saucer or bowl, as well as being soaked from above, to allow complete saturation once again. Some of the smaller plastic pots have a detachable transparent base to contain water, while the opaque upper compartment ends in a conical projection downwards, to act as a wick and conduct water slowly up into the medium. This helps to avoid the problems of drying out, as the level of remaining water is visible at a glance. These pots are still available second-hand, but unfortunately the manufacturer has stopped making new ones.

The choice of material

The material from which the pot is made is a very important factor in the choice of a pot. Inferior plastics that broke up after exposure to ultraviolet light have influenced many gardeners' attitudes to plastic. But modern flexible black plastic pots, made from polypropylene (recycling number 5), are well priced (about $3), and they will last 30 years or more. These plastic pots are generally preferable to terracotta because they are not porous, and lose much less water over the life of the plants. Injection-moulded plastic pots are lighter and stronger than terracotta, and less prone to fracture. They also require less energy to make, and so contribute much less to industrial carbon dioxide emissions. The drainage holes can be cut vertically into the wall of a plastic pot, as well as through the base, so these pots will actually drain even if the base is flush with a flat surface. Smaller pots are also being designed with uneven bases, so that drainage is possible under all circumstances.

The colour of the plastic is also important. Black is fine for winter-growing peas (see Figure 42) and cool-weather beans, when extra warming of the pot is helpful. But for plastic pots exposed to the summer sun, black is not appropriate because it absorbs heat too strongly. A lighter colour will help to reduce any heat stress to the root system, although in my experience, coloured pots are not as durable as black pots, and I have found it preferable to persevere with the black pots. Coloured pots made from ultraviolet-stabilised polyethylene may do better (Thomas, 2005).

There was a fad for concrete pots a while ago. They are still available, sometimes painted to resemble terracotta. Many are thick, awkward and cumbersome, heavier than terracotta, and so more difficult to move about. The great virtue of pots is their portability, and if that is taken away, the pot is not as useful as it would first appear to be. However, there are some new lighter pots available made from fibreglass and concrete (Thomas, 2005). These are about two-thirds the weight of fully concrete pots, and stronger. Some smaller concrete pots might suit the herbs that require an alkaline pH, certainly until they age and stop leaching alkali into the soil they contain. Besser masonry blocks with hollow spaces can be used inventively, too, and suitably arranged to form small herb gardens in the tops of walls.

Replaced concrete laundry tubs (double, with plugholes), and old overhead toilet cisterns, which have already been extensively rinsed in the course of their working lives, can readily be adapted for herbs such as mints (see Figure 35). Often their origin can be disguised

by positioning them behind other pots, unless you want to display your prowess in recycling. Forget about using sunken rusted-out buckets, however, because the open base is no challenge to any self-respecting mint.

Half-barrels, sliced and sold off by many wineries when the extraction of oak tannins by the enclosed wines is practically complete, are very useful as containers for small fruit trees. Made from either European or American oak, half-barrels are sturdy and long-lasting in the garden. Just make sure that the carpentry includes drilling holes for drainage through the bottom, otherwise you will have a water-garden.

Despite these various options there is a strong and persistent tradition matching authentic terracotta with herbs and ornamentals. The slight variations in colour of ageing terracotta cannot be duplicated by any alternative material, and many gardeners will continue to choose terracotta because it looks good. Appreciation of the craftsmanship involved in making the pot is one aspect of this preference. 'To have such a thing in my garden is a pleasure in itself', is how Trevor Nottle (1996) defends his handmade terracotta pots. A wide variety of individual pots in various square, rectangular or bowl shapes (see Figure 39) can be found, often with classic Greek and Roman decorations. Many have stubs or feet, which ensure that they will drain properly.

It is also possible to have the best of both worlds: the modern plastic with its water-saving potential, and ancient terracotta, with all its aesthetic appeal and associations. This can be done simply by standing the plants in plastic pots inside terracotta pots, and padding the gaps with coconut fibre. As an added bonus, this also provides extra insulation in the summer.

Terracotta strawberry pots, with four or more pockets, are very attractive. Herbs as well as strawberries can readily be grown in these pots, and they make excellent presents for the gardening friend or relative 'who has everything'. Any mutual antagonism among plantings would surely be noticeable, but most culinary herb combinations seem congenial. Some writers advise against including mints in such pots because of their aggression, and the fact that the mint will remain supreme when the annuals die off. It depends how much of each herb is likely to be needed. If a mint is to be included, rotate the pot so that the mint gets least direct sun, and be prepared to thin ruthlessly when harvesting.

Put the herbs requiring most water, such as basil, coriander, mint or Vietnamese mint, around the lowest pockets. Vietnamese mint (*Persicaria odorata*, Polygonaceae) belongs to a different family from ordinary mints (see Chapter 9), but nevertheless needs lots of water. The best way to plant in the pockets is not by insertion from outside after the pot is completely filled, but by threading the plant into the pocket from the inside while the pot is being filled, as recommended by Margaret Davis (1973). Fill, pack and water lightly between plantings, using the materials described in the next section. Chives, garlic chives (*Tulbaghia violacea*), with spectacular mauve flowers, or thyme will do very well in the central top position (see Figure 40) that drains more freely, and receives the most sunlight. Umbellifers (see Table 12 on page 81) are unsuitable for growing in strawberry pots, as they grow too tall when they eventually run to seed. When purchasing these pots, make sure that they do have a drainage hole cast into the centre of the base. Beware of unsaleable imports without a drainage hole.

Pots with the appearance of terracotta but with all the structural advantages of being plastic can also be purchased. Some have reservoirs in the base, with cut-away access from outside for refilling. The main disadvantage of these pots is that the water level is not visible. However, if the pots are sometimes watered from above, any surplus will drain through and be held in a position where it is available to the plants later on. More expensive replica pots come with concealed internal reservoirs and 'smart' valves that admit water only when the soil is dry. Consider these for featured fruit trees, such as kumquats, or dwarf forms of apples and stonefruits.

Getting pots ready

It is perfectly in order to use pots again and again. Basic cleanliness is all that is required — a scrubbing brush and a jet of water from the hose. It is pointless attempting to sterilise pots, given that they are going to contain a medium that hopefully will be teaming with all the microbial life-forms that contribute to healthy plant growth. My usual pot is the 30 centimetre size, holding about 15 litres of soil. This measurement refers to the uppermost internal diameter. This size allows seven pea seeds to be planted in a ring about 8 or 9 centimetres apart (see Figure 42). Put no more than four bean plants in a pot of this size, and only single plants of tomato, eggplant or capsicum. A larger pot, with upper internal diameter of 36.5 centimetres, can accommodate nine or ten pea plants.

Commence filling each pot by placing a piece of crock (broken terracotta pot) or a stone over each drainage hole, without completely blocking the hole. Follow this with clean gravel or smaller stones, or shed leaves that are not fully broken down, and a coarse, partly broken-down fraction sifted from the compost heap. At this point, decide whether to try a high-quality purchased potting mix (premium grade rather than regular), or your own soil enriched with fully developed compost, exactly as for the preparation of garden beds (see Chapter 4), and mix these components together as the pot is filled. Some garden soil should be added towards the top, with about 2 centimetres left unfilled.

As well as blending in some aged horse manure, a small quantity of Dynamic Lifter can be included, unless you are growing herbs that prefer soils that are not enriched in nitrogen, or plants that prefer an acid pH. Some vermiculite (exploded mica or magnesium silicate; see Figure 41) would be useful in this case, improving drainage and water-holding capacity, and breaking down very slowly. So-called 'water crystals' are short-lived by comparison. The name is a misnomer, like chicken 'nuggets'. 'Water crystals' are not crystals at all, but fragments of desiccated polyacrylamide gel, with an unknown content of carcinogenic acrylamide monomer. Labels do not reveal the identity of the 'crystals', and falsely claim that the product is safe. The only warning is to 'keep out of the reach of children'! This material is useful in the laboratory for electrophoretic analysis, and should be kept there. But polyacrylamide is too dangerous, too expensive and too ineffective to be recommended for potting media.

Another worthwhile option is to add some Sungro sterile rice husks (bracts). Like vermiculite, they have good porosity and break down slowly, but they are organic in composition, and a renewable by-product of rice-grain harvesting. Currently more than 100 000 tonnes of Sungro rice husks are being produced per annum.

If Dynamic Lifter is to be included in the mixture, and this is recommended before planting peas or beans, blend it in well, and allow about three weeks to pass before planting. Under no circumstances use any fresh manure or other fertiliser very high in nitrogen content, such as ammonium sulfate.

Water the filled pot, and keep it moist until planting. Rotate a handfork through the surface material from time to time, to even out dry and wet patches. Once the pot mixture is able to hold moisture uniformly, it is ready for planting. There should be no need for wetting agents other than those already present in the compost, such as saponins from the bark of native trees.

When pots are placed on top of discarded roof tiles, or two or three bricks, drainage from the holes in the undersurface of the pot becomes assured, and a guarded space is provided for trapping snails (see Chapter 16). At less than $1 each, second-hand bricks are much cheaper than specially made terracotta 'feet', which are very much overpriced. Raising the pots also prevents their invasion by exploratory tree roots or grass runners, which can happen if they are in direct contact with the ground.

Keeping pots going

Annuals in pots do not generally require more nutrients than those committed to the soil during preparation. Exceptions include tomatoes and capsicums, which should be given more nutrients as the fruits begin to set. Calcium deficiency, which leads to blossom-end rot infection of tomatoes, can be avoided by incorporating extra compost at this stage, well before there are any overt symptoms. Peas and beans benefit from extra potassium just after flowering begins. Wood ash is recommended, as it is a rich source of potassium and other cations, but contains no nitrogen, so it lacks any ammonium ions that would reduce the uptake of potassium by direct competition.

Perennial herbs kept in pots will need supplementary additions of nutrients. The occasional addition of a little compost mixed into the surface is a wise precaution even if you do need to increase the size of the pot, which then allows the addition of more potting mixture while scaling up. Perennial herbs should be repotted after two years, even into a pot of the same size, as the medium will have shrunk perceptibly. This is because much of the original supply of organic material has been converted to carbon dioxide. By repotting, a fresh supply of compost can be used to make up the space that was gradually lost. Take care not to cover any stems above their previous junction with the soil, and do not overwater. A small quantity of water applied several times is better for the roots than a one-off flooding. Repotting also gives the opportunity to remove any root congestion at the bottom of the pot by pruning. Adjust the pH upwards again, with a sprinkle of ash, lime or dolomite, mixed thoroughly.

Fruit trees in pots should rarely need repotting, as the size of the pot should be chosen in the first place according to the anticipated size of the tree. Top-dress with a mixture of compost and Dynamic Lifter about twice a year, and encourage companions such as sweet alice, clovers or violas as groundcover. These pots should also have a priority in the allocation of cooking and rinsing water from the kitchen (see Chapter 7), or suspended yeast lees from bottles of home-brewed beer, liquids that convey valuable nutrients in addition to water.

Worms in pots

Some writers want to preclude worms from your pots. They imagine that worms somehow damage the plants. Let me assure you that worms in pots are a good thing. They will commence the breakdown of mulching materials, mix organic materials and aerate the soil. Between crops, use a hand-fork to explore your pots, and lift any worms out of the way when adding compost and Dynamic Lifter. Put them back after mixing. The fact that they can survive in your pots is a good indication that you have an appropriate amount of organic matter in the soil.

6.
Plant propagation

'Instead of dirt and poison we have rather chosen
to fill our hives with honey and wax; thus furnishing
mankind with the two noblest of things, which are
sweetness and light.'

Jonathan Swift, Preface, *The Battle of the Books*

Day-length and control of flowering

Sweetness and light are inextricably linked. Day-length controls flowering in the vast majority of the plants that we want to grow. If the day length is right, flowers will form, and bloom, not to waste their sweetness on the desert air, but to have it appreciated by honey bees, other useful insects, and the attentive gardener. To flower at appropriate times, the plants must have been growing for a suitable period, or they would lack the accumulated reserves needed to sustain fruit and seed production. This applies especially to annuals and biennials. Accordingly, seeds must normally be planted in seasons approximating to autumn or spring.

Many garden plants proceed to flower as the day lengthens again after the winter solstice. These 'long day' plants include *Pelargonium tomentosum* (see Figure 107), the grasses responsible for hayfever (see Chapter 2),

oregano, potato and 'bolting' types such as parsnip, radish (see Figure 101), turnip (see Figure 119), beetroot, fennel (see Figure 89), dill, carrot (see Figure 94), basil, cat mint, lettuce (see Figures 43 and 45) and yarrow. All of these have commenced flowering by early summer. There is no absolute value of day length that triggers flowering. A 'long day' plant is one that flowers when the day length exceeds some critical minimum value. This might be anything from 11 to 14 hours.

Strictly, it is the uninterrupted period of darkness, or the 'night length', that is the key determinant of flowering. The ratio of darkness to light period is registered in the leaves of the plant by a copper-containing pigment, phytochrome, present in minute concentrations. Interrupting the dark period with a few minutes of white light (or just red light) is enough to convert a long night into a short night, and upset the normal flowering pattern. As noted in Chapter 1, the light of the full moon is not sufficiently intense to pass the threshold for detection by this system.

There are fewer 'short day' plants. These proceed to flower as the day shortens again after the summer solstice, and include chrysanthemums, tansy, zonal pelargoniums, *Crassula arborescens* (jade plant), violets and possibly orange mint (see Chapter 9). The 'night length' detection system is the same, except that the flowering response is geared to increasing duration of the dark period rather than a shortening. The remaining flowering category consists of 'day neutral' plants, where flowering is conditional on complex temperature and day length interactions. Peas, beans, maize (see Chapter 13) and fruit trees (see Chapter 14) generally belong to this grouping. Occasional cultivars exist of species that are usually 'long day' or 'short day', but which have lost their photoperiodic control. A good example is the carrot All Seasons.

Managing pollination

Where crossing is not wanted, it is simplest to grow only a single variety of the plant in question; for instance, parsley (see Chapter 9). Precautions to be taken when two or more varieties are to be kept genetically unaltered (except for chance mutations) include spacing, bagging and caging. The distances suggested for separation are usually impracticable in a typical suburban garden. Bagging is a chore, but manageable, and useful after a deliberate introduction of pollen, as with pumpkin flowers (see Figures 129, 130, 131 and 132), or after collecting pollen from the male flowers of maize (see Figure 136), and coating the silks with it. Bagging prevents any uncontrolled introduction of pollen by insects afterwards.

Caging, which can be done with capsicums, eggplants or crucifers, is definitely for the enthusiast (see Figure 44). The stigma of the capsicum flower is receptive for only one day,

so when several fruits have set on a plant, the cage can be removed promptly and used elsewhere. Later flowers can be nipped off until the fruits have developed to a stage when subsequent flowers fail to set. Deterrent plants are also a simple but valuable precaution; for example, garlic chives or garlic with runner beans (*Phaseolus coccineus*) or lima beans (*Phaseolus lunatus*), as noted in Chapter 2.

Saving and storing seeds for future planting

Spring, summer and autumn will bring a succession of maturing fruits. Dry pea pods will be followed by *Nigella* capsules, then parsley heads, then fennel or dill seeds. Lettuce seeds and freesia capsules can be ready in midsummer, and so too beans. Allow these fruits to dry fully — do not enclose them in plastic or paper bags. This may involve hanging inflorescences or pods under protective cover, or placing them in baskets, or on open-mesh cane-work (see Figure 48). Put these in warm locations such as the top of the hot water tank, or even the television set. Position flakes of naphthalene amongst the fruits and seeds to discourage the approach of insects. This has been its traditional function in herbarium boxes. Naphthalene is not carcinogenic, and does not actually kill insects — it acts simply as a deterrent.

Fleshy fruits mostly come later, from summer into autumn. A single fruit will often provide more than enough seeds for the next planting; for example, a capsicum (400 seeds) or a cucurbit (70–300 seeds). Fruits that are normally eaten immature, like cucumbers and zucchinis, are surprisingly large and almost unrecognisable when allowed to mature fully. Make sure that the fruits reserved for seed production are selected from the very best ones. Marking, tagging or bagging will help to prevent accidental premature harvest.

Seeds to be kept for replanting are generally separated from the mature fruits, and kept dry. Naturally dry seeds are easiest to handle. Breaking up material by hand, and catching seeds and debris is straightforward. The debris can be separated by blowing, or 'yandying', an Aboriginal term for shaking and allowing seeds to fall to the bottom. Large seeds like peas or beans are readily shelled from dry pods. Some bean pods even begin to open at one end while drying out. Lima bean pods have a sharp point, so to open these, put the pods in full sunlight. They will open by themselves.

In an emergency — for example, if rain sets in before bean pods have completely dried out (see Figures 148 and 149) — the seeds can be removed and spread out to dry. They will shrink in just a few days (see Figure 51).

Some seeds need to be recovered from a pulpy surrounding tissue, as in cucurbits and passionfruit. Push the seeds from the pulp using a wire kitchen sieve and fingers. Rinse, suspend the pulp, and rescue the seeds. Spread them out to dry on paper. When dry, scrape them off and leave them to dry longer than you think is really necessary. Eggplant seeds are mainly concentrated in the base of the fruit. They are easily separated by pushing with a finger, then rinsed and dried on paper. For tomatoes, squeeze out the gel that surrounds the seeds, and incubate this with a little water for two or three days (see Figure 52). This allows the gel to partly break down, liberating the seeds. Rinse to remove any pulp fragments and then spread the seeds on absorbent paper towel to dry for several days. Separated dry seeds are then more easily sent to other gardeners, simply by cutting out pieces of paper and writing labels on the back. Some authors (for example, McLeod, 1994b) recommend a warm-temperature treatment with the incubation to discourage tomato diseases (about 55°C), but this is risky if your temperature control is not accurate.

Alternatively, keeping seeds inside the fruit is sometimes useful. A convenient method of storing tomato seeds, and those of similar fleshy fruits like tomatillo and eggplant, is simply to allow the mature fruits to dry out. This may go through a messy, smelly stage, so do it in the laundry, the workshop, or outside somewhere under shelter. Small glass jars, labelled and open to the air, are ideal. They may be colonised by banana flies (*Drosophila melanogaster*), but these red-eyed flies are harmless, and should not be confused with the fruit flies that grow inside developing fruits. The dried tomato fruits can be left under ambient conditions until the time comes for planting out the seeds. I prefer this method, because the seeds are left in contact with their protective gel until the time comes to encourage germination.

To recover the seeds, suspend one or two of the dried fruits (according to size) in water. After preliminary soaking, break up the fruit by hand, pushing the pieces of pulp to liberate individual seeds. Suspend the slurry with plenty of water and then pour off the surplus as the sound seeds gravitate to the bottom of the jar. Suspend the seeds in fresh water several times, pouring away the fruit fragments and surplus liquid each time. After about one day of occasional rinsing, tip the seeds over the surface of a prepared pot or tray, and cover them lightly with the same potting material. Water thoroughly, and keep well watered. The seeds can germinate once the natural inhibitors that surround them are rinsed away. After several days, small seedlings with two finely shaped cotyledons should appear (see Figure 55). If not, keep watering. The method just described suits the smaller mature fruits obtained on visits to other gardeners, or varieties that you intend to maintain in your own garden.

Even when seeds are recovered from dry fruits, it is difficult to be sure the seeds are dry enough to store in an airtight container.

Getting it wrong means that fungus may grow inside the container and ruin that particular batch of seeds. This is where granules of silica gel containing cobalt chloride as an indicator are indispensable (see Figure 49). When blue, the colour of the indicator cobaltous chloride ($CoCl_2$), they are capable of absorbing moisture. When pink, the colour of the hydrated form $Co(H_2O)_6{}^{2+}Cl_2{}^-$, they need to be replaced. Put the seeds into a container with plenty of spare room and fill the extra space with blue silica gel. When the gel has changed colour completely to pink, replace it with blue gel. Beans are more difficult than most other seeds, and will normally need three changes of gel before they are dry enough to store in a permanently closed container.

There are many possible containers, so choose according to the number of seeds to be stored. Plastic film canisters are excellent, and should be labelled both inside and out. Recently these have changed from black plastic to translucent white, but this does not alter the usefulness of the container. Scaling up, baby-food jars are excellent. Mini-jam jars, the smallest of instant coffee jars, and vegemite jars are also useful.

Silica gel can be regenerated by spreading it out and heating it for half an hour in a low oven, at about 120°C. Tip the gel into a lidded can while it is still hot. Use a curled piece of paper as a funnel. Put the lid on the can, and do not use the gel until it has cooled down. Silica gel is sold by the Seed Savers' Network (see Useful Addresses) and can be used over and over again.

To avoid extremely high temperatures, store seeds in the coolest part of the house. I use the southeast corner of the house (the laundry) as well as the southeast corner of my workshop. The seed containers are totally enclosed in drawers, and absolutely inaccessible to rodents (see Figure 50). Some people use the refrigerator or the freezer for seed storage, but several precautions are necessary (Fanton and Fanton, 1993; Murray, 1996a, 1999). The low temperature will kill any insect eggs present, as well as prolonging the storage life of the seeds — provided all surplus water was removed from the seeds beforehand. We know that 100% germination is still possible after frozen storage of bean seeds for eight years, and of chickpea seeds for nine years (see Figure 54). An experiment with mung bean seeds, also commenced in 1991, is continuing. Prior to storage, the water contents of these chick pea seeds and mung bean seeds were 8.0% and 9.5%, respectively. Mature pea seeds normally have 10% water content. At the Tamworth Centre for Crop Improvement in New South Wales, cereal grains have been found to germinate in high proportion after 30 years of frozen storage. When taking seeds out of a container that has been stored in the cold, always let it equilibrate to room temperature before opening. Be careful of any condensate coming into contact with the seeds, and renew the accompanying silica gel before returning any seeds to storage.

Germination of seeds

It is rarely necessary to buy seedlings of the plants you want to grow. Most garden plants can be grown readily from seed, and there is no reason why a novice cannot get results that are just as good as those of the seasoned practitioner. High germination percentage and vigorous seedling growth depend on the quality of the seeds. This is determined mainly by storage conditions and age. Commercially produced seeds are often sold in foil packets that have been vacuum sealed to exclude damaging oxygen, but many kinds of seed will last three to five years even without this precaution, provided they are kept absolutely dry and free from seed-eating pests.

The size of the seed often determines whether seeds are placed exactly in the positions where the seedlings are wanted, or first planted in a seedling tray or pot. Small seeds like catmint, tomato or capsicum are difficult to handle one by one, and end up thickly sown in temporary quarters. The seedlings should then be transplanted as soon as they are big enough (see Figures 56 and 57). Larger seeds that can be handled individually, like pumpkins, peas or beans, can be properly spaced and planted at once. A useful rule of thumb is to plant the seed at a depth three times the length of the seed, or three times the diameter if the seed is round.

Some seedlings are better not transplanted. Parsnip (see Figure 46), carrot and caraway are best sown where they are to be grown, then thinned down to the final number. Members of this family (see Table 12 on page 81) often develop the taproot as a major storage organ, and this is particularly sensitive to disturbance, even at young stages. Exceptions to this general rule are found among the parsleys. These can be transplanted at a very young stage, at the appearance of the first true leaf. Just take care to keep the whole root in contact with the soil it has commenced to grow in. The length of a typical trowel is adequate for this purpose. At this juncture it is worthwhile commenting on the myth that parsley seeds are difficult to germinate. I don't know where the myth started, but it is demonstrably untrue. When the Australian Consumers' Association tested commercial seed germination many years ago (Choice, February 1983, pages 26–31), they found a germination rate of 72 to 88 per cent for the parsley samples. Any writer who repeats the myth that parsley seeds are difficult to germinate has obviously never grown parsley from seed.

Coatings of inert materials can be used to artificially enlarge the seed, but the additional cost means that it is always cheaper to use unpelleted seed and waste some. Paper strips with seeds embedded but widely separated can also now be purchased, but this is just a trendy means of selling highly priced paper to the truly lazy gardener. An economic method of sowing small seeds involves prior mixing with dry sand or sandy soil. The mix is run into a row or scattered on the top of the ground, with the sand diluting the frequency of the resulting seedlings. Thinning may still be necessary, but the wastage of seeds is much less than if seeds had been sprinkled onto the ground straight from the packet.

Avoid seeds coated with pesticides, such as the dithiocarbamate fungicide thiram. Although intended to prevent loss of seedlings to damping-off fungi, thiram has disastrous effects on seedlings of many kinds. The germination rate is lowered, the growth rate is slowed, and the leaves are malformed. Thiram can be rinsed off larger seeds, but this is not always a practicable solution. Fortunately, seeds kept from thiram-affected pea plants that have struggled to maturity yield plants that grow faster on the next occasion the peas are sown.

If there is a need to sterilise the seed surface — for instance, if there is an obvious trace of fungus in the container where the seeds were stored — a rinse with hydrogen peroxide is helpful. First dilute to a 1 per cent solution from a 6 per cent or 3 per cent stock solution, which can be purchased cheaply. From a 6 per cent starting solution, measure a volume with a medicine glass into a small jar or glass tumbler, add five times this volume of water, and mix by swirling. Keep the seeds immersed in this solution for no more than 30 minutes and then plant them. Using hydrogen peroxide instead of sodium hypochlorite (as in bleach) avoids the possibility of damaging chlorinated compounds being formed. The breakdown products from hydrogen peroxide are water and oxygen. We have come along way from using mercury salts, which were recommended for sterilising the seed surface from the 1940s to the 1960s.

The germination medium, when this is needed, should be very similar to the prepared soil that the seedlings will be growing in. Half compost and half garden soil, well mixed, is an ideal medium. Provided the garden soil has a reasonably open texture there is really no need for anything very different, and once again the old recipes can be thrown away. Put the mixture into a box or tray, about 8 centimetres deep. Position or scatter the seeds, and cover them with a little of the same mixture, to a depth of two or three times the length of the seed.

There is no need to sterilise the seedbed with formalin, a solution containing formaldehyde. Although Norman de Vaus (1976) described formalin as 'one of the best and simplest materials to use', the three-week waiting period before planting into a formalin-treated seedbed must have been extremely irksome, and it would have been very dangerous to have bottles of formalin around the home. Formaldehyde is not selective. It would kill every soil organism it came into contact with, beneficial micro-organisms included. This simple organic compound should remain in laboratories and museums, where it is used as a preservative.

An overlay of sifted manure for seedbeds was often recommended in the past. There is no harm in doing this with horse manure if the manure is properly aged, but never overfertilise any medium that seeds are to germinate in. As noted in Chapter 3, excessive nitrogen will damage seedlings. Remember, too, that all common seeds except those of orchids carry some reserves inside, either in the endosperm (see Figure 53), or in the plant embryo itself, usually in the cotyledons. For large seeds like peas, these stored reserves are sufficient for the seedling's growth for at least three weeks without any new input from the root system. This is known from experiments where seeds are placed to germinate in vermiculite, and provided only with deionised water and illumination (see Figure 41). In practice, the seedling begins to take up new supplies of minerals as soon as the primary root has broken the seedcoat and entered the soil. Taking this point one step further, it is possible to use an overlay of vermiculite itself. Care must be taken not to overwater.

Suitable temperatures

The temperature range that seeds are exposed to on germination does not have to be exactly at the optimum for that particular plant. For temperate or subtropical species, adopt a range of 10–20°C. The classic advice here is not to sow 'until all danger of frost is past'. This is clearly desirable, and for legumes it is imperative that temperatures do not fall below 7°C, otherwise nodulation of the roots will be inhibited. Tropical species do well between 20°C and 30°C, and a rule of thumb for something like common beans is not to plant unless the minimum temperature is at least 15°C.

What matters is the duration of exposure to potentially adverse temperatures, rather than fleeting dips below the recommended minimum. Different varieties can tolerate lower ranges than others, and this should be taken into account when starting to plant. Among bush beans (*Phaseolus vulgaris*), Staley's Surprise and Hawkesbury Wonder can be planted early, when night temperatures are still touching 9°C or so. The Redlands series was bred to be grown through the northern New South Wales–Queensland winter. The choice of cultivar is critical when trying to extend a garden's productive period by avoiding peak times for known pests (see Chapter 16).

To know how the temperature changes in different parts of the garden, a robust maximum/minimum thermometer is a useful tool. Always keep records of the date that you plant something, for future reference. A separate calendar is handy, or a gardening notebook.

Label the seedlings, so that when the time comes to consider saving seeds again, there is absolute certainty about what is being saved.

Planting out seedlings

Home-grown seedlings will soon reach a size that allows them to be planted to the next stage, perhaps individually into small pots, or spread out in larger pots (see Chapter 5), or into the open garden. Use a trowel to make the spaces that will receive the seedlings before beginning to separate them, and keep as much of the original medium around the roots as possible. After transfer, pack around them gently, and water the surface directly, without knocking any seedlings over. Provided due care is taken, almost all seedlings transplant readily. Most prohibitions on transplanting result from the incompetence or sad experiences of individual writers, rather than from any inherent inadequacy of the seedlings.

When choosing seedlings, or indeed any plants at all in nurseries, look for obvious signs of nutrient deficiency, such as yellowing leaves, shed leaves, and stunted or uneven growth. Never be tempted to buy herbs or vegetable seedlings in poor condition. They are usually incapable of recovery, and if diseased, they are not even fit for the compost heap.

Herbs or vegetables bought in punnets or pots from nurseries should be planted out immediately. In the nursery they are often oversupplied with water, regardless of labels, because watering is something that happens routinely in nurseries. A related problem is starvation. This problem is widespread and stems from inadequate medium composition, compounded by overwatering. There is often too much filler in potting media — for example, white, hydrophobic polystyrene beads — which are a total waste of space. Polystyrene can be distinguished from perlite (which is useful) by its compressibility when squeezed. The manufacture of polystyrene has caused enormous environmental damage, and because of their very low density, polystyrene beads easily escape into aquatic habitats. Compounds like polystyrene have no place in ecologically sustainable horticulture.

Always rescue new purchases by planting them out at once. If the garden is not yet ready to receive them, at least increase the size of the pot, filling the extra space with appropriate compost or potting material (see Chapter 4), so that the plant can begin to compensate for any subliminal deficiencies.

Seedlings from cuttings

Many plants can be grown from cuttings (see Figure 58). Healthy shoots with two or three nodes and with the bottom leaves trimmed off make good candidates. Allow the cut surfaces to dry in the air for about one hour before positioning the cutting in a pot. Use a potting medium prepared for growing seedlings from seed, and ensure that it is never too wet. The time of the year may be important, and failure to strike can be blamed on the attempt being made at the wrong time. Plants like pelargoniums seem to strike whatever the season. To improve the chances of successful root development, a rooting powder, which contains a synthetic plant hormone preparation, can be employed. This works by increasing local auxin concentration, shifting the balance of growth substances in favour of root initiation. Just dip the end of the cutting into the powder before planting.

Seedlings from vegetative reproduction

A number of plants can reproduce vegetatively, whether or not they produce seeds. Plants that persist as bulbs often produce a series of smaller bulbs divided off the original. The pregnant onion is spectacular, as the new bulbs form under the outer skin and then break through. Zygocactus (see Table 9 on page 68) has flattened stem segments (cladodes) that often break off and take root — and pieces can be broken off deliberately. *Kalanchoe* can produce new plants from buds in notches around the edge of a shed leaf (see Figure 59). The crucifix orchid (*Epidendrum species*) produces red, orange or mauve flowers for most of the year. As well as setting capsules containing very fine seed, it routinely produces new vegetative plants along the stem. The walking iris (*Neomarica gracilis*) sends out strappy shoots that each produces a flower subtended at the same node by a new plant. When this touches the ground, it takes root and grows independently. The flowers open for one day only and then shrivel, but the new plants advance.

Tradescantia virginiana has jointed stems, readily broken, and where these touch the ground, roots are formed and the adjacent shoot becomes a new plant. Hoverflies, native bees (*Amegilla* species) and European honey bees take pollen from the violet-purple flowers, which are produced year-round. It is quite different from the much-reviled *Tradescantia albiflora*. Every long-established university in Australia has a plot of this plant, to service practical classes. The cells in the staminal hairs show cell structure and cytoplasmic streaming beautifully, usually in the first microscopy class of an introductory botany or biology subject.

Both tall bearded iris and Louisiana iris spread from rhizomes (creeping stems), and often this is symmetrical, with buds on opposite sides of the rhizome developing simultaneously. The 'increase' can be separated using clean secateurs, and repotted. Many weeds display very effective vegetative means of reproduction, and it is well to be aware of their potential for spreading (see Chapter 7).

Do-it-yourself grafting

Kits for grafting tomatoes, eggplants or capsicums are sold by New Gippsland Seeds & Bulbs (see Useful Addresses). Grow the plants that are to provide the root stock at the same time as those to be grafted (the scions). The rootstock variety is resistant to *Verticillium* and *Fusarium* pathogens, but would have inferior fruits compared to the varieties preferred as scions (see Chapter 13). Tomato seedlings make ideal subjects when they are about 10 centimetres tall. Make angled cuts with a sterile razor blade, position the scion against the stock, and then hold them together with grafting tape and a clip. Keep the plants unstressed until a graft union has formed. The whole plant will then continue to grow. Practice makes perfect. To graft camellias, see Savell and Andrews (1982), and for fruit and nut trees, see Alexander (1990).

Setting up a nursery area

It is a good idea to lay claim to a sheltered, sunny spot as somewhere suitable to line up seedlings in their pots and trays while they are beginning to grow. Frames or covers with glass panes sound old-fashioned, but these methods are still useful in the coldest parts of the country. Gaps behind garages and sheds are sometimes suitable, depending on available light. Small platforms, perhaps shielded with a frame and shadecloth, are ideal (see Figure 60). Having seedlings well above ground level is a sound strategy for foiling hungry slugs and snails. Depending on the scale of operations, consider whether a small plastic igloo or glasshouse might be desirable, according to how badly the weather misbehaves. A dedicated protective structure gives good control over rain, wind, humidity, temperature and light, and need not be too stark and unsightly if partly covered by climbing plants.

7.
Wind, water and weeds

'One year's seeds, seven years' weeds.'

Traditional rhyme

Connections

The three factors wind, water and weeds are closely interconnected, and not simply because weed seeds can be transported by the elements. First, there is what plant physiologists call the transpiration compromise. Whenever plants open the pores (stomata) in the leaf surface that allow carbon dioxide to enter and become assimilated through photosynthesis, they inevitably allow some water vapour to diffuse out. Most plants do this in the daytime. Rapid air movement takes away saturated air from the leaf surface more rapidly, instigating faster evaporation from the interior gas space of the leaves. This is replaced by water ascending through the capillaries of the xylem. So under windy conditions, plants need to transmit more water from the roots, through the stems, into the leaves. If the supply of water in the soil is insufficient, the leaves wilt, and may suffer heat stress. This could happen because normal evaporation has a very strong cooling effect, keeping the leaves up to 10°C below air temperature, and if transpiration is prevented, the internal leaf temperatures must rise. Far from being a necessary evil, the loss of water through open stomata has a vital part to play

in allowing photosynthesis to proceed at all.

Mulching is often employed to cut down the direct evaporation of water from the upper soil, retaining more for transpiration by plants, and keeping the temperature more stable around the roots. But so much depends on the skill of the gardener. Weeds can either be suppressed or assisted by mulch, and the choice of mulching material poses major dilemmas for the truly organic gardener.

Windbreaks

Windbreaks are fundamentally important to cover those occasions when the wind blows strongest. Winds may be seasonal, and more or less predictable, or sudden and unexpected. For example, in the Illawarra we expect about eight days per year to be extremely windy, at most 120 to 140 kilometres per hour. Take advantage of boundary fences. If solid, they can block the wind. If they are lattice materials like weldmesh, then encourage strong vines to grow through them. These can be introduced species like jasmine (*Jasminum officinale*), *Solanum jasminoides* or passionfruit (see Chapter 15), or ornamental natives, such as

Pandorea jasminoides, *Hardenbergia violacea* or *Kennedia rubicunda* (see Figure 10). On a smaller scale, collars of broken drainage pipe are useful with newly transplanted seedlings if the weather suddenly turns windy (see Figure 61). These valuable fragments can be left in place, providing shade to the central root zone until the seedling is established.

Protection and support

Twigs and stems, fallen in the wind, or deliberately cut from trees and shrubs, are useful for protecting newly planted areas from inadvertent feet, or pet cats and dogs. Most vegetables and herbs growing in a proper depth of well-prepared soil need no extra support. Those that sprawl, like potatoes and dwarf beans, should be allowed to do so, because this results in better exposure of the lower leaves to light. For plants that do need support, prepare stakes from plants like bamboo, sacred bamboo, *Indigofera australis*, or even mulberry prunings, dried for two months so that they are unlikely to strike and resprout. Wire hoops are useful for supporting the early stages of vines such as cucumbers or zucchinis (see Figure 64). Larger tomatoes, peppers and eggplant should be supported as a precaution against stems breaking under the weight of fruit (see Figures 37 and 176). Tie the stems onto stakes with old nylon stocking. Most gardeners acquire an inexhaustible supply of this paradoxical material. As intact garments, nylon stockings last no time at all, yet nylon is practically indestructible in the garden, providing the flexibility that prevents injury under stress.

Hardwood stakes bought from a nursery should be reserved for supporting wire or string mesh for climbing peas or beans, or passionfruit vines. In this way a few stakes support many plants, and they can be reused many times. Whenever possible, encourage some plants to support others; for instance, put tall peas or climbing beans in positions close to an established passionfruit vine, so that the annuals can grip the perennial. Strings can also be led from nearby shrubs or trees.

Take advantage of opaque boundary fences by covering these with supporting mesh, and allow plants to cover the mesh. This approach can be extended logically to include the walls of the house (see Figures 62 and 63). As noted by Tim North (1999), architects are beginning to promote this idea, because a close covering of plants can keep a house up to 12°C cooler in summer, and reduce heating costs substantially in the winter.

Watering

When using a hose, aim to water the ground without wetting the leaves, especially if watering is being done in full sunshine. It is not always possible to water thoroughly in the cool of the evening, or early in the day, but if plants are wilting, this is a clear sign that more water is needed in the soil. For garden beds, install drip lines or feeders either above or below the soil surface, or use a soaker hose left on dribble. It is more efficient in the long run to keep the soil moist, rather than attempting to re-wet a soil that has dried out excessively. Narrow jets from coffee pots or kettles also give better precision for watering the soil around plants in pots than do the conventional 'roses' attached to watering cans, which wet foliage as well.

Gardening does not consume as much mains water directly as water supply authorities like to pretend. Water use in the garden has been unfairly targeted as restrictions have tightened. It is more 'essential' to support the production of food and honey than it is to allow second-hand car dealers to hose their vehicles every day. At last, as level 3 restrictions are imposed in New South Wales, such profligate waste will be confined to one day per week. On the plus side, I don't have an in-ground swimming pool to maintain, and I don't have a dishwasher. Why shouldn't I choose to water my plants instead?

Rosemary Morrow (1993) recommended doing a water inventory to find out where it all goes. Most of the water consumed from the mains supply in many households goes on washing and rinsing clothes, towels and bedding, followed by the amounts used for showers and baths. Washing water is too alkaline for continual use in the garden, and may also contain unwanted sodium or borate. Adopt a washing powder with low phosphorus content, so that it is possible to use the final rinse safely on plants that normally grow in the pH range 6 to 7; that is, most garden plants (see Chapter 4). In this way, 60 to 80 litres of water per wash can be used twice over. A word of warning: if you collect the final rinse in 10 litre buckets as I do, then dispense the water immediately. Such water left standing around can culture mosquito larvae and bacteria, presenting an unnecessary health hazard. It is also possible to treat shower, kitchen and laundry grey water to the point where it can always be used safely on lawns and gardens (for example, the Nature-Clear system, see Savannah Environmental Ply Ltd under Useful Addresses).

A simple measure such as washing hands outside after gardening, before returning to the house, will avoid a significant quantity of water being consigned to the sink. Cold water and a brush will get most of the dirt off, and then the saved water can be applied to the garden. Similarly, when harvesting root or stem vegetables, clean them outside. As much soil as possible should stay in the garden, and not end up needlessly down the kitchen sink.

Water for the garden does not always have to come from the mains supply through the hose. Leaving a bucket at the overflow outlet from my electric off-peak water heater means that 5 litres per night is rescued from the drain and goes onto pots the next day. This may not seem much, but it all adds up — this modest bucket represents more than 1800 litres per year. Keeping a bucket in the shower recess catches water while the temperature is equilibrating. The kitchen, too, is a great place for salvage. Water from the steamer saucepan or from boiling eggs, and rinsing water from rice or legumes, should be carried out to the garden, because soluble or suspended nutrients are saved as well as the water itself.

Home-brewed beer is another excellent source of suspended nutrients, because the discarded yeast lees from each bottle are rich in nitrogen and minerals. If the red wine bottle has a crust, then shake some water in the bottle to resuspend the tannins and tartaric acid crystals before pouring the lot onto a pot. Make sure the contents of any spoiled wine bottles are also directed to the garden. But there is no need to emulate Aristoxenus, the epicurean philosopher and musician, who is supposed to have watered lettuce plants with his best wine. Was that before or after drinking it?

Instead of directing rainwater to the stormwater system, run-off from the roof of the house can also be a boon for the garden. It is possible to position tanks either above or below ground level to receive rainwater, which can be disbursed into the garden later on. Above-ground tanks are now encouraged, and there is a partial rebate from state governments. In many areas rainwater tanks are mandatory for all new dwellings; for instance, in New South Wales, such a measure helps new homes comply with BASIX targets for water conservation (see Useful Addresses). Most of these tanks are made from polyethylene. A variety of shapes has evolved, so that it is possible to choose a tank to fit awkward spaces, such as between the house wall and a fence. For example, the Waterwall measures 2.4 m x 1.8 m x 33 cm and holds

1200 litres. Suppliers of tanks and auxiliary equipment have mushroomed — see your local Yellow Pages telephone directory. Some will supply free pumps.

Having to renew my house guttering several years ago provided an opportunity to plan what would happen to the rainwater that fell on the roof. An underground retention tank now receives the run-off from 80 per cent of the roof area, releasing the water slowly under an area close to all the backyard gardens and several fruit trees. It also supports a small fibreglass pond that has allowed frogs to breed successfully, and provides drinking water for birds. Recently, as leakage became significant, this pond was lifted and rubber sheeting placed underneath it (see Figure 65). This method of handling run-off does not give the control that an above-ground tank would, but neither does it impose on lawn or garden space. In fact, the resulting mound of clay over the tank has gradually been converted into a new garden bed that now contains sweet potato, parsley, fennel, *Echium fastuosum*, pelargonium, rocket, broad beans, tomatoes and tall-bearded iris.

Choosing plants that need less water

Beans are plants that I consider need a lot of water. Growing thirty 30 centimetre pots of beans over a 90-day summer at an average of 2 litres of water per pot per day requires a total of 5400 litres. But this is no more than 1 per cent of my total mains consumption over the same period, about 600 litres per day. Beans grown through autumn use about half the water needed through summer (when maximum temperatures are sometimes 40°C). This difference reflects the stronger rate of evaporation from the soil surface in the hotter season, and a greater rate of transpiration for cooling the interior of the leaf. Even so, the

quantities in either season are not prohibitive.

Plants with lower water requirements than beans can be deliberately chosen as a further step towards minimising the amount of water used in the garden. Many Australian native shrubs require little or no water once established. Quite a few plants from South Africa come to mind, such as *Agapanthus*, *Gazania* (see Figure 66), *Clivia miniata*, African daisy (see Figure 67), *Strelitzia reginae* and pelargoniums. One particular group avoids the hot summer altogether: plants such as jonquil, daffodil, freesia, rain lily (see Figure 68) and naked lady (*Amaryllis*) all resprout from bulbs in late summer or autumn, then flower from autumn to spring. Many members of the iris family are hardy, including the pink-flowered *Gladiolus carneus* (a weed in Western Australia) and *Dietes* species.

There is another group of plants that avoids opening stomata (pores) in the heat of the day, opening them by night instead. These are generally succulents, and most belong to just a few families: the Cactaceae, Crassulaceae, Agavaceae, Aizoaceae, Euphorbiaceae, Liliaceae, Asclepiadaceae and Bromeliaceae. Because their stomata are closed for most of the day, they lose little water.

Since their carbon dioxide fixation has to occur mainly at night, they also have a more complex mechanism of photosynthesis, termed Crassulacean Acid Metabolism (CAM). This involves the assimilation of carbon dioxide into malic acid and storage of this acid overnight. Next day, in the light and with stomata closed, carbon dioxide is released from the malic acid and refixed into sugars via a more normal pathway of photosynthesis. With adequate soil moisture, the stomata will begin to open in the late afternoon, enhancing productivity.

But with little or no water available, succulents will subsist for long periods with the water and substrates they have stored. Pieces of the notorious prickly pear (*Opuntia*

TABLE 9. A SELECTION OF SUCCULENTS AND EPIPHYTES

Aechmea fasciata	*Epiphyllum* hybrids
Aloe vera	*Kalanchoe tomentosum*
Ceropegia woodii (chain-of-hearts)	*Ornithogalum* (pregnant onion)
Crassula arborescens (jade plant)	*Peperomia* species
Crassula multicava	*Schlumbergera* (zygocactus)
Dendrobium speciosum (native ground orchid)	*Sedum morganianum* (donkey tail)
Echeveria elegans (pearl echeveria)	*Tillandsia usneoides* (Spanish moss)

stricta) are said to remain viable even after hanging on barbed wire fences for many months, if not years.

Table 9 lists a number of succulents and epiphytes (plants that grow on other plants) that have become popular garden or indoor subjects (see Figures 69 to 72). None of these has thorns or sharp spines, and most have attractive flowers that appear for several months. Some suit hanging baskets, a situation that generally exacerbates loss of water from the medium. On the other hand, ventilation is enhanced, thus avoiding high humidity that could assist unwanted diseases. In a wire frame, I use paper bark as an outer shell, enclosing a free-draining mix of soil, compost and vermiculite. It is important that these plants are not subjected to situations where they will receive too much water, so they need to be protected from normal rainfall. My 'semi-arid zone' is the ledge of the front verandah, plus the branches of an adjacent frangipani (*Plumeria*) for hanging baskets. When watering these plants, a spray-pack gives excellent control, whereas pouring or sprinkling would apply too much water at once.

Tillandsia usneoides is an exceptional epiphyte, as it lives only on dew or rainwater while draped over other plants. This plant has no roots. Tiny scales move in response to moisture, allowing water uptake together with dissolved nutrients. It is hard to believe that Spanish moss belongs to the same family as pineapple — Bromeliaceae.

Mulching

Mulching is the most abused procedure associated with organic gardening. Mulch is often applied too thickly, with a heavy and enthusiastic hand, without thought for all of the consequences. Once the ground dries out underneath, the lack of moisture cannot be seen, so the first inkling of a problem is the wilting collapse of plants in the garden. Many gardeners assume that weeds will not penetrate the mulch, and give up weeding once the mulch is in place. Wrong: they will. Weeds will start growing from seeds dropped into the mulch by birds, or spread with the mulch itself. Privets often accompany the street tree trimmings produced by electricity providers. Weed seeds may accompany lucerne mulch, although this is less likely with baled pea straw, or cereal straw. Lack of diligence allows many weeds to flourish through mulch, and splendid specimens they are too! Routine cultivation will cut them off as seedlings.

The choice of mulching material presents a major problem. Who can guarantee that any purchased 'organic' mulch is free of pesticide residues or too high a content of heavy metals or salt? Do the various woodchip mulches on sale represent genuine waste from selective logging procedures, or the obscene fragments of trees clear-felled just for chipping? This is unwarranted vandalism. Trees, wherever they may be, are best left alive, otherwise there is no chance of halting the inexorable increase in atmospheric carbon dioxide concentration that will undermine food quality in the forseeable future (Murray, 1995, 1997b).

The question of ecological sustainability hangs over all commercially available mulches. Yes, they are 'organic', in the carbon-chemistry sense, and yes, they are renewable, because the material they are prepared from can theoretically be grown again. But are they 'organic' in a holistic sense? If these mulches are so good, why are they not being returned to the soil where the originating plants grew? What is being added back to compensate for the removal of so much of the previous crop?

The key to mulching is to find an acceptable clean source of mulch. Occasionally you will see a television demonstration of mulching with freshly cut grass, or of someone just leaving it on the ground where it is cut. This is not a good idea, because it deprives the underlying plants of light, and creates patches of dead lawn. The temperature increase discussed earlier may also contribute to this process. Never pile freshly cut grass against any plant that really matters — put it in the compost where it will do most good (see Chapter 3).

Sungro mulch prepared from rice husks is weed-free because it undergoes a high-temperature treatment, at 130°C. Tea tree mulch has also been through a high-temperature treatment, necessary to distil off the oil. Sugarcane mulch has only recently appeared in the marketplace, because cane farmers used to flame the tops when harvesting the stems. At 60 litres for $10 to $15, it is competitively priced.

Cereal straw needs to be clean at the outset. If what is on offer is already spoilt by rain and fungus, then reject it. My wheat straw comes from a produce store at $3 per bag, and lasts for several years. To apply sound straw to bean pots in a very thin layer, the length needs to be reduced with sharp scissors.

Ultimately, the best mulches are leaves, stems and bark obtained from plants in your own garden. In many locations my gardens and pots receive a 'default' mulch, arising from natural shedding, which I then have to thin down or remove altogether. A thin layer of mulch in summer will help reflect heat and conserve moisture within the soil, while allowing water to penetrate the soil surface on watering (see Figures 14 and 74). A summer mulch will partly break down, and this is why having a legume straw with plenty of residual nitrogen is advantageous, avoiding microbial nitrogen 'draw down' close to non-legumes. I also use home-grown pea straw, legume pods, or saved peanut shells as a 'sandwich' mulch. When these are available, I pull back the coarser materials around my citrus trees, interpose the light-weight leguminous material, then replace the heavier outer layer (see Figures 73, 77 and 78).

Do not allow mulch to accumulate too close to the house in bushfire seasons. Several years ago (2002), I had to dispose of such flammable material near my garage and workshop by scraping it up and burning it. At the same time, we removed a bed of fishbone fern (*Nephrolepis cordifolia*) in the front of the house, because its wiry, brown residues are too slow to degrade naturally and present a fire hazard.

Never mulch where seedlings are emerging, because many mulch materials release compounds that inhibit germination and

TABLE 10. GARDEN PLANTS WITH INVASIVE POTENTIAL NEEDING EXTRA VIGILANCE OR COMPLETE REMOVAL

VINES	OTHERS
Ipomoea indica (morning glory)	*Agave americana* (century plant)
Ipomoea carica (mile-a-minute plant)	*Alstroemeria pulchella* (New Zealand Christmas bell)
Araujia hortorum (moth vine)	*Cestrum parqui* (green cestrum)
Caesalpinia decapetala (Mysore thorn)	*Chlorophytum comosum* (ribbon plant)
Cardiospermum grandiflorum (balloon vine)	*Chrysanthemoïdes monilifera* (bitou bush)
Anredera cordifolia (Madeira vine)	*Cortaderia selloana* (pampas grass)
Lonicera japonica (Japanese honeysuckle)	*Genista* species (broom)
Jasminum polyanthum (jasmine)	*Hypericum perforatum* (St John's wort)
Thunbergia alata (black-eyed Susan)	*Bougainvillea* (bougainvillea)
Protasparagus plumosus (climbing asparagus)	*Bryophyllum tubiflora* (mother of millions)
Myrsiphyllum asparagoides (wedding creeper)	*Ochna serrulata* (Mickey Mouse bush)
Delairea odorata (Cape ivy)	*Oxalis corniculata* (yellow wood sorrel)
Hedera helix (English ivy)	*Oxalis latifolia* (fish-tailed oxalis)
TREES	*Oxalis pes-caprae* (soursob)
Ligustrum lucidum (large-leafed privet)	*Protasparagus aethiopicus* (asparagus fern)
Ligustrum sinese (small-leafed privet)	*Cytisus scoparius* (Scottish broom)
Cinnamomum camphora (camphor laurel)	*Oenothera stricta* (evening primrose)
Phoenix canariensis (Canary Island date palm)	*Crocosmia x crocosmiiflora* (montbretia)
Senna pendula (cassia)	*Tradescantia albiflora* (wandering Jew)
Erythrina crista-galli (cockspur coral tree)	*Verbena bonariensis* (purpletop)

seedling growth. This is why Roman farmers flamed their cereal stubble. The larger fragments of mulch also conceal slugs and snails. The safest places to mulch are underneath trees (see Figure 74), keeping the root zones free of vigorous grasses, and amenable to occasional additions of fertiliser. But do not allow any mulching materials to pile up against the trunk, or rots may gain entry. The organic gardener who knows when to use mulches and when not to will avoid many bitter disappointments.

Weeding

Vigilance and timely action to remove unwanted plants will keep your gardens always under control. Never let a weed flower and run to seed. The number of seeds produced by a single plant can sometimes be several thousand. Even seven years is a conservative estimate of future supply once these dormant but viable seeds enter the soil's repository or seed bank, and 30 to 60 years is nearer the mark for some. Plants such as *Stellaria media* (chickweed), *Capsella bursa-pastoris* (shepherd's purse), *Amaranthus retroflexus* (redroot), *Ambrosia artemisifolia* (a ragweed), *Lepidium virginicum*, *Plantago major* (plantago or large plantain), *Polygonum hydropiper* (smartweed), *Brassica nigra*, *Rumex crispus* (curled dock) and *Verbascum thapsis* (great mullein) gave evidence of their considerable longevity in Dr Beal's buried seed experiment, dating from 1879 (Bradbeer, 1988; Murray, 1994, 1996b). The longevity record for some of these seeds is 80 to 100 years. It is truly amazing that seeds can survive for so long in a hydrated state, with fluctuating rather than uniform soil temperatures, and no way of coping with oxygen-induced damage to cell constituents except enzyme-catalysed repair.

Take especial care to eliminate plants that might harbour pests over winter, such as lantana (white fly), nasturtium (cabbage white butterfly, *Pieris rapae*) and milk thistle (leaf-miners). Keep other garden plants free of leaf-miners by detaching affected leaves and squashing them. There is no need to blast everything in sight with herbicides when physical methods are not only sufficient, but also highly specific. Milk thistle can also harbour lettuce necrotic yellows virus (Whittet, 1968). Similarly, dandelion (see Figure 84) and cat's ear (*Hypochoeris radicata*, see Figure 76) can host cucumber mosaic virus, and *Solanum nigrum* can host three tomato viruses as well as root-knot nematodes.

Clovers in the lawn, or in the garden, are not weeds. Like peas and beans, they will fix atmospheric nitrogen in their root nodules, supporting their own growth, as well as that of other plants. They are often the greenest plants in the ground, and being shorter than most grasses, they can flower successfully before mowing resumes in the spring, and between mowings. This ensures that they set enough seed to perpetuate themselves. White clover (*Trifolium repens*) has also been shown to exert allelopathic effects against some allergenic plants definitely not wanted in the lawn, such as *Plantago lanceolata* (lamb's tongue) and *Rumex acetosa* (sour dock) (Harborne, 1982). With clover about, you should never need to use any kind of nitrogenous fertiliser on the lawn. In fact, no one should feed their lawn anything: it is an absolute waste of fertiliser. The sky will not fall if you give the lawns nothing; grasses will continue to grow by deriving their nutrients from soil particles and rainwater.

Whether clover is encouraged or not, the numbers of rosette weeds in lawns can be lowered by never allowing the grass to be cut shorter than 2.5 millimetres. This will reduce the opportunity for their seeds to land on the soil surface and germinate. Seedlings that do begin to grow have their leaves forced to work at an angle, rather than being able to absorb maximal light set flush to the ground. Cut off their flowers on sight, and dig them out before you forget where they are. There is a special hand tool for this, comprising two prongs set above a 'rocker', on which the whole lifting action can pivot. This should loosen the roots and allow them to be lifted out cleanly. Simply cutting the tops off with a trowel runs the risk of regrowth from the roots. A few minutes' attention each day can eliminate thistles, dandelions, cat's ear, dock, fleabane, plantago and bindi-eye (*Calotis hispidula*), even if your neighbours encourage these plants by cutting their lawns too short. This weekly suburban scalping of grassed areas is deeply ingrained in the Australian psyche, and is analogous to overgrazing in pastures. The ecological consequences are the same.

Keep garden beds free of weeds in places where newly sown seeds have germinated and seedlings are appearing. Pull weeds out by hand, or cultivate with an old cutlery spoon or fork. Once the seedlings are clearly established, leave behind some of the innocuous volunteer plants recommended as groundcover in place of mulch (see Table 2 on page 22). This is fighting weeds with 'weeds'. The growth of these chosen plants will retard the growth of any newly emerging weeds beneath them.

A good way of cutting down the amount of time spent on weeding is to target overly vigorous garden plants and progressively get rid of them (or avoid acquiring them in the first place). Table 10 (page 70) contains a list of troublesome plants to avoid (and see Figures 75, 81, 85, 90 and 113). Some of these have tenacious root systems, and every fragment needs to be removed. Many have been given the noxious weed classification W4 in various municipalities in New South Wales, which means that they should no longer be sold, propagated or knowingly distributed. You may also be obliged to prevent them from spreading to adjoining properties, and for plants like the privets, to stop them from flowering and fruiting. Some of these plants have been 'cottage garden' items since halfway through the nineteenth century (Cuffley, 1989; Nottle, 1997), but science has a habit of providing us with very clear hindsight. For further information on potentially invasive plants, see the book by Suzanne Ermert (2001) and the website for Australia's Cooperative Centre for Weed Management (in Useful Addresses).

8.
Botany, herbs and herbalists

'What a shame that thee should have been employed
so many years tilling the earth and destroying so
many flowers and plants, without being acquainted
with their structure and uses.'

John Bartram, 18th-century American farmer

Botane and botany

Herbs are prominent among those companion plants likely to assist other plants (see Chapter 2) and their cultivation probably extends back at least 12 000 years. The science of botany developed from ancient studies of herbs and the compilation of herbals, which were illustrated lists of plants and their uses. 'Botany' itself is not a Latin word, but comes from *botane*, a Greek word meaning herb. 'Herb' comes from *herba*, the Latin for grass. This term is supposed to apply generally to softer-bodied plants that lack much secondary thickening in their stems, but in practice the term is a misnomer. None of our traditional herbs comes from the grass family (Gramineae or Poaceae), and many have firm, woody stems, even soft-leaved annuals like sweet basil.

It is an extraordinary fact that most of the long-cultivated herbs belong to just three families of flowering plants or Angiosperms.

This is remarkable given that there are more than 300 Angiosperm families containing more than 200 000 species. The most commonly grown herbs are considered here in their family groups (see Chapters 9 and 10). The advantage of remembering which family a plant belongs to is that we can immediately assume some of its general properties, just by knowing something about other family members.

Herbs as weeds

Among common names, the suffix 'wyrt' or 'wort' is derived from an Anglo-Saxon word for herb, which in turn has given rise to 'weed'. This label was not always as pejorative as it is now. Although herbs have been grown for thousands of years, they are generally not domesticated in the same way as fruit trees or vegetables. For most herbs there are very few recognised varieties or cultivars. Two notable exceptions are lavender (*Lavandula* species) and thyme (*Thymus* species). In each case, interspecies hybrid crosses have been made, and at least 100 cultivars are known. Many herbs are inclined to grow thickly and to take over any area they are given. Mostly they are well adapted to continual harvesting of leaves and stems, which mimics consumption by herbivores under natural conditions. It is a good idea to confine 'aggressive' herbs to beds in competition with similar assertive plants, or in some cases to pots, as already recommended (see Chapter 5).

An example of balanced competition is provided by a clump of oregano (*Origanum vulgare*) that has maintained itself near my letterbox at the front gate for 25 years. Although pushed aside by sprouting jonquils in winter, this clump holds its own with the short, pink-flowered succulent *Crassula multicava* for the rest of the year (see Figures 87 and 88). Oregano requires nothing but dead leaves, including those from the jonquils that lie dormant through the summer. Very few weeds appear in this part of the garden. Sometimes the odd runner of kikuyu grass (*Pennisetum clandestinum*) comes through from the lawn, or other single plants appear that are easily spotted. This is a low maintenance area — taking advantage of the herb's competitive abilities.

It is very useful to have plants that will perpetuate themselves in a garden setting. Some plants can do this because they are prolific seed producers. The innocent sweet alice (*Alyssum maritimum*, Cruciferae) has tiny seeds that break free and lodge in crevices everywhere. This plant can be encouraged in places where no one would waste time trying to plant the seeds. It flowers throughout the year, providing nectar to hoverflies and other insect visitors.

The Italian or flat-leafed parsley (see Table 12 on page 81) in my back garden has come entirely from self-sown plants over more than

26 years. It is no trouble to harvest whole parsley seedlings from places where they are not wanted, taking them straight to the kitchen. Others can be left to grow where they are, forming a natural border on the edge of the lawn, or in the mulch around fruit trees.

No one would suggest that sweet alice or parsley are weeds, but there are several herbs that are such serious pests once escaped from a garden that they are candidates for declaration under weeds legislation. Horehound (*Marrubium vulgare*) is one of these. Although valued as a traditional ingredient for cough medicines, and listed as a companion plant for tomato by some writers, horehound is notorious as a widespread weed of overgrazed pasture. Its hooked calyx means that seeds are easily spread by sheep. Of course, one solution to the perception of horehound as a weed is not to allow overgrazing, and to resow with perennial grasses. But even in city situations, another reason not to have horehound in your garden is that it can attract the horehound bug (*Agonoscelis rutila*), a large purplish shield bug that soon spreads to other ornamentals.

Wild fennel (*Foeniculum vulgare*) is another herb that really is a weed, too extensively spread to be declared noxious, but visually attractive along the roadside, providing a splendid aroma, good support for honey bees (see Figure 89), and preferable by far to toxic plants such as Crofton weed (*Eupatorium adenophorum*) that is spreading unchecked along NSW roadsides. Fennel is a plant whose introduction to Australia can be traced back to Governor King, who obtained seeds of various herbs and vegetables from Sir Joseph Banks before his return to New South Wales in 1800. In a garden situation, it can easily be controlled. Its seedlings are readily identifiable, and should be transplanted or removed.

St John's wort (*Hypericum perforatum*, see Figure 90) was growing in Melbourne

Botanical Gardens in 1857, but appears to have escaped into the countryside since its reintroduction as a garden plant by a German settler in the Ovens Valley, Victoria, in the 1880s. With two 'races' distinguished by size, this plant is a declared noxious weed in many rural parts of New South Wales — in more than 80 shires. At flowering, the hypericin content of the plant is maximal, and the toxicity for stock animals is greatest. However, because of their contents of hypericin and related compounds, preparations from St John's wort have definite medicinal value, replacing antidepressant drugs such as Prozac.

In New South Wales, approval has been given by the Minister for Agriculture for the harvesting of St John's wort plants in areas where it is declared a W3 noxious weed, but not in areas where it is a W2 noxious weed. Conditions apply to this approval; for instance, the areas to be harvested must be nominated in advance, and deliberate spreading of seeds is not permitted (Fisher, 1998).

The obligation to control the plant in unharvested areas also still applies. This approval to harvest means that fewer seeds will be produced, because plants will be removed before seeds have a chance to form. So harvesting is a measure that should retard the further uncontrolled spread of the plant. The size of the first harvest was estimated to be 500 tonnes (dry).

Caution should be exercised in taking any preparation from this plant, as photosensitivity or dermatitis are common side-effects. Professional guidance should always be sought. Nevertheless, confidence in this natural antidepressant is growing, and in Germany the number of people taking Prozac has contracted to be many fewer than those taking St John's wort preparations. Traditionally, St John's wort was able to chase out evil spirits — it now seems to be doing just that.

Herbals and the medicinal value of herbs

Herbs were not grown just to encourage bees, or to garnish staple foods. Some were grown to sweeten the air, to mask more offensive odours, and were classified as 'strewing' herbs. Many, however, were deemed to have medicinal value in their own right, or in addition to their culinary and aesthetic values. There is sometimes a firm basis to claims of medicinal properties or benefits from traditional uses of herbs, because these have been confirmed by the isolation of active compounds, and clinical trials. A good example is the isolation and use of a range of cardiac glycosides from foxglove (*Digitalis purpurea*), where the amounts that stimulated heart function were sometimes close to fatal doses. Another is the bark of willow, *Salix alba* and other species, from which came acetyl salicylic acid (aspirin). Equally, there is no foundation for many claims, such as those for orris 'root' (see Chapter 10). Another complication is that there are individual differences in thresholds for effectiveness, so for some people there is a benefit, but for others no effect is apparent at all. Opposing views of the efficaciousness of herbal remedies may sometimes both be correct, for specific individuals.

Herbalists were people who prepared compilations of what each plant was supposed to be useful for. If we look at the track record of individual herbalists, we find a great diversity of competence. Hippocrates, the famous Greek physician from Cos (460–375 BC), compiled a list of remedies that included many based on plant preparations, and on honey, which we now know to contain useful antibiotics, some of them effective against so-called 'superbugs', bacteria that are resistant to all standard antibiotics. The ancient theory of illnesses being based on four 'humours', as promulgated by Galen, is of course totally inadequate. But the remedies of Hippocrates often worked regardless. At the centre of his teaching is the idea that the physician should assist the body to heal itself, and in this respect he was absolutely right. Kos or Cos (where the cos lettuce also originated) became one of two chief centres of medical education in Greece, and Hippocrates was still widely read centuries later.

De Materia Medica was the title of a book written by Dioscorides (an army surgeon) in about AD 50. This title survived in the name of a subject for students of pharmacy at the University of Sydney at least until the 1960s. The Italian botanist Fabio Colonna (1567–1650), who devised the term 'petal' (Latin *petalum*) for the description of flowers, unfortunately suffered from epilepsy. He studied Dioscorides carefully, and decided that valerian (*Valeriana officinalis*), often used to prevent cramps, would be beneficial for preventing seizures. He evidently found it to be effective. Valerian root is still useful as a sedative.

Dioscorides had better adherence than Theophrastus (370–286 BC), regarded as the founder of botany as a science. This is because what Theophrastus wrote was lost from general sight for close to 1200 years, until translated into Latin by Theodoro Gaza in 1483. Theophrastus was remarkably perceptive, concluding that pollen transfer was necessary for fruit development in date palms and figs. Dates and figs were especially important in the ancient world because they could be dried and stored.

After Roman government waned in Britain and Europe, the detailed knowledge of herbs used medicinally was maintained by Christian communities living in monasteries. The Benedictines have a strong record in this area. The remarkable Abbess Hildegard von Bingen (1098–1179) gained a reputation for healing and recorded the names of the herbs grown at Rupertsberg and their possible uses in at least

three of her books — *Physica, Causae et Curae* and *Lingua Ignota* (Bobko, 1995; Hozeski, 2001). Certain monasteries also planted extensive orchards and vineyards, providing a living herbarium for varieties of edible fruits (McLeod, 1994b).

About 1000 plants had been named by the advent of the printing press, when botanical publication flourished, although erratically. For example, the sixteenth-century plant illustrations of the Swiss naturalist Konrad Gesner were not published in his lifetime. Some were used without acknowledgment by Joachim Camerarius, but they were eventually acquired and published as Gesner's work by the Nuremberg physician and botanical enthusiast Christoph Jakob Trew, between 1751 and 1771 (Sarton, 1955; Mondadori, 1984).

The herbalists, botanists and horticultural writers who published in England in Elizabethan and Stuart times (see Table 11) had to contend with increasing numbers of new plants as samples were brought back from places near and far. It is hard to imagine an England where such common fruit trees as apricot and pomegranate were novelties, but this was the case. The pomegranate (*Punica granatum*, Figure 92) came with Katherine of Aragon (1501), and the apricot (*Prunus armeniaca*) later still, by 1580. Both would have been grown 'against walls' (Bingley, 1831), indicating their need for extra warmth. Many new plants from the Americas were introduced during the sixteenth century, and these generally came via Europe first. As yet there was no systematic way of dealing with plant names and relationships. Latin binomials were not widely adopted until Linnaeus coined them so abundantly about the middle of the next century.

These writings (see Table 11) are a splendid mix of first-hand observation and fantastic fairytale. John Gerard actually grew many of the plants mentioned in his herbal, but even in

TABLE 11. SOME OF THE MAJOR PUBLICATIONS BY NOTABLE ENGLISH HORTICULTURAL WRITERS, BOTANISTS AND HERBALISTS OF THE 16TH AND 17TH CENTURIES

Name	Year	Title
William Turner	1551–68	*New herball* (three volumes)
Thomas Hyll	1568	*The profitable arte of gardening*
Thomas Tusser	1573	*Five Hundreth Pointes of Good Husbandrie*
Thomas Hyll	1579	*A profitable instruction of the perfite ordering of bees*
William Langham	1579	*The Garden of Health*
John Gerard	1597	*Herball or general historic of Plantes*
Francis Bacon	1597, 1612, 1625	*Essays: Of Gardens*
Richard Gardiner	1603	*Profitable Instructions for the Manuring, Sowing and Planting of Kitchin Gardens*
William Lawson	1618	*The Country Housewife's Garden*
William Lawson	1618	*A New Orchard and Garden*
John Parkinson	1629	*Paridisi in sole Paradisus terrestris*
Gervase Markham	1631	*A Way to Get Wealth*
Thomas Johnson	1634	*Mercurius botanicus Vol. 1*
Thomas Johnson	1640	*Mercurius botanicus Vol. 2*
John Parkinson	1640	*Theatrum botanicum*
Nicholas Culpeper	1653	*The Complete Herbal*
Robert Sharrock	1660	*A History of the Propagation and Improvement of Vegetables by the Concurrence of Art and Nature*
Charles Cotton	1661	*The Planter's Manual* (2nd edition)
John Evelyn	1664	*Sylva*
John Ray (Rea)	1670	*Historia plantarum generalis*
J. Worlidge	1677	*Systema horticulturae*
Moses Cook	1679	*The Manner of Raising, Ordering and Improving Forest and Fruit Trees*
John Evelyn	1699	*Acetaria: a Discourse on Sallets*

his own time was criticised for using other people's material without acknowledgment. The cobbled descriptions had come in a roundabout way, from an English translation of a French translation of the original Dutch text (1578) by Rembert Dodoens (Dodonaeus). The drawings were taken mainly from a German collection of woodcuts made by Jacob Theodore of Bergzabern, although in mitigation it was the printer John Norton who purchased these, and expected to use them as he saw fit. Gerard's plagiarism was quickly recognised by a friend of Dodoens, Matthieu de l'Obel, who had migrated to England, and become botanist to King James I. After John Gerard's death in 1612, Thomas Johnson was enlisted to correct the numerous mistakes in the Gerard herbal, the printer aiming to gain more sales in advance of the completion of a rival work by John Parkinson, *Theatrum botanicum*. This was very carefully prepared from the outset, with descriptions of nearly 3800 plants, and 2600 illustrations.

Much of what Nicholas Culpeper wrote was exaggeration and invention, and every activity in the garden was subordinate to astrology. You could not even pick a leaf unless you had the correct star sign for harvesting that plant. One explanation for this attitude is that a young lady he was planning to elope with was struck by lightning and killed (Leighton, 1970). He fled Cambridge, and rather than return to university, apprenticed himself to an apothecary in St Helen's Bishopsgate, where he imbibed the teachings of Galen. Ultimately, he surpassed Galen, and had much of his fantastic output pirated by others. Like Gerard, Culpeper wrote in English instead of Latin, with the aim of being more widely read. In

this, both were very successful, appealing to the superstitious and the gullible. This is where biodynamics comes from (see Chapter 1). The Gerards and Culpepers of botanical publication are ever with us.

Herbalists did not necessarily deal with the public. This was the role of the apothecary, and also the squire, who had to be his own apothecary (for example, Nicholas Blundell; Dwyer, 1978). Apothecaries were the pharmacists of their day, acquainted with the contents of the herbals, and with their shelves stocked accordingly. Thomas Johnson and John Parkinson were both apothecaries. The importance of accuracy in identifying plants that were to be used medicinally was obvious to these men, although not to some of their contemporaries. It was this need that led the Society of Apothecaries to establish the Oxford Physic (or Physick) Garden in 1636, a place where newly introduced plants could be grown, studied and described, and from where they could be disseminated. The Chelsea Physic Garden followed in 1673. It was to retain these functions until William Aiton moved from Chelsea to Kew in 1759.

In the eighteenth century, we find the link between botany and herbs suggested at the beginning of this chapter personified in the lives of those who studied plants because they were familiar with herbs (see Glossary and Biographical Notes). So often we read that some important botanist was 'the son of an apothecary', and with good reason. From childhood they would have been steeped in knowledge about plants and their healing applications. What could have been more natural than to continue a journey of discovery into the wider botanical world?

9.
Three prominent families

'What's in a name? that which we call a rose
By any other name would smell as sweet.'

William Shakespeare, *Romeo and Juliet*, Act 2, Scene 2

Umbelliferae forever

This family of approximately 3000 species was recognised centuries ago as a clearly defined natural group, because of the arrangement of the flowers, and the peculiar structure of the fruit, usually a schizocarp that splits into two flattened 'seeds', readily dispersed by the wind and the rain. An umbel is an inflorescence in which the flower stalks are arranged like the spokes of an umbrella. In this family, the tiny flowers are usually grouped in a compound umbel: an umbel of smaller umbels. This striking arrangement gave rise to the family name Umbelliferae, devised by the great French botanist Pierre Magnol in 1689.

Taxonomists have done well when they feature some prominent or distinguishing characteristic in a formal name. However, the thought-police of plant taxonomy have recently insisted on Apiaceae instead, after the alleged 'type' genus *Apium* (celery). But caraway, dill, fennel, anise, coriander, cumin,

parsley, carrots, parsnips, lovage and hemlock all belong to this family (see Table 12 on page 81), belying the undue prominence given to a single genus. This kind of arbitrary name change is resented by gardeners, which is why it has been strongly resisted ever since John Lindley suggested it in 1836 (for example, Ingram, 1998). 'Apiaceae' has also been rejected by the more perceptive botanists, who realise that such a change is the very opposite of what a phylogenetic classification of plants should be aiming for. Despite the abundance of information on DNA base sequences for a variety of important genes and non-coding sequences, there is no evidence that any species of *Apium* is the ancestor of all the other genera in this family. This is what is implied by the proposed name change.

The cultivated plants in this family are usually biennial or perennial, not flowering in their first growth season. When flowering does occur, the main stem reaches heights from about 1 metre (for example, parsley) up to

79

2 metres (for example, fennel). Although each flower is small and inconspicuous, there are so many flowers clustered together that they become a very popular nectar source for innumerable insect visitors, including flies, hoverflies, beetles and honey bees. Even ants, which rarely bring about pollination because they exude compounds toxic to pollen, seek nectar from parsnip flowers (see Figure 93).

Some botanists have described this family as 'promiscuous' because of this apparent lack of specificity in pollination vector, but this is an overly anthropomorphic interpretation of plant development and insect behaviour. Human eyes see the flowers as white (see Figure 94), pale pinky-mauve, pale yellow, or sometimes bright yellow (see Figures 89 and 93), but insects perceive these flowers in much greater contrast. Their ability to see in the ultraviolet region of the spectrum means that the five individual stamens stand out as radiating, interrupted spokes. To insects, the whole inflorescence presents a dazzling mosaic, signifying abundant food supplies.

ANISE, DILL AND FENNEL
All three share a strong anise or licorice flavour, but most gardeners find just one of these herbs sufficient. Fennel repays cutting back hard after seed maturation in the autumn. It will usually resprout, for at least 10 years. In addition to the leaves, the roots of fennel are also edible, in soups and casseroles (Mackenzie, 1980). Florence fennel, with massively swollen leaf bases (see Figure 95), is often preferred to the wild form, because the base of these plants can be sliced and eaten as a delicately flavoured vegetable, either raw in salads, or steamed. Known as *finnochio dolce* in Italian, this is one of the favourite vegetables brought as seeds by Italian immigrants to Australia.

It is interesting how similar flavours can turn up in quite unrelated plants. The anise or licorice flavour is also found in star anise

(*Illicium verum*, from China), in the roots and rhizomes of the licorice plant (*Glycyrrhiza glabra*, a legume), in the leaves of tarragon (Compositae), and the rare Australian native tree *Backhousia anisata* (Myrtaceae). The onslaught of bushfood enthusiasts further jeopardises the survival of this plant in its original habitat. Little do restaurant customers know, however, that they are also eating the scale insects that normally frequent these leaves.

PARSLEY
Parsley was a herb associated with funerals in Ancient Greece, and there are many superstitions surrounding its culinary use. Scottish lore forbids accepting parsley as a gift; a token coin must always be given in payment. There is a widespread but mistaken view that parsley did not arrive in Britain until 1584, coming then from Sardinia. The Italian flat-leafed form made a much earlier appearance, and evidently came to Britain with the Romans. By the fourteenth century, parsley featured in shredded greens, in soup with leeks, in sauces to accompany salted fish, and as green food colouring (Attwater, 1964; Dawson, 1994; Innes and Perry, 1997).

As noted early in Chapter 8, flat-leafed parsley is often much easier to grow than the crinkly-leafed type, which developed more recently. Burr (1865) confirms this lack of hardiness, and describes how the curly-leafed forms had become fashionable in the United States by the middle of the nineteenth century because of their 'superior excellence for garnishing'. But they were an absolute pain to grow, being transplanted up to four times to enhance the curliness! This is the kind of cultivar we can afford to lose.

Parsley will manage with an indifferent soil, but will do better if the soil is occasionally fertilised with compost. 'Peruvian' parsley is also a flat-leafed type, and the leaves stay sweet (not bitter) for a long time into autumn.

Its flowering is about one month out of phase with the Italian version, as it proceeds to bolt in late winter, flowering in early spring. Italian parsley flowers later. This would help considerably in avoiding natural crosses, provided later flowers are religiously removed from Peruvian parsley before they open. If growing and maintaining more than one kind of parsley, keep them well apart, or grow different kinds in different years, and recover all the seeds. This is sound advice for all members of this family.

TABLE 12. HERBS, WEEDS AND VEGETABLES: ALL MEMBERS OF THE UMBELLIFERAE

Angelica	*Angelica archangelica*
Anise	*Pimpinella anisum*
Caraway	*Carum carvi*
Carrot	*Daucus carota*
Celeriac	*Apium graveolens*
Celery	*Apium graveolens*
Chervil	*Anthriscus cerefolium*
Coriander	*Coriandrum sativum*
Cumin	*Cuminum cyminum*
Dill	*Anethum graveolens*
Fennel	*Foeniculum vulgare*
Great burnet	*Pimpinella major*
Hemlock	*Conium maculatum*
Lovage	*Levisticum officinale*
Parsley	*Petroselinum crispum*
Parsnip	*Pastinaca sativa*
Spignel	*Meum athamanticum*
Sweet cicely	*Myrrhis odorata*

GOTU KOLA

Gotu kola (*Centella asiatica*, formerly *Hydrocotyle asiatica*) from India is reputed to ward off rheumatism if two leaves per day are consumed. However, gotu kola causes adverse reactions in many people. Celery is much safer. Gotu kola can also host green aphids in the autumn.

The mint family: Labiatae

This family of more than 3200 species also has two names: Labiatae, referring to the lobed floral tube, and Lamiaceae, a phylogenetically inaccurate name featuring a genus few Australian gardeners have ever seen. *Lamium amplexicaule* (deadnettle or henbit) is a weed of farmland, and may cause 'staggers' in sheep and other stock animals. Nevertheless, *Lamium album* (white deadnettle) has useful medicinal properties, apparently reducing benign prostate enlargement (Ody, 1998).

In this family, numerous flowers are formed on a terminal inflorescence that projects clearly above the leaves, and which is often incorrectly described as a spike. This inflorescence is not a spike, because each flower has a tiny stalk, and in a spike all the flowers sit abruptly against the stem without stalks. This arrangement is much more complex. It may be condensed and spear-like, as in lavender, or sparse and spread out, as in sweet basil. In lavender, many of the bracts that subtend small groups of flowers become petal-like, and take on a lilac or purplish shade, quite distinct from the blue colour of the flowers. These bracts are especially prominent in 'topped' lavender (*Lavandula stoechas*), hence this common name.

Flowering may continue for a period of many months. The individual flowers are usually zygomorphic, with just a single plane of symmetry. Lavender, however, is more regular than most, with five tiny lobes, fairly equal. Some flowers are white, but most are coloured in the violet-blue-lilac-mauve-purple range. The size of the flower also varies widely. This can influence which insects visit, and how they feed. Honey bees and larger native bees (*Amegilla* species, and their predator, the domino cuckoo bee, *Thyreus lugubris*) forage from all, but damsel flies like lavender, and butterflies seem to prefer sweet basil and catmint.

The stem is generally square in cross-section. The leaves are usually simple, not overly large, perhaps even tiny (thyme), but occurring in opposite pairs that alternate at right angles with each successive pair along the stem. All are replete with oil glands that produce and store the mix of essential oils that we associate with each species or variety. When compounds contributing to aroma or flavour were first isolated and described, they were given names corresponding to source; for instance, thymol from thyme, menthol from mint (*Mentha*).

MINTS

The mints are deservedly very popular. They are easily grown, prospering in sunny, damp conditions. The flavour is commonly associated with peas, pineapple, or summer fruit-juice drinks. When identifying a mint plant, it is important to know that varieties cannot be categorised by leaf shape alone, because this is so variable. Most mint plants pass from one gardener to another after the leaf has been tasted. A 'transplant' can be taken just by severing shoots from a clump.

Spearmint, with its crisply embossed leaves, is *Mentha spicata*; peppermint is *M. piperita*. The name *M. viridis*, as used on labels sometimes, corresponds to *M. spicata*. Orange mint (*M.* x *piperita* var. *citrata*) has very attractive lilac flowers, and may produce these from axillary as well as terminal shoots. The scent from its soft leaves would suit an

aftershave lotion. This plant is quite short, about 40 centimetres at most, but very expansive. From a pot it can send out runners and invade the lawn on all sides, providing a fragrant alternative to grass. It flowers in mid to late summer.

Pennyroyal (*M. pulegium*) is definitely a mint, although *Pulegium* was once the name of the genus. The Romans first claimed that this herb banished fleas (Latin *pulex*, hence *pulegium*, of the fleas). Pennyroyal is still promoted as a natural way of killing fleas on dogs. Be assured it does not. Pennyroyal irritates the genital or urinogenital tracts, and its main herbal use in Australia has been to precipitate abortions. Dioscorides listed it correctly for this purpose.

A tight-knit groundcover plant with small leaves, pennyroyal is sometimes suggested as a lawn substitute. It needs protection against snails to become established. Despite its propagation by gardeners throughout the world, and status as a noxious weed in Western Australia and New Zealand, pennyroyal is fast disappearing from areas where it previously occurred naturally. In the United Kingdom, it is now found wild only in the New Forest (Hampshire), and on the western shores of Lough Beg in Northern Ireland (Everett, 1999).

BASIL

Sweet basil (*Ocimum basilicum*) is very like mint in needing plenty of water and full sunshine but, unlike mint, basil is usually an annual, and is best grown from seed sown each spring. The leaves are picked from established plants as they are needed. The common kind has crumpled green leaves, and white flowers. Far more attractive are the purple-veined types, with more colour also in and around the flowers. One from Taiwan (imported as seeds by the Minara Company) has flat leaves with purple veins, plus mauve flowers and purple subtending bracts. Another known as Thai basil is similar to this, but with even more pronounced colour in the stems. Ultimately, there are varieties with fully purple leaves, such as Dark Opal and Purple Ruffles. Flowering continues throughout summer and autumn. Always let some plants flower and produce seeds. In my experience, perennial basil does not produce any seeds.

ROSEMARY

Rosemary (*Rosmarinus officinalis*) is a woody perennial, which lasts for many years. It flowers for almost the entire year. The leaves are an exception to the general kind, about 1–2 centimetres long, very narrow, and with distinctly rolled-over edges. The underneath is whitish compared to the glossy green on top. Other plants are named as having 'leaves like rosemary' (*rosmarinifolia* or *rosmariniformis*). Propagation of rosemary is easy. Stems that dip downwards can be deliberately buried in the soil until roots have formed, and then new plants can be snipped free and moved about. Rosemary is for remembrance, as it was once supposed to aid the memory. It is more reliable in the treatment of migraine headaches.

SAGE

Sage (*Salvia officinalis*) is a plant that prefers drier conditions. The name *Salvia* comes from Latin, and connotes health or strength. The texture of the dark green, elongated leaf is interesting, and the flavour is characteristic. The flowers are violet, appearing in midsummer. Sage plants may protect other plants against aphids, but like most others in this family, fail to deter white fly. Many *Salvia* species of medicinal rather than culinary application are currently attracting interest in Australia (see Figure 2). Ornamental species have also been popular, such as *S. splendens* (red flowers).

THYME

Thyme, *Thymus vulgaris*, is a small plant that prefers drier conditions. It has very small leaves, and tends not to be long-lived. As already noted, there are many cultivars.

LAVENDERS

Lavenders are perennial plants that can be left in suitable positions for some years. Assume they will reach 1 metre over their first two or three years, with a similar spread. The leaf is more complex than the general kind, and the edge can be ornate, simple or mixed. The naming of lavenders was initially very muddled (McLeod, 1994a, 2000), and the names adopted here are the stable ones. *Lavandula angustifolia* or narrow-leafed lavender is also known as English lavender, although it was probably a Roman introduction to Britain. French lavender, *L. dentata*, has a crennelated leaf edge that enhances the attractiveness of the foliage. *L. stoechas*, topped or Italian lavender, sometimes runs amok, and has weed status in Victoria. All of these can be grown en masse for the production of oil by steam distillation, as in Tasmania, Jersey and Provence.

Many parts of Australia are not cold enough for some of the classic European species. On the coast near Sydney in New South Wales, French lavender will flower profusely, but English lavender is most reluctant. Be on the lookout for novel kinds, many of which have been bred for warmer or more humid conditions. Examples are Silver Feather, derived from a cross of *L. pinnata* and *L. canariensis*, and Sidonie, of unknown parentage, but in view of the dissected leaf shape, possibly also involving *L. canariensis*. Sidonie flowers well in warm, humid climates, but its leaves are lacking in oil. Since the lavender perfume comes mainly from the oil glands in the leaves and bracts, this is a serious deficiency. *Lavandula* Walberton's Silver Edge, with variegated leaves, has recently been released in the United Kingdom. It will be interesting to see how it performs in Australia. There are variants in inflorescence colour too, including white, green and pink. Swan River Pink is apparently the first pink Italian lavender, and is an Australian variety that was found growing near Perth, Western Australia.

Lavender plants may protect other plants against aphids, while the cut, dried leaves have been used for generations to deter clothes moths by placing them in sachets with stored linen or clothing. Whether lavender leaves are effective deterrents for other household pest insects and silverfish is a matter for conjecture.

Lavender leaves are edible, providing an attractive, complex flavour. Elizabeth I, who ruled England between 1558 and 1603, was more astute about dietary matters than her father. She was very keen on lavender as a staple garnish with food, and as a tisane, or tea blended with honey. She did indeed have 'the heart and stomach of a king'. Elizabeth's lavender was *L. angustifolia*, but English lavender is not the only edible type. *L. dentata* yields a lavender vinegar that is both visually attractive and delicious (see Figure 192).

LEMON BALM

Melissa officinalis tells all in its name: it is attractive to bees (Greek μελι *meli*), and preparations from the plant were to be found at the apothecary's. The plant may reach 1 metre, and it spreads well. There is a variegated form, which is not as vigorous. Flowering is late, from summer to autumn, and the pale flowers are held in the axes.

The leaves are lobed around the edges, but are shaped more like those of catmint than peppermint. The leaf can be used for every conceivable culinary purpose, as for mints, except that the lemony flavour of the leaves is distinctive, and they serve as a lemon substitute. This source of lemon flavour is much to be preferred over lemon grass (*Cymbopogon citratus*), because the latter's sharp-edged leaves cut young hands. The fresh shoots of lemon balm makea tasty herb vinegar. Medicinally, extracts can be used for

painful swellings or bites. But forget about claims that lemon balm aids the memory, or restores lost youth.

SAVOURY

There are three species that might be encountered: summer savoury (*Satureja hortensis*), an annual; winter savoury (*S. montana*), which is much taller, and *S. repandens*. They have small leaves and, like sage, are very sensitive to poor drainage. The alleged superiority of summer savoury comes from Culpeper, but this opinion is rightly disputed (Reid, 1992).

OREGANO

The perennial or wild oregano is *Origanum vulgare*, whereas the annual, sweet marjoram, is *O. majorana*. The wild form is a plant that looks after itself (see Figures 87 and 88). The leaves have a delightful, strong flavour, so very few are needed. This herb is at its best with scrambled eggs or omelettes, or with cheese sandwiches. Flowering occurs in early summer.

HYSSOP

The modern plant of this name (*Hyssopus officinalis*), a strewing herb, is not the biblical hyssop. This could have been any one of several plants, including oregano (Hepper, 1994).

BERGAMOT

Most familiar members of this family come from around the Mediterranean, but bergamot (*Monarda didyma*) comes from the United States. It was used by the Oswego Indians of New York to prepare tea, hence the common name Oswego tea. The flavour is pleasant, but not as rich as oil of bergamot, which is obtained from a species of citrus and named for Bergamo in Italy. John Tradescant the younger introduced bergamot to England, possibly in the enormous batch of plants he brought over from Virginia in 1638. It has large leaves, about 10 centimetres long, and usually has clusters of striking red flowers, but pink, mauve, violet and white are also possible. The flowers are edible. Plants grow readily from seed, and do well with partial shade. If planted in spring, they can be cut and dried at the time of flowering, in summer.

The daisy family: Compositae

This is an enormous family, the largest among flowering plants, ranking ahead of grasses and legumes. It comprises 13 tribes and roughly 20 000 species. Despite the numbers, this is a readily distinguished natural group because the inflorescence is a composite head or capitulum of small flowers, hence Compositae. The collection of 'florets' mimics the appearance of a large flower, the result of convergent evolution. This resemblance is accomplished by some of the flowers on the edge (the ray florets) producing a petal-like flap which is directed away from the centre of the disc. The small tubular flowers (disc florets) comprise the majority. The floral tubes of all florets are formed by the fusion of five petals, and the edges of these are often distinct.

A spectacular sunflower head (*Helianthus annuus*) can produce more than 1000 florets, spirally arranged, maturing and progressively opening from the outside towards the centre. Most species of Compositae produce fewer than this, and at the other extreme, yarrow (*Achillea millefolium*) might have as few as 20 florets per head.

These arrangements effect pollination brilliantly, since finding one flower means finding many, and visiting insects know they have hit the jackpot, day after day, as new florets open. As each one matures, the pollen is released and presented first, then the style grows upwards and the stigma or receptive surface is revealed. This sequence ensures crosspollination as insects move from one inflorescence to another. In many species of Compositae, crosspollination is essential for fertilization to occur, and for seeds to be produced.

Most of the important herbs or companion plants in this family belong to one tribal grouping — the chrysanthemum tribe, or more formally, the Anthemideae (see Table 13 on page 86). *Chrysanthemum cinerareaefolium* has been mentioned in Chapter 1 as the commercial source of pyrethrum. We are lucky to have kept the name *Chrysanthemum*. The normal rules of priority have been set aside in order that the name should still apply to the cultivated plants gardeners are used to calling chrysanthemums, rather than to a couple of obscure wild plants known only to specialist taxonomists. When brushed, the leaves of members of this tribe produce a range of characteristic scents broadly reminiscent of varnish. The scent of *Chrysanthemum* itself is divisive, prompting infatuation or revulsion according to individual taste and sensitivity.

CHAMOMILE

The garden form of this plant is more vigorous than the lawn form, so before you are tempted to dig up the grass and replace it, remember that you must be prepared to spend the time necessary to keep a chamomile lawn free of weeds. The leaves of Roman chamomile are harvested, dried and used to make a soothing tea.

German chamomile has been known by several names. It is difficult to believe that this plant could have grown so luxuriantly as to help cover the Somme battlefield only a year after the devastation (*Plant Talk* 16, 1999, page 44). It flowers yellow and white in spring, but is prone to powdery mildew. It does much better in the open garden than in a pot, and is recommended as a companion for Cruciferae, onions and potatoes (see Figure 115).

ARTEMISIA

The genus *Artemisia* is named for Artemis, the herbalist wife of Mausolus (he of the mausoleum). Four common species (see Table 13) provide a variety of flavours. Wormwood is bitter, and also known as vermouth. It is an ingredient in this liqueur, and very good for digestive upsets. Southernwood, or lad's love, tarragon and mugwort can all be eaten in small quantities with greens, or as culinary herbs. Tarragon has a complex flavour, and there are great arguments about whether French, German or Russian tarragon is the best. As companion plants, try any *Artemisia* with other members of the same family, Cruciferae and cucurbits.

ACHILLEA

This genus is named after Achilles, who is supposed to have used yarrow leaves to treat wounds. Remembering what happened to Achilles, we should not rely on this property, nor on this plant providing a cure for baldness. It does, however, play a valuable role as a companion, and the dried leaves have a more attractive scent than many in this group. The flowers, too, have an excellent honeyed scent. Despite a reputation for aggression, and the English worrying about its weed potential, yarrow marks time throughout the winter, and is easy to accommodate on the edge of a mixed garden bed.

The two common colour forms in Australia have either white or magenta flowering heads appearing in early summer. The colour range has been expanded dramatically by recent breeding programs in England, Holland and Germany (Thornton-Wood, 1999).

The Caucasian species *Achillea filipendulina* has yellow flowering heads, and hybrids formed with *A. millefolium* have produced some interesting orange shades and combinations. One of these, Terracotta, is available from Diggers' Seed Club (see Useful Addresses).

TABLE 13. HERBS BELONGING TO COMPOSITAE

ANTHEMIDEAE

chamomile		
Roman		*Anthemis nobilis*
German		*Chamomilla recutita* (*Matricaria chamomilla*)
chrysanthemum		*Chrysanthemum cinerareaefolium*
feverfew		*Tanacetum parthenium*
mugwort		*Artemisia vulgaris*
southernwood		*Artemisia abrotanum*
tansy		*Tanacetum vulgare*
tarragon		*Artemisia dracunculus*
wormwood		*Artemisia absinthium*
yarrow		*Achillea millefolium*

OTHER TRIBES

coltsfoot	*Tussilago farfara*
purple coneflower	*Echinacea purpurea*
dandelion	*Taraxacum officinale*
lettuce	*Lactuca sativa*
marigold	*Calendula officinalis*, *Tagetes* species

Another attractive newcomer is Inca Gold, which commences bright yellow with orange tips, fading gradually to yellow. These hybrids are stable provided the plants are propagated by division. How adaptable they are remains to be seen.

TANACETUM

Tansy has attractive, feathery leaves (see Figure 97), and yellow flowers. It is not the ogre sometimes portrayed, and is stopped in its tracks by winter. Numerous leaf-eating caterpillars and snails also control it. Feverfew has a leaf that is not as finely divided as that of tansy, hence the name. Feverfew is possibly useful for migraine headaches.

MARIGOLDS

Confusion reigns. The so-called African and French marigolds both came from Mexico: *Tagetes erecta* and *T. patula*, respectively (see Figure 96). These marigolds have the ability to deter root-knot nematodes (eelworms), a property that was evidently discovered in the Netherlands (Carson, 1962). However, *T. patula* supports mealy bugs in summer, and my preferred substitute is cobbler's peg, *Bidens pilosa*. For planting in pots or gardens, I have selected a dwarf form, which rarely exceeds 60 centimetres in height, and is usually much shorter (see Figure 98). To prevent *Bidens pilosa* becoming a 'weed', control the number of seeds produced by trimming off flowers (see Figures 99 and 100).

Other useful species of *Tagetes* are *T. minuta*, or 'khakibos' in Africa, and *T. filifolia*, the Irish lace marigold, with ferny leaves. *T. minuta* leaves are extracted and used against aphids.

The standard English or pot marigold *Calendula officinalis*, may be no use against nematodes, but its flowers support newly emerged hoverflies in late winter to early spring. Orange and yellow forms are both available. To keep marigolds in the garden, simply break up dry flower heads and toss the seeds around.

DANDELION

Dandelion (*Taraxacum officinale*) is named from the French *dents de lion* ('lion's teeth'), referring to the shape of the leaf outline. This rosette plant is a traditional leafy green, but bitter, and not to everyone's liking. It should not be confused with cat's ear, *Hypochoeris radicata*. The latter has a branched stalk with several flowering heads (see Figure 76), but the dandelion has only a single flowering head on each straight stalk (see Figure 84). Take particular care to prevent dandelion flowers from maturing and releasing their pervasive seeds. Tea or wine can be produced from the dried leaves.

LETTUCE

Lettuce (see Chapter 12) is included in Table 13 because there have been times when it was regarded as a soporific and healing herb. Its Greek reputation was that it robbed men of desire, but there seems little evidence of this.

ECHINACEA

Purple coneflower (*Echinacea purpurea*) is the latest cure-all. The claims made for its benefits are greatly exaggerated, but seeds will continue to fetch high prices while the craze lasts. Grow it for fun, or out of curiosity, because it is an attractive garden subject.

10.
More familiar herbs

'Geraniums were the only flowers I saw grow in the drought
out there. I remembered this woman had a few dirty grey-green
leaves behind some sticks against the bark wall near the door;
and in spite of the sticks the fowls used to get in and scratch beds
under the geraniums, and scratch dust over them — and ashes
were thrown there — with an idea of helping the flowers
I suppose; and greasy dish-water, when fresh water was scarce —
till you might as well try to water a dish of fat.'

Henry Lawson, 'Water Them Geraniums'

Mustard and cress

Certain edible members of the family
Cruciferae (Brassicaceae) have long been
consumed as herbs or condiments. Apart from
the mustards, which are herbs or spices
according to whether leaves or seeds are
prepared, the herbs in this family include
rocket (*Eruca sativa*), and cress of two kinds:
salad cress (*Lepidium sativum*) and watercress
(*Nasturtium officinale*) (see Table 14). The
pungent spicy or peppery flavours of leaves
and seeds alike are caused by glucosinolates,
compounds that contain glucose and sulfur as
well as nitrogen. They can be converted to
isothiocyanates, typical of mustard oils, by
removal of the glucose sugar.

The cruciform flower is regular, with two
pairs of sepals forming the calyx, then four
petals forming one 'cross', and four prominent
stamens another. The petals are often yellow.
Self-incompatibility of pollen and stigma is
common in the family, with mandatory
outcrossing achieved by insect visitors. A
twofold stigma is connected to the ovaries,
which consist of two compartments with
ovules attached by short stalks around the
perimeters. Ultimately the fruit is a silique: a
dry pod with two parallel compartments
containing small seeds formed from the ovules.
Sometimes the pod wall is thick and pithy —
for instance, radish (see Figure 47) — and

sometimes the pod is short. The seeds contain little or no endosperm, with oil as a major energy reserve, stored in the embryo.

Despite the production of glucosinolates by these plants, some are very sensitive to toxic compounds produced by other plants. Salad or garden cress is so sensitive that it is used in a standard bio-assay of allelopathic compounds. Accordingly, companion planting for cress is generally restricted to a few plants from the same family, such as radish and horseradish, plus lettuce.

Borage, comfrey and the viper's brood

These plants are among about 2000 species given family status as Boraginaceae, but they are very close relatives of Labiatae. The flower may be actinomorphic ('star-shaped'), as in borage, but in others such as *Echium* the flower is zygomorphic, like most members of Labiatae (see Chapter 9). The leaves are mainly alternate beyond the first pairs, rather than opposite, sometimes forming a rosette, as in *Echium*. The position of the micropyle in the ovule — the opening through which the pollen tube gains entry — is usually different. This is at the top in most Boraginaceae, but at the bottom in Labiatae, and in the Heliotropium group within Boraginaceae. These differences are fairly trifling in developmental and genetic terms, and it is difficult to seize on a single reproductive character that always distinguishes members of Labiatae from Boraginaceae. A phylogenetic classification might well include these two families in the one superfamily.

BORAGE

Borage (*Borago officinalis*) is an untidy annual of variable height, with shoots producing a succession of bright blue-purple flowers (see Figure 103). I say untidy because it flops

TABLE 14. HERBS, SPICES AND VEGETABLES BELONGING TO CRUCIFERAE	
black mustard	*Brassica nigra*
brown mustard	*Brassica juncea*
brussels sprouts	*Brassica oleracea*
cress	*Lepidium sativum*
horseradish	*Amoracia rusticana*
kale	*Brassica oleracea*
pak choi	*Brassica campestris*
radish	*Raphanus sativus*
rocket	*Eruca sativa*
swede turnip	*Brassica napus* (also called rutabaga)
tatsoi	*Brassica campestris* (rosette form of pak choi)
turnip	*Brassica rapa*
watercress	*Nasturtium officinale*
white mustard	*Sinapis alba*

about and changes direction, even with adequate water supplies. The flowers are sometimes used to decorate salads, but you will have to fight the bees for them. Pick early or late in the day, when the bees are least active. The leaves must be crushed in order to release their flavour, which is often likened to cucumber. Seeds that are left to be shed will germinate readily, and perpetuate the plant automatically. Borage is supposed to be the best companion plant for strawberries, and certainly its root system operates at a deeper level. However, strawberries will prosper with many different companions (see Chapters 2 and 5), and so will borage (see Figure 168 and Chapter 1).

COMFREY

Comfrey (*Symphytum officinale*) is a perennial, with pink or similar coloured flowers that hang in small clusters, and are attractive to bees (see Figure 106). Because of its deep roots, it has a useful role as a pioneer, but in well-prepared garden soil it will undermine its neighbours and deprive them of nutrients. Its multitude of handsome leaves will shade them, too. Comfrey is fine by itself, like valerian, but objectionable as a companion. If you have this plant, manage it ruthlessly, and do not be taken in by the 'need' for comfrey leaves as an accelerator for compost production. Mown grass is far more useful (see Chapter 3).

Root preparations of comfrey were traditionally applied to broken bones, and one common name was 'knitbone'. The leaves of comfrey are still valuable applied externally to strained muscles or injured joints, and likely to be useful in the treatment of arthritis. Handle the leaves with gloves, as they cause dermatitis in sensitive people. Avoid taking any preparation from comfrey internally, as this may injure the liver.

CHINESE FORGET-ME-NOT

The leaves of this plant (*Cynoglossum amabile*) are reminiscent of comfrey, but this annual is much more willing to share resources. Blue star flowers on an upright inflorescence are produced from April right through until summer, and are frequented by hoverflies and flies. This is a good companion in any garden. One irritation is that the seed cases are covered with tiny hooks that cling to clothing and to dogs. The solution is to cut off the inflorescence after flowering has finished.

ECHIUM

Echium vulgare (viper's bugloss, see Figure 105) has a long tradition in herbal medicine, for ailments such as fevers and headaches, as a diuretic, and as a supposed cure for snakebite. *Echium* comes from the Greek word for snake or viper, reflecting this reputation. It was once commonly imagined that plants bore some resemblance to the condition that the plant could cure (the 'doctrine of signatures'). Hence 'viper' as part of the common name refers to this imagined likeness of the flower to a snake's open mouth, with protruding tongue.

Echium plantagineum (salvation Jane or Paterson's curse) is believed to have escaped from Elizabeth Macarthur's garden near Camden, New South Wales, by about 1840. More recently, attention has focused on its toxic alkaloids. The plant is certainly poisonous to horses and pigs, but less so to cattle and sheep, unless it predominates in their diet. Well-fed horses have the good sense to ignore it.

Concern for its effects on human health has been greatly exaggerated. The presence of trace amounts of alkaloids in honey was used as a pretext to have this species declared a noxious weed at a time when the species contributed substantially to the production of honey — at about $5 million per annum (Briggs, 1985). Strategically, because of its early flowering time, this plant helped the numbers of bees to build up at the beginning of the season, so it had a significance to honey production that was not simply related to the monetary return from the high quality light-coloured 'curse' honey. The protein content of the pollen is clearly adequate for the needs of an expanding bee population. Furthermore, the name 'salvation Jane' indicates the value of the plant as drought fodder, certainly in South Australia.

Having such a useful plant declared as a weed has been extremely counterproductive. This notorious misapplication of science reflected the political dominance of pastoral interests in the early 1980s. Neither *E. plantagineum* nor the closely related perennial *E. vulgare* are weeds of capably managed pasture, although their small, black seeds may be dormant for at least five years. The answer, as usual, is to sow a diversity of perennial grasses that have a competitive advantage, then not allow stock animals to destroy this advantage.

An attractive species for the garden is *E. fastuosum*, which comes from the Canary Islands. This hardy perennial forms a bush about 2 metres tall, and the same around. In spring it products striking club-like inflorescences packed densely with bee-attracting blue flowers (see Figure 104).

BLUE HELIOTROPE

Common blue heliotrope (*Heliotropium europaeum*) comes from the Mediterranean region. The leaves are decorative, neatly embossed, and alternate. The flowers have a strong perfume that is unique; to say it is musk-like does not do it justice (hence the common name 'cherry pie'). Flowering from summer to spring, this plant is an asset to any garden (see Figure 91). Its close relative, the prostrate *H. amplexicaule*, falls foul of noxious weeds legislation in certain districts as it is toxic to stock animals.

Orris and iris

There are more than 250 species and natural hybrids of Iris, many of horticultural interest originating in or near Georgia (Caucasia). Iris is named for Orris, the angelic golden-winged sister of the Harpies, who ran messages for Hera between Olympus and Earth. The rainbow is supposed to have come from her multicoloured cape, streaming out behind her. Iris flowers do indeed display the colours of the rainbow, and many more besides. The name was originally given by Theophrastus (Simpson, 1985).

The powdered rhizome (orris root) has been used as a herbal preparation for more than 2000 years. Once believed to cure practically every known ailment, orris today is used to 'fix' the scent in potpourri mixtures. The violet-like scent of orris develops during drying and storage of rhizome slices. The cultivation of tall bearded iris and extraction of the rhizomes became an important industry in Florence, whose coat of arms displayed a white iris on a red field. The Florentina iris is a form of *Iris germanica*, and is sometimes called *I. florentina*.

This industry spread to France. The heraldic or French fleur-de-lys dating from the twelfth century is obviously an iris, not a lily (which would be *lis*). The source of confusion appears to be John, Duke of Bedford, who in his *Book of Hours* (about 1415) put forward the legend that a cloth embroidered with three fleurs-de-lys was brought by an angel to a hermit, who gave it to Clotilde, wife of Clovis, in return for alms (Evans, 1969). Iris were grown abundantly on the banks of the River Lys, and hence were referred to as 'the flower of the Lys'. Thomas Hyll (1579) wrote 'flouredeluce', and William Shakespeare wrote 'fleur-de-luce' or 'flower-de-luce' on different occasions. There is no mention of *lis* here.

Not only do tall bearded iris have beautiful flowers, but their scent, which is often overlooked, is magnificent: something like the much-prized black jelly beans fondly remembered from childhood days. Flowering from spring to summer (see Figures 3, 108, 111 and 112), iris is an excellent source of food for honey bees. As a companion for vegetables and herbs, a few iris plants provide stability in the landscape. Keep the old, dead leaves pulled away from the rhizome to enhance the plant's appearance and remove pests. Irises should be divided and moved every two or three years in the autumn, discarding the oldest parts of the rhizome that have already flowered. Take the opportunity to lime their soil, as they prefer a neutral to slightly alkaline pH. When repositioning the rhizomes, use a small rock to hold each rhizome in place, otherwise new root growth will pull the end with the leaf bases underground and encourage rot. The replanted rhizomes should never be totally covered by soil, as this will prevent flowering.

Tall bearded irises (in the germanica group) are still most popular, but the widening scope of available species and cultivars can best be appreciated by consulting books by Gwendolyn Anley (1946) and Graeme Grosvenor (1984, 1997).

Pelargoniums and geraniums

Geranium is an ancient name, coming from the Greek *geranos* for crane, based on the resemblance of the dry fruit to the crane's bill. The name is attributed to Dioscorides. The geranium of later herbals is herb Robert, *Geranium robertianum*, but these days the name 'geranium' is often misapplied to species of *Pelargonium*.

Before 1789, geraniums and the plants now called pelargoniums were all classified together as *Geranium* in the family Geraniaceae. Many had been brought to Europe from their countries of origin in southern Africa, via Cape Town. The flowers of *Geranium* are sym-metrical. However, in *Pelargonium* the flowers are irregular (zygomorphic), and they have a floral tube capable of holding nectar. The inflorescence is likely to be an umbel, whereas the flowers of *Geranium* are single or held in pairs. So an observant gardener only has to look at the flowers to tell the difference at once.

Another feature that can be used to differentiate the two, provided the flower is fertile, is the mechanism of seed dispersal. In *Pelargonium*, the drying fruit splits open, revealing an array of tufted seeds, ready to be dispersed by the wind. *Geranium* seeds are not tufted. The parallel name pelargonium is from pelargos, Greek for stork, again likening the fruit shape to the bill of a bird. The botanist who first made these distinctions was Charles Louis L'Heritier de Brutelle, the same capable

Frenchman who coined our genus name *Eucalyptus*.

Horticulturally, *Pelargonium* became extremely popular in the nineteenth century, as many interspecies hybrids formed readily, and these could be maintained by growing plants from cuttings. An ability to cope with short-term water shortage made pelargonium the ideal pot plant. They are often featured on windowsills in the Beatrix Potter illustrations from her Peter Rabbit books (1904–13). However, it is extremely doubtful that Mr McGregor ever employed them as companion plants in his famous vegetable garden. Did they perhaps stop flies from coming through the windows? The strongly perfumed scent of pelargonium foliage suggests this possibility.

There are now several thousand cultivars of *Pelargonium*. Avoid those with complex double flowers for companion planting, because insects cannot gain access. Try the typical zonal types with variegated leaves, and be on the lookout for those with distinctive leaf aromas; for example, nutmeg (*P. fragrans*), lemon (*P. crispum*) and peppermint (*P. tomentosum*). Beware of overwatering, as this can diminish production of the volatile compounds contributing to the scent. Pelargoniums prefer a soil pH in the range pH 6.5 to pH 7, and all grow readily from cuttings at most times of the year. Some will also grow from seed. *Pelargonium tomentosum* flowers in spring (see Figure 107), overlapping the autumn and winter-flowering zonals. One plant can spread very widely over several years, providing an ideal setting for other pot plants. Trimming will keep it within bounds. This species has been in Australia since 1857 (Nottle, 1997).

Pelargoniums help to deter white fly (Murray, 1999), and possibly also fruit fly. However, the correct type must be chosen. The Stellar group of zonal pelargoniums, named for the jagged leaf outline and originally bred in Australia, is particularly effective. According to Blaise Cooke (1998), these arose from a cross of *P. staphysagroides* and *P. × hortorum* made by Ted Both. My Stellar plants originated from May Barrie's property, Callemondah, described in an article by Mare Carter (1995). The petals in this form are jagged in outline, resembling the leaves (see Figures 109 and 110), but their uniform colour distinguishes the flower from previously described cultivars. Ironically, white fly are pests of two other distinct groups — the Unique and Regal cultivars. Their breeding history is quite different. For further information, see the books by Llewellyn, Hudson and Morrison (1981), Delamain and Kendall (1987), Stockton, Stockton and Mason (1996) and Blaise Cooke (1998).

I must disagree with some of the advice proffered by Stockton, Stockton and Mason (1996, page 96): 'It is a good idea to spray occasionally whether your plants need it or not'. This is not really a good idea. First of all, it is wasteful of whatever is being sprayed. Second, the adverse side-effects of spraying will occur more frequently, whether this is death of beneficial insects or slow poisoning of oneself. The list of pesticides these authors had in mind to spray included fungicides such as Benlate, Baycor and Zineb, all of which are worthy of avoidance. Pelargoniums are hardy plants, and I have yet to meet the pelargonium that needs any help at all from synthetic pesticides. The key to avoiding fungal diseases is never to overwater.

Do not be in a hurry to trim off the brown stalks and drying fruits. They are useful as camouflage for net-casting spiders.

Sweet violets

Some of the fancy violas (pansy, painsease or hearts-ease, *Viola tricolor*) are prone to powdery mildew and snail attack, but the introduced European species *V. odorata* and the native violet, *V. banksii* (formerly *hederacea*), are robust, and seem to be impervious to most pests and diseases. The plants are very short, with long leaf stalks radiating from a very compact stem. Runners form new plants readily. Flowering occurs in late autumn, continuing throughout the winter into spring, filling a vital niche for nectar-seekers. *V. odorata* is almost pure colour, but *V. banksii* is delicately marked with several shades, and partly white. This flower lacks the spur typical of *V. odorata* and *V. tricolor*. Nectar is produced by glands on two of the stamens, collecting in the base of the flower, and accessible only through a narrow opening.

V. banksii is a coastal species indigenous to New South Wales and Queensland (up to Brisbane), whereas the true *V. hederacea* was first described from Tasmania, occurring also in Victoria, inland New South Wales and South Australia (Thiele and Prober, 2004). Although excellent in the lawn as a grass substitute, *V. banksii* needs to be kept out of gardens, as its runners extend quickly and are easily overlooked until it is too late. Both *V. banksii* and *V. odorata* are ideal as pot specimens, or as groundcover in controlled locations. Put them in damp positions, or keep them well watered.

Dried flowers or leaves from *Viola* species can be used for the preparation of washes, creams or poultices for the treatment of skin rashes, eczema or boils, and even skin cancers. Internally, syrups prepared from the flowers with honey have long been used as an expectorant. In the 1930s, before more effective alternative treatments were developed, syrups were also taken for internal cancers (Ody, 1998).

Miscellaneous herbs

ALOE VERA
This short succulent plant (see Figure 69) produces a soothing gel. Just break a leaf and apply it directly to insect bites or skin irritations. It really works.

EVENING PRIMROSE

Evening primrose (*Oenothera biennis*) is an erect plant up to 1 metre tall, and its yellow flowers attract bees very early in the morning (see Figure 113). This plant has become noticed in Australia because the seed oil is beneficial for premenstrual stress. Most of this oil is presently imported from Canada, but the plant could certainly be grown in abundance here. It has quickly become a roadside weed throughout the Blue Mountains, west of Sydney, so care is needed.

FOUR-O'CLOCK (MARVEL OF PERU)

This plant (*Mirabilis jalapa*, Nyctaginaceae) forms a bush about 70 centimetres tall, and can be grown from black, barrel-like seeds, or after the first year, from dormant tubers. The leaves are handsome and opposite, with a rank smell when crushed. The flowers have a tube at their base, amplified into a prominent fan, with orange anthers held outwards (see Figure 114). The flower colours are white, yellow or magenta, and sometimes variegated yellow and magenta. Not only do they open in the late afternoon, they remain open overnight, well into the next morning, closing in response to full sunlight. The seeds may be collected over a period of many months, from summer into autumn. As remarked upon in Chapter 2, four-o'clock does well when planted with tomatoes (see Figure 37). This makes sense, as both come from Peru. In late autumn to early winter, the whole plant senesces and collapses, the stem segments disarticulating at nodes that look like knee-joints.

NASTURTIUM

Nasturtium, *Tropaeolum majus*, is from Mexico. The common name comes from the Latin words for nose-twisting, a reference to its strong and 'different' aroma. The young leaves provide a peppery tang to mixed salad greens. Flowers appear from winter to spring, with colours ranging from red to golden yellow, and sometimes mixed. Tim North (1999) notes that there used to be white and purple nasturtiums too, and questions what became of them. The petals are edible, and provide excellent colour to herb vinegars.

Nasturtium is generally recommended as a groundcover and companion for a wide range of vegetables. The fruit is a schizocarp (a fruit that breaks into pieces). In this instance there are three pieces, each containing a seed, so the plant propagates itself readily. Watch out for leaf-miners and snails, and be aware that the larvae of the cabbage white butterfly (*Pieris rapae*) can consume these leaves as a substitute for brassicas (see Figure 178).

VALERIAN

Valerian (*Valeriana officinalis*) is a perennial of variable height, producing clusters of deep pink flowers attractive to bees in spring. Valerian has a tendency to dominate, but this is not a problem when companions are well matched for vigour. The roots are the source of the medicinal preparations discussed in Chapter 8.

11.
Root vegetables and tubers

'Knowing where a plant comes from is not just an academic exercise; it can help you work out the best growing conditions for that particular variety.'

Michael Bailes

Fads and fashions

Root vegetables in general were despised by the English aristocracy during the reign of King Henry VIII (1509–47), because of their intimate contact with the soil. Henry boasted that he had no equal on Earth, but his food snobbery was to bring him undone. The seasonal lack of fresh greens and fruits every winter, plus reluctance to eat these lowly alternative foods, led to Henry's malnutrition. His symptoms, including leg ulcers that would not heal, are entirely consistent with a lack of vitamin C. Henry also had gout, the formation of crystals of uric acid in the joints due to incomplete breakdown of purines from excessive nucleic acid consumption. Henry's disease was venal, not venereal, and his unbalanced diet an object lesson in how not to eat well despite every advantage.

In contrast to these strange English attitudes, Europeans welcomed potatoes when they first arrived from the New World. According to one tradition, the potato was taken to Europe by the Spanish conquistadors, who obtained samples from Colombia in the late 1530s. An alternative tradition is that Christopher Columbus brought some back on one of his four voyages. Either way, the potato reached Europe long before Sir Francis Drake or Sir Walter Raleigh had the opportunity to import them. The latter are often wrongly credited with introducing the potato to England. This misconception, like many, springs from John Gerard (see Chapter 8). He included the potato in his 1597 herbal, but muddied the waters by naming it as though it had come from Virginia.

Parsnips and carrots

Umbellifers generally have strong, central taproots (see Chapter 9), with a storage function, well enhanced in parsnips and carrots. But these roots are not starchy. They are sweet because they retain significant quantities of sugar. In his essay on parsnips, Roger Swain (1981) describes how to cook them, and how to grow them. Never mind rows. Planting in a hexagonal grid gives the maximum yield, with each plant the farthest distance possible from each other member of its cohort.

This equidistant principle makes a lot of sense, but has never made the transition from research finding to gardening practice. It applies to growing many kinds of plant together (see Chapter 1), as the wide and wasteful spacing between rows is avoided. An easy way of achieving hexagonal spacing is to make the distance between rows the same as the distance between seeds, then to stagger each second row. However, because germination of parsnip seed can be fairly uneven, it is difficult to plant parsnips in hexagons. Throw the seeds in patches, cover them finely, and look after what comes. Thin them progressively, and fill any large gaps with suitable companions.

Hollow Crown is a popular variety of parsnip that has been grown in Australia for many years, and one which gives good germination provided the seeds are no more than one year old. Hollow Crown dates from the 1820s, and was so named because of the depression in the top of the root immediately surrounding the area where the leaf stalks join. Other varieties of parsnip have no such depression, and look more like carrots. The Reverend William Bingley (1831) relates that the coquaine type was much favoured for feeding dairy cattle on the Channel Islands, Jersey and Guernsey, contributing to the richness of their milk and butter. Melbourne

Whiteskin is the standard market garden variety.

'Garden carrot (*Daucus carota*) is a plant too well known to need any description', says Bingley (1831), but a description always helps. Wild carrots are white, and the cultivated forms used to be purple rather than orange. Yellow forms probably originated in Afghanistan. A more orange-coloured type was selected from these yellow forms in the Netherlands in about 1600. Modern orange carrots, of whatever shape, have descended from these. Recent breeding criteria include uniform distribution of orange pigments (carotenes), and reluctance to 'bolt' when plants are exposed to long days. Seed should generally be sown in early spring, although I have on occasion tried winter carrots.

Yates Garden Guide (1971, reprinted 1975) recommended eight varieties, from which Chantenay and Topweight stand out. Chantenay epitomises French breeding efforts, and has good strong flavour. Topweight is resistant to virus infections, the root reaching 20 centimetres in length. All Seasons is a selection from Topweight, and as the name implies, can be grown year round without bolting.

Turnips and radishes

These vegetables belong to the Cruciferae (see Table 14 on page 89). The conventional companion plant for turnips of all kinds is the leek (see Chapter 12). Turnips need cold weather during maturation to develop their best flavour, and should be sown in late summer to early autumn. The classic turnip is represented in Britain by the Norfolk white, although the turnip was widely grown in other parts of Britain for many centuries before it became prominent in Norfolk, during the seventeenth century. Turnips probably came from northern France to England in Roman

FIGURE 1 Box hedges in formal herb gardens need trimming too often.

FIGURE 2 An assembly of salvias in Daisy Burton's garden, Adelaide.

FIGURE 3 A tall bearded iris (Wedding Vow) with garlic chives, spring onions, rhubarb and yarrow (foreground).

FIGURE 4 A net-casting spider with American cockroach prey.

FIGURE 5 A hoverfly sipping nectar from a tomato flower.

FIGURE 6 The St Andrew's Cross spider (underview) is one of the orb-weaver group.

FIGURE 7 The praying mantis is a useful predator.

FIGURE 8 At last, the secret of the organic vineyard revealed.

FIGURE 9 A medieval harvest – note the clover at the base of the wheat sheaf (Notre Dame Cathedral, Paris).

FIGURE 10 *Kennedia rubicunda* (running postman) is attractive on weld-mesh fences.

FIGURE 11 The much maligned rue, seen here as the understorey to crepe myrtle.

FIGURE 12 Onions with beans – why not?

FIGURE 13 An ancient American guild: maize with cucurbits, beans and other plants.

FIGURE 14 Basil growing with the climbing bean Blue Lake.

FIGURE 15 Get rid of castor bean (*Ricinus communis*), a noxious weed in every sense.

FIGURE 16 Morning glory cuts off light to other plants.

FIGURE 17 A poppy flower – plenty of pollen, but no nectar.

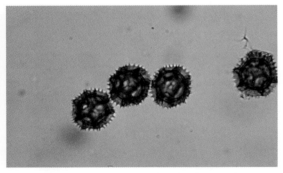

FIGURE 18 Pollen grains transferred by floral visitors have a rough exterior, often with spines, as in *Hypochoeris radicata* (Compositae)

FIGURE 19 *Robinia pseudoacacia* – autumn colour, but the flowers produce toxic nectar.

FIGURE 20 Flowers of *Grevillea banksii* – leave them for the birds.

FIGURE 21 Tomato plants given a zero-sulfate medium, with the oldest leaves showing signs of sulfur withdrawal.

FIGURE 22 Michel Fanton turning over a batch of coffee grounds.

FIGURE 23 With sufficient moisture, white mites commence the breakdown of fallen leaves.

FIGURE 24 Leaves of native species such as flame tree (*Brachychiton acerifolium*) are valuable for compost.

FIGURE 25 Rhubarb leaves, one day after placement on the compost heap.

FIGURE 26 After four more days, the rhubarb leaves have practically disappeared except for the major veins.

FIGURE 27 A barrow-load of cut grass with a thermometer reveals how hot it gets.

FIGURE 28 Leopard slugs on the compost heap (photographed with flash, at night).

FIGURE 29 A mature centipede, confirming the need to wear gloves when handling compost.

FIGURE 30 Two blue flower wasp males fighting, oblivious to the photographer.

FIGURE 31 Save the scarce Australian snail on the left, but keep the European snail moving.

FIGURE 32 Cicada cases can benefit the compost heap, or the garden directly.

FIGURE 33 Choose garden locations with plenty of direct sunlight. Terracing is a good idea on slopes.

FIGURE 34 Signs of magnesium deficiency in a leaf of *Pelargonium tomentosum*.

FIGURE 35 Mint in early spring shows the benefits of yeast lees from the previous summer.

FIGURE 36 Peas growing with a single parsley plant, plus a few hangers-on.

FIGURE 37 Pots galore: an eggplant (left), plus an early tomato, with four-o'clocks starting later from tubers (right).

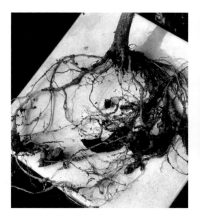

FIGURE 38 The 'tuberous' roots of this tomato result from root-knot nematodes (eelworms).

FIGURE 39 Terracotta is very desirable for ornamental pots.

FIGURE 40 A 'strawberry pot' after assembly, with garlic chives (*Tulbaghia violacea*) on top.

FIGURE 41 Vermiculite is durable in pots and holds water. This 17-day-old pea seedling in vermiculite is a yellow mutant incapable of photosynthesis.

FIGURE 42 Eureka pea seedlings, seven plants per 30 cm pot.

FIGURE 43 On flowering, lettuce clearly indicates that it belongs to the daisy family (Compositae).

FIGURE 44 Cages are sometimes used at SSN headquarters to prevent any chance of crosspollination.

FIGURE 45 A cos lettuce plant 'bolting' in response to increasing day-length (early October).

FIGURE 46 These two parsnip plants are the same age, but the one in the foreground was transplanted.

FIGURE 47 Developing radish pods – hard work for seed removal.

FIGURE 48 Pods and seeds should be left open to the air while drying.

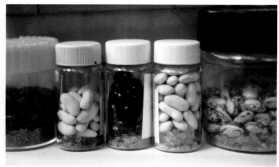

FIGURE 49 Blue silica gel stored with seeds absorbs water vapour and turns pink.

FIGURE 50 Enclose your seed containers again for extra protection and insulation.

FIGURE 51 Bean seeds can be dried for storage from the shelling stage onwards (left). Seeds shrink and coat colours intensify (right). This is the Frost Bean.

FIGURE 52 Stir the tomato pulp and discard the rinse as soon as most seeds have settled to the bottom.

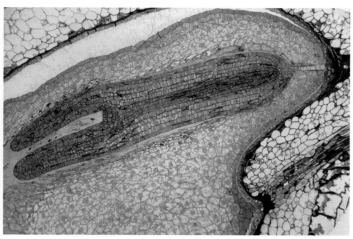

FIGURE 53 Section of a maturing seed of *Solanum nigrum*, showing the embryo (forked) attached to its suspensor and surrounded by endosperm.

FIGURE 54 Chick pea seedlings from seed stored at -18°C for nine years (1991–2000).

FIGURE 55 Eggplant seeds are large enough to space properly in a nursery pot.

FIGURE 56 The same eggplant seedlings being moved to individual pots.

FIGURE 57 Tomato seedlings should be potted on from a seedling tray or pot.

FIGURE 58 A new plant of blue heliotrope (*Heliotropium europaeum*) from a cutting taken two months before.

FIGURE 59 New plants of *Kalanchoe* develop vegetatively from leaf notches.

FIGURE 60 This nursery in Sue McGregor's garden is suspended above ground level and protected from full sun.

FIGURE 61 Support your recent transplant with broken drainpipe, very stable in the wind.

FIGURE 62 Jude and Michel Fanton covered most of their house with meshes and climbing plants, including choko and lima bean.

FIGURE 63 Loofah (*Luffa cylindrica*) and a climbing snake bean on bamboo lattice against a wall of the Fantons' house (Byron Bay, NSW).

FIGURE 64 Not Rodale 'electroculture' but wire hoops, used to raise and support a zucchini vine.

FIGURE 65 This small pond (about 80 cm across) close to the exit from an underground rainwater tank supports tadpoles periodically.

FIGURE 66 *Gazania* is a hardy plant.

FIGURE 67 African daisies (*Osteospermum ecklonis*) are also hardy and flower from autumn to spring.

FIGURE 68 *Zephyranthes candida* (rain lily) from South America flowers in late summer to early autumn.

FIGURE 69 Flowers of the succulent *Aloe vera*.

FIGURE 70 Donkeytail in a hanging basket, flowering.

FIGURE 71 The ground orchid, *Dendrobium speciosum*.

FIGURE 72 The zygocactus 'Bridgeport'.

FIGURE 73 Shelled bean pods.

FIGURE 74 Pea straw mulch, set around the 'drip-line' of a Eureka lemon tree.

FIGURE 75 *Chlorophytum comosum* has tuberous roots that crowd out other plants.

FIGURE 76 *Hypochoeris radicata* differs from dandelion in having branched flowering stalks.

FIGURE 77 Pea straw used as the inner layer of a 'sandwich' mulch around a young lime tree.

FIGURE 78 A heavier layer of local leaves placed over the pea straw (Figure 77).

FIGURE 79 Flowers and young fruits of onion weed. Don't let this happen!

FIGURE 80 If glyphosate is sprayed on onion weed in lawn, the onion weed survives.

FIGURE 81 *Tradescantia albiflora*, an unwanted groundcover that gives dogs dermatitis.

FIGURE 82 Onion weed uprooted to show bulbs and bulbils.

FIGURE 83 It is easier to remove *Conyza* plants when they are as small as this one.

FIGURE 84 Dandelion, a classic weed, disperses seeds in the wind.

FIGURE 85 Balloon vine also disperses seeds in the wind.

FIGURE 86 A potato plant suffering from the attention of the 28-spotted lady beetle.

FIGURE 87 Jonquils, *Crassula multicava* and oregano (*Origanum vulgare*): midwinter view.

FIGURE 88 The wheel turns: jonquils senescent, with oregano dominant, four months later.

FIGURE 89 A honey bee collecting from wild fennel flowers.

FIGURE 90 St John's wort (*Hypericum perforatum*).

FIGURE 91 Blue heliotrope (*Heliotropium europaeum*) supports beneficial insects.

FIGURE 92 Pomegranate (*Punica granatum*): a late arrival in Britain.

FIGURE 93 Flowers of parsnip (*Pastinaca sativa*) attended by ants.

FIGURE 94 Carrot (*Daucus carota*) setting seed.

FIGURE 95 Florence fennel (*Foeniculum vulgare*), in Italian called *finnochio dolce*.

FIGURE 96 The 'French' marigold from Mexico (*Tagetes patula*), growing with strawberry and rhubarb.

FIGURE 97 Tansy (*Tanacetum vulgare*).

FIGURE 98 *Bidens pilosa* (centre) is a better companion for beans than *Tagetes patula*.

FIGURE 99 Flowers of *Bidens pilosa*.

FIGURE 100 Seed heads of *Bidens pilosa*.

FIGURE 101 A radish (*Raphanus sativus*) flowering.

FIGURE 102 For sweet alice, having white flowers is important in selecting insect visitors.

FIGURE 103 Borage (*Borago officinalis*) has flowers that hang downwards.

FIGURE 104 *Echium fastuosum* from the Canary Islands.

FIGURE 105 Viper's bugloss (*Echium vulgare*) in flower.

FIGURE 106 Comfrey used as a border.

FIGURE 107 *Pelargonium tomentosum* flowering.

FIGURE 108 Flower of a Louisiana iris, Brookvale Brocade.

FIGURE 109 The jagged leaves of the Stellar pelargonium that deters white fly.

FIGURE 110 Flowers of the same Stellar pelargonium, originally from Callemondah.

FIGURE 111 Flower of a Louisiana iris resulting from a cross of yellow and white varieties (Dinah Miller).

FIGURE 112 A tall bearded iris, Wedding Vow.

FIGURE 113 Evening primrose (*Oenothera biennis*) has a narrow floral tube behind this flourish, but is also favoured by honey bees.

FIGURE 114 The four-o'clock is an ideal companion for tomato.

FIGURE 115 German chamomile grown with potatoes protects against scab.

FIGURE 116 A selection from the many kinds of potato tuber.

FIGURE 117 A plant of Sebago, showing early signs of senescence.

FIGURE 118 The yield from potatoes is hard to better (same plant as in Figure 117).

FIGURE 119 A swede turnip flowering, with *Tradescantia virginiana* in the background.

FIGURE 120 A sugarloaf cabbage.

FIGURE 121 Chinese cabbage and sunflower (rear) growing in the author's front garden.

FIGURE 122 Leaves can be picked from a young cos lettuce without the loss of the whole plant.

FIGURE 123 Endive (blue flowers) with shorter mixed herbs.

FIGURE 124 The spreading onion (*Allium fistulosum*): no storage needed.

FIGURE 125 The flower of eggplant (*Solanum melongena*) shows clear affinities to potato and tomato.

FIGURE 126 Eggplant fruits are not necessarily purple.

FIGURE 127 Asparagus eventually rewards those who persist.

FIGURE 128 Tomatoes with trusses of small fruits are easiest to grow.

FIGURE 129 The female flower of pumpkin has a convoluted stigma in the centre.

FIGURE 130 The male flower of pumpkin has fused anthers in the centre.

FIGURE 131 The base of the female flower shows marked swelling only four days after fertilization.

FIGURE 132 Developing pumpkin fruit (same as in Figure 131), 18 days after fertilization.

FIGURE 133 Yellow squashes and zucchinis show that *Cucurbita pepo* is a species with 'polymorphic' fruits,

FIGURE 134 More cucurbits (from left): Table Queen, Sweet Dumpling and Baby Blue, about 1 kg each.

FIGURE 135 Crystal Apple cucumber growing with sweet potato.

FIGURE 136 Male flowers at the top of maize plants shed pollen that must be received by the silks of female flowers for kernels to form.

FIGURE 137 Sweet Dumpling at maturity, three months later than in Figure 134.

FIGURE 138 Dry maize cobs, including Strawberry popcorn (right).

FIGURE 139 The roots of a broad bean plant (*Vicia faba*) showing pink nitrogen-fixing nodules.

FIGURE 140 The King snow pea flowering.

FIGURE 141 Flowers of Avalon, a semi-dwarf snow pea derived from a cross of Carlisle River snow pea with garden pea Melbourne Market

FIGURE 142 New powdery mildew-resistant semi-leafless pea, Medusa.

FIGURE 143 Broad bean plants rarely need support.

FIGURE 144 Flowers of broad bean.

FIGURE 145 Dwarf butterbean, Stella Bianca, flowering.

FIGURE 146 Heirloom Ukrainian runner bean, Bullabun, with typical red flowers.

FIGURE 147 Ralph's Runner, with unusual orange and white flowers.

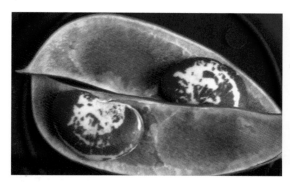

FIGURE 149 Christmas lima bean seeds at shelling stage.

FIGURE 148 Developing pod of Mammoth Golden Cluster climbing butterbean.

FIGURE 150 Asparagus pea (*Lotus tetragonolobus*), flowering.

FIGURE 151 A 25-year-old dwarf crab apple in flower.

FIGURE 152 The fruits of the wild pear, *Pyrus caleryana*, are tiny and tough, but still sought by birds.

FIGURE 153 A typical peach (*Prunus persica*) has reddish skin and yellow flesh.

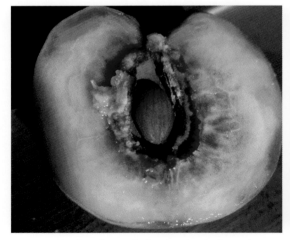

FIGURE 154 Section of a peach showing the single seed enclosed by a stony layer inside the flesh.

FIGURE 155 Nectarines are smooth like plums.

FIGURE 156 Mangoes growing in a Sydney suburban garden.

FIGURE 157 Unprotected persimmons are popular with birds.

FIGURE 158 Lemons (Eureka), ready to pick.

FIGURE 160 A handsome bunch of bananas growing in Port Kembla, NSW.

FIGURE 159 Babaco (*Carica pentagona*) suits cooler climates.

FIGURE 161 Flowers of the tree tomato, *Cyphomandra betacea*.

FIGURE 162 Tree tomato fruits.

FIGURE 163 Flower of the common purple passionfruit, *Passiflora edulis*.

FIGURE 164 Flower of *Passiflora coccinea*.

FIGURE 165 Flower of the 'banana' passionfruit, *Passiflora mollissima*.

FIGURE 166 Flower of *Passiflora laurifolia* ('leaf like a laurel').

FIGURE 167 The choko is often picked too late (as on the right).

FIGURE 168 Borage makes a suitable companion for the grapevine.

FIGURE 170 The green vegetable bug was once a major pest of beans and tomatoes.

FIGURE 169 Romano bush beans planted on 1 February yield abundantly in autumn.

FIGURE 171 The undersurface of a bean leaf infested with white fly and two-spotted mite.

FIGURE 173 The adult of the bronze orange bug (*Musgraveia sulciventris*) is purple

FIGURE 175 Another useful predator—the robber fly.

FIGURE 172 Passionvine leaf-hoppers.

FIGURE 174 Newly hatched young of the bronze orange bug are well camouflaged.

FIGURE 176 The fruits of this grafted Grosse Lisse tomato have been protected with jackets made from old nylon stockings.

FIGURE 177 White cabbage moth caterpillars can strip a tatsoi plant in no time.

FIGURE 178 Beware: white cabbage moth caterpillars like nasturtium leaves, too.

FIGURE 179 A green looper caterpillar running out of cover.

FIGURE 180 Spare the last green loopers, because they will be parasitised; they can spin a cocoon, but never emerge.

FIGURE 181 The adult green looper has a distinctive profile.

FIGURE 182 Powdery mildew coating a tomato leaf.

FIGURE 185 A lady beetle on a powdery mildew-infested pea plant.

FIGURE 186 Powdery mildew and numerous lady beetles on cucurbit leaves.

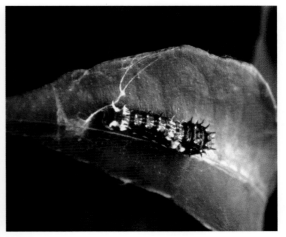

FIGURE 183 The orchard butterfly caterpillar is unmistakable.

FIGURE 184 A dead female orchard butterfly.

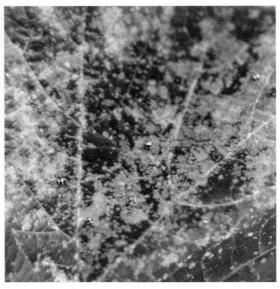

FIGURE 187 Asparagus pea, with black aphids farmed by ants.

FIGURE 188 A pupa of the orange and black lady beetle, *Hippodamia variegata*, with aphids on fennel.

FIGURE 189 White 'rust' on a rocket leaf.

FIGURE 190 The equipment needed to prepare and spray an extract of casuarina needles.

FIGURE 191 A bean plant seriously affected by a virus.

FIGURE 192 Herb vinegars prepared from lavender and fennel.

times. They were grown specifically for animals to eat, and could be stored in the ground throughout the winter until needed. However, Bingley (1831) reminds us of the value of turnips during famine. Bread was made by mixing equal parts of turnips and cereal flour in England in the famine years 1629, 1636 and 1693. A combined mash of turnips and potatoes is very tasty.

The swede turnip or rutabaga (*Brassica napus*), with its characteristic purple/yellow colour scheme, resulted from the spontaneous hybridisation of *B. campestris* and *B. oleracea*. This plant has definitely arisen during cultivation, probably in European gardens where turnip and kale were being grown together. How many times this happened is not certain. The current favourite in Australia is Purple Top, and I recommend harvesting when they have just reached a diameter of about 10 centimetres, before they become old and horrible. The young greens make an excellent addition to soup.

The radish (*Raphanus sativus*) is a plant well known to the ancient Egyptians, from as long ago as 2700 BC. Radishes should be planted as the weather warms up in spring, since rapid growth gives best results. However, the full heat of summer should be avoided. The seeds are big enough to plant directly. When the seedlings emerge, it can be seen that the cotyledons are unequal in size, one folded around the other. As they expand and make the transition from storage organs to functional leaves, they even up. This sequence of events can be guaranteed to fascinate young gardeners, and so radish is one of the best plants to give children to grow.

A great many shapes and colours of radish have been grown at different times. The now standard globose red forms first appeared in the eighteenth century. The most popular kinds in Australia, including French Breakfast, Long Scarlet and Long White Icicle, have been here more than a century. More than 30

varieties have been listed in *The Curator*.

The large, white Daikon radish should be planted in autumn. This has an exceptionally mild flavour, provided it is not grown in the summer. Evidently, it came with the Chinese to the goldfields in 1852, hence the early description 'White Chinese'. Seeds were also sent to Mr Henry Moore from Japan in 1864 (Smith, 1995). Today in Japan there are nine distinct Daikon varieties.

Beetroot

The beetroot (*Beta vulgaris*) is easy to grow in soil that is not too rich. Small-scale sowing every few weeks over spring and summer will provide a succession. Any not harvested should flower in their second year. Boiled and sliced, beetroot has long been a traditional summer salad ingredient. Crimson Globe (Yates' Derwent Globe) and Obelisk, with a more elongated shape, have been popular since the 1930s. Cylindrica is a more recent variety resembling Obelisk.

Potatoes

The edible potato, *Solanum tuberosum*, belongs to a large genus with about 1500 species. *Solanum* began to evolve in Gondwanaland in the southern hemisphere, continuing to produce most of its different species in South America, followed by Australia, as these continents finally severed their Antarctic connection. The edible potato was domesticated in the Andes, where related wild species were to be found in abundance until recently.

When potato plants flower and fruit, remember that the fruits are poisonous, because they contain the alkaloid solanine. This same compound is produced in tubers that have turned green because of exposure to light. Allowing tubers to green before planting is supposed to enhance their disease resistance, but there seems little substance to this claim. Genetics is more important. When large tubers are cut before planting, the pieces should be allowed to dry quickly in well-ventilated conditions, so that new skin (epidermis) may form. It is not necessary to rub the cut edges in ash, as many earlier writers have recommended.

Yates Garden Guides from 1952 to 1975 dismiss the growing of potatoes in the home garden: 'The planting of potatoes may not be warranted in very small gardens because other vegetables would be likely to give much better returns for the space available'. This neglect is all the more amazing because it is well known that the potato can outproduce most annual food plants on an area basis. It is reasonable to expect at least a fivefold return on the size of the tubers planted. Moreover, the potato was one of the most reliable food sources for colonists in New South Wales, producing very well within nine to twelve weeks of planting. Convicts in service to landholders were allowed to grow potatoes and other vegetables in their own plots. Even arrogant landholders like John Macarthur did not disdain to grow potatoes. Macarthur wrote in 1794 that he had '20 acres of fine wheat growing', and '80 acres prepared for Indian corn and potatoes'.

Compare the yield of one 30-centimetre pot of peas, approximately equivalent to the area occupied by one potato plant. Suppose six semi-dwarf plants produced an average of 10 pods each, with six seeds per pod at 400 milligrams per seed at maturity. This amounts to 400 x 6 x 10 x 6 milligrams per pot, which is 144 000 milligrams, or 144 grams. The yield from a single potato (about 350 grams) planted and grown under the same winter to spring conditions (4 to 5 months) would be measured in kilograms, not grams. If eight potatoes were produced at 350 grams each, the yield would be 2.8 kilograms. This is so far in front, I don't even have to correct for the different water contents of potato tubers versus mature pea seeds to make my point.

Although the identities of the varieties grown initially in Australia are uncertain, this information is academic following the catastrophic late blight (*Phytophthora infestans*) in Europe, Britain and Ireland (1845–50). Pre-famine potatoes in Europe and Australia were mostly blight-sensitive, and are now rare or extinguished. One exception is Manistee Earliest of All (Early Manistee), which was introduced to the islands in Bass Strait and grown by convicts early in the nineteenth century. It proved to be blight-resistant in New South Wales, and was still being recommended to the home gardener by Brunning as recently as 1964.

Most varieties developed since the famine are blight-resistant. In the United States, Early Rose became an important variety shortly after 1861, when a grower passed on a 'seed ball', a potato fruit produced on a Garnet Chili plant, to Mr Albert Bresee of Vermont. Early Rose was chosen for uniformity of tuber, as well as producing early in the season. The Garnet Chili had been selected from the Rough Purple Chili, brought back from South America by the Reverend Chauncy Goodrich in the late 1840s.

In turn, Early Rose gave rise to Early Ohio, released by James Gregory in Massachusetts in 1875; Magnum Bonum, bred by James Clarke in the United Kingdom; Russet Burbank, Luther Burbank's famous enlargement; and Rosette, a beautiful, rounded, pink-skinned potato with white flesh, bred in France (Vilmorin-Andrieux, 1885). Like Albert Bresee, Luther Burbank recognised the importance of a 'seed ball': 'I planted the seeds in that ball. I had twenty-three seeds and I got twenty-three seedlings. From that whole number, although there were many that were an improvement on any potato then grown, I selected two that were amazing, valuable, and a distinct type'

(Burbank and Hall, 1927). Russet Burbank and Magnum Bonum were both released in 1876.

Other James Clarke potatoes include Best of All (1887) and Epicure (1897), while later derivatives of Magnum Bonum include King Edward, and the Arran series, all popular in the United Knigdom. Albert Bresee developed at least half-a-dozen contemporaries of Early Rose, from the same unknown cross, including his King of the Earlies, Peerless and Prolific. In France, Prolific was more highly regarded than Early Rose, as it was found to keep better. In Australia, Prolific was known as Coronation, suggesting a late arrival in 1902.

Independently, in about 1870, E.S. Brownell released Vermont Beauty (Brownell's Beauty), also a good keeper. Brownell's Beauty was a main crop potato in Tasmania, and recommended for the home garden by P.J. Hurley (1949, 1956). Then came Green Mountain (1885), known in Australia as Carman. The latter developed two forms: the early (No. 1) and late (No. 3). Both were often recommended for the home gardener by Brunning (1952, 1964).

Even allowing for synonyms, hundreds of new kinds of potato have been bred since the Irish famine. An inventory listing about 500 varieties known in Australia has been published in *The Curator* (Hankin and Schmetzer, 1996). Some now have characteristically Australian names, such as Dandenong Blue, Dargo Goldfield and Tasmanian Pink Eye. But the zenith of potato breeding has clearly passed, and only about 20 varieties are currently grown in commercial quantities. There has been a strong revival of interest in trying out different potatoes in recent years.

What are the best kinds to grow? Find out first what your taste preferences are. Look at the differences in skin colour and texture, flesh colour, tuber size and shape, and whether the eyes are deeply recessed (more waste on peeling) or shallow. Some of the small,

knobbly ones are arduous to peel, and the solution is to cook them whole, then cut and peel them on the plate. There was a time when potatoes that were not perfectly white inside were looked down on (the Romans had the same attitude to bread), but now it is generally realised that yellow flesh indicates a waxy texture. This is often preferable for the potato that is steamed and eaten hot as a vegetable, or cold in potato salads. The whiter potatoes are generally better for roasting (in the skin), baking, frying (as chips), or mashing after steaming. There are exceptions to these generalisations, and every variety should be assessed after growing under local conditions. Many varieties not profiled here are available from the potato enthusiasts who belong to the Seed Savers' Network (see Useful Addresses).

Potatoes sold for eating are not certified free of common potato diseases, and are riskier to plant and grow, but the last potatoes from the bag are often good space-fillers if the eyes have already sprouted and the tubers are sound; for example, Sebago is always reliable. To play safe, certified seed potatoes can be purchased from the larger retail outlets, such as hardware stores and some nurseries. They are generally very small, so do not expect yields as high as those anticipated from a tuber weighing 350 grams. Planting as soon as possible, in winter or spring, should ensure maturity by late spring to early summer, well before leaf-mauling pests become too abundant.

Potatoes can be planted with onions and peas. A floral companion that appears to protect tubers against diseases like scab (*Streptomyces scabies*) is German chamomile (see Chapter 9; Figure 115). Potatoes are not suitable as 'the first crop in new ground', as claimed by *Yates Garden Guide* (27th edition, about 1957, repeated until the 41st edition, 2002). I can assure you that if you plant them in soil with too much clay and inadequate drainage, they will rot. The soil that potatoes should be planted in must be well worked, friable and conditioned with compost and horse manure. Do not provide too much nitrogen, and avoid alkaline manures or dressings.

Plant and cultivate according to Hurley (1949, 1956, 1970). Instead of perpetually hilling the plants as they grow, plant them deep enough in the first place, about 20 centimetres down. Leave a shallow depression on top to collect water and conduct it through to the roots. Once shoots have appeared, growth is rapid, then the plants tend to sprawl. This is the stage to hill. Cover any tubers that push above soil level so that they do not turn green. Wait for the plant to show signs of yellowing and permanent wilting, then the tubers should be ready to lift (see Figures 117 and 118).

CROOKWELL CARMAN
Crookwell is a famous, frost-prone, potato-growing town west of Goulburn in New South Wales. This potato is large and lumpy, with patchy light brown skin (see Figure 116), and white flesh. It might be a version of Carman No. 1, which was certainly one of the top-yielding potatoes grown in Crookwell early in the twentieth century (Makin, 1918). For mashing, this potato is superb.

DESIREE
Bred in the Netherlands in the 1970s, Desiree is a smooth, purple-skinned, medium-sized potato (see Figure 116), with yellow flesh and waxy texture. An excellent general-purpose potato, it is currently very popular, and has displaced Pontiac. It is also superior to Symfonia. Although Symfonia was bred from Desiree, it lacks the shallow-set eyes that minimise waste on peeling.

KATAHDIN
This white-skinned variety was bred in the United States and released in 1932. The flesh is white, and the tuber round. Good for

steaming, mashing or baking. This variety is pivotal to modern US breeding programs, becoming a parent of Pontiac, Sebago and Sequoia, all released later in the 1930s.

KENNEBEC
Another light-skinned, round potato with white flesh. Although grown commercially for processing as crisps or chips, it is good steamed or baked. Kennebec was introduced from the United Staes soon after its release in 1948.

PINK EYE
Tasmanians are one-eyed about Pink Eye, which they have recently adopted as their own. But Keith Smith (1995) records that it came as Lancashire Pink Eye from the United Kingdom, and has been well known in various parts of mainland Australia since the 1860s. The name refers to the splash of colour around the eye. The flesh is yellowish, and the texture waxy. In the southern United States, Pink Eye was displaced by Early Rose.

PONTIAC
Produced in the 1930s in the United States from a cross of Triumph and Katahdin, and grown in Australia soon after release. My grandfather (G. Douglas Murray) grew Pontiac from 1937 onwards. The pinkish skin conceals yellow flesh, and waxy texture. Still popular, although superseded by Desiree, which has eyes less deeply recessed.

ROYAL BLUE
A small oblong tuber, with striking blue-purple skin (see Figure 116), and flesh that is remarkably yellow. Its virtues include brief cooking time, and delicate flavour and texture. Steam whole, and peel on the plate.

RUSSET BURBANK
This classic (see Figure 116) accounts for an enormous proportion of total potato

production both in the United States and in Australia by virtue of having been selected by McDonald's for their French-fries production. This is an incredible ranking for an heirloom potato more than 130 years old. Such dominance is a concern for the sustainability of large-scale potato cultivation, but compare this situation with what befell Magnum Bonum: viral degeneration, loss of its blight-resistance in France, and extinction in the world at large. Forget French fries; Russet Burbank is good steamed, but better mashed.

SEBAGO
A medium-sized, well-rounded tuber (see Figure 116), with thin white skin and white flesh. Another descendant of Katahdin — derived from a cross of Chippewa and Katahdin in 1938. Sebago has been justly popular with Australian gardeners for many years, as it yields reliably under a wide range of circumstances. Excellent steamed or mashed.

SEQUOIA
A light-skinned, rounded tuber, with white flesh. Derived from a cross of Carman (Green Mountain) with Katahdin in 1939. Sequoia is not as large and lumpy as Carman No. 3 (photo in Brunning, 1952) and produces early, like Carman No. 1.

SNOWFLAKE
Released in 1874 by Bliss & Sons of New York, the name refers to both the skin and the flesh. But the Australian version now appears to differ from the American in several respects. Here Snowflake is a late main-crop variety, with long, rounded, white-skinned tubers, and the flower colour is 'pale purple' (Hankin and Schmetzer, 1996). Snowflake is also 'a noted heavy cropper'. In contrast, Weaver (1997) records that his version has white flowers and is 'the least productive' of those American heirloom varieties that he describes. This may be related to a preference for sandy, open soil textures, or it may reflect a genetic divergence following geographic separation over more than 120 years. Recommended by Brunning (1952), and still available through the Seed Savers' Network (see Useful Addresses).

TOOLANGI DELIGHT
This potato was bred by Roger Kirkham at Toolangi, near Melbourne in Victoria, and released in 1987. Its small round tubers have purple skin and white flesh. Except that the eyes are too deeply recessed, it resembles Rosette. Popular with gardeners in Victoria, it is an early variety that suits every form of cooking.

Sweet potatoes and yams
Widely distributed in the tropics, sweet potato (*Ipomoea batatas*) has a highly nutritious tuber. In the 1920s there were about 20 kinds in New South Wales, but many varieties are now coming to light through the efforts of gardeners like George Bollen (Bowen) and Wally Bergmann (Mackay). The nature of the plant encourages replanting at the time of harvest. The leaves can be simple or beautifully lobed, like one variety currently available through SSN that tastes like chestnuts.

Yams (about 10 species of *Dioscorea*) are also tropical. Yams are a rich source of phyto-oestrogens, now regarded as very important in controlling extreme symptoms of the menopause. Many species require extensive detoxification treatments (slicing, washing, shredding, rinsing and cooking), but one species found in southern Queensland and New South Wales, *D. transversa*, gets by with just cooking. The tubers are 'pencil-like' (Cribb and Cribb, 1975).

12.
Leaf, bulb and stem vegetables

'The time has come,' the walrus said, 'to speak
of many things — of shoes — and ships — and
sealing wax — of cabbages — and kings.'

Lewis Carroll, *Alice in Wonderland*

Kale and colleagues

My old genetics lecturer, Professor Spencer Smith-White, would always launch one of his lectures with this quotation, asking his students what it was that cabbages and kings had in common. The answer was genes and chromosomes, of course, but now I appreciate that cabbages can do quite a few things with their genomes that kings cannot.

'Polymorphic' species — having many forms — are common in *Brassica*. The ultimate polymorph is *Brassica oleracea*, which encompasses kale, collards, cabbage (see Figure 120), kohlrabi, brussels sprouts, cauliflower and broccoli. How can plants that look so different belong to the same species? As with the multitude of pod and seed differences in common beans (all *Phaseolus vulgaris*), the genetic differences are very slight, involving alternative forms (alleles) of just a few genes, or alterations in their mode of expression, so that different parts of the plant become compact and adapted for storage. These different 'morphs' certainly do not warrant trinomials, or ranking as subspecies. The common names are sufficient to indicate the form.

Cabbages, kale and most of these prefer cool climates and a fairly rich supply of nutrients. They need more sulfur than many other plants, one reason for this being the nature of the flavour compounds (see Chapter 10).

Kale is easier to grow than cabbage, being less susceptible to caterpillars (there are fewer places to hide). The frilly leaves can be eaten young and raw in salads, or older and cooked in soups. True to its common name, brussels sprouts did arise during cultivation in Brussels, in about 1750. This new vegetable became

102

well known in France and England from early in the nineteenth century. Its chief appeal for many gardeners is the potential for continuous harvesting.

Lettuce and endive

An excellent history of lettuce (*Lactuca sativa*) is given by Weaver (1997). The genus name refers to the milky sap. Here in Australia we have passed through the 'iceberg' age, and rediscovered cos (see Figure 122). The advantage of cos forms over hearting forms is that leaves can be harvested as needed without destroying the whole plant and leaving a mighty gap in a hot, midsummer garden. Cos lettuce plants gradually increase in height (see Figure 45), eventually flowering (see Figure 43) to produce abundant seeds that can be kept, or sown at once. The seeds will wait until the right time to germinate. About 30 kinds of lettuce are listed by Seed Savers' Network.

Endive (*Cichorium endivia*) is a biennial plant closely related to chicory (*C. intybus*) and they are sometimes difficult to tell apart. Both appear to be of Caucasian origin. The edge of the leaf, either crinkled or smooth, is the chief distinction between Greek and Italian forms. The flowers are blue (see Figure 123). The flavour of the leaves is more bitter than lettuce.

Bulb vegetables

A bulb is a storage organ constructed of swollen leaf bases, enclosing axillary buds as well. Bulbs allow plants to die back, survive an inclement period (which may be summer rather than winter), then resprout and grow under more advantageous conditions. Some irises form bulbs instead of rhizomes, but the bulb-forming plants that are most familar

belong to the genus *Allium* (see Table 15 on page 105). Many have originated in the Near East, or central and eastern Asia.

These species of *Allium* plus others like *Tulbaghia violacea* (garlic chives) from South Africa are considered by some botanists to comprise their own family, the Alliaceae. Before this distinction they were placed in the Amaryllidaceae. They have much in common with other members of Amaryllidaceae, including the formation of bulbs, and on flowering, they produce an umbel of flower buds completely enclosed by a spathe (bract). Biogeography and biochemistry provide most of the reasons supporting a distinction at family level. The rank sulfur-rich compounds they produce include antibiotics, long valued for their contribution to human health.

Onions, garlics and leeks were known to the Egyptians as early as 3200 BC, and to other Mediterranean cultures thereafter. Onions were clearly in evidence on the island of Thera, the lost bastion of Minoan civilisation destroyed in a massive volcanic eruption around 1520 BC (Marinates, 1972). Variations in shape, size, colour and intensity of flavour were remarked upon by Hippocrates and Theophrastus. Before it was obliterated in the explosion of Vesuvius in AD 79, Pompeii was famous among other things for the quality of the cabbages and onions grown there, and in the surrounding district of Campania. The Roman writer Columella recorded that one variety of onion was named after Pompeii (Descoeudres, 1994).

MODERN ONIONS

Since the 1920s, the main onions grown in Australia have included Early Barletta, Silver Skin (also early), Hunter River Brown Spanish and Odourless, a mild brown onion. Early Barletta is white, but has a flattened shape, approaching a discus, with a diameter sometimes as great as 15 centimetres. From the Hunter River Brown Spanish an early strain was selected by Mr A. McKimm of Bulwarra (Douglass, 1927), and this was released by Yates in 1930. Yates' standard form of Hunter River Brown went by the name of Derwent. The early form produces well by December if sown in March, whereas the Derwent is long-keeping, and should be sown later. Ailsa Craig, a large, light brown onion from the United Kingdom, has also been popular, although it tends to bolt in warmer areas. Since the 1970s, a brown onion called Pukekohe (Creamgold), originating in New Zealand, has done well. 'Spanish' currently applies not to brown-skinned onions, but to a brilliant purple bulb, which is so mild it can be eaten uncooked in salads.

Various globe onions such as Southport White Globe and Golden Globe are generally regarded as not keeping well, but the key to keeping quality is to plant early enough, matching the kind to the climate. This involves a great deal of trial and error. Frosts can promote bolting, but too far north, where the weather is not cold enough, onions cannot be grown at all because the development of bulbs is not triggered.

Never put onions (or garlics) in soil enriched with too much nitrogen. Excess nitrogen has long been known to induce over-large, soft bulbs of very poor keeping quality, likely to succumb to pathogenic fungi. Organic methods are ideal, with compost and aged manures gradually providing everything that is needed. Steady growth helps the more compact bulb to resist fungal diseases: during growth, at maturity and during storage. Never attempt to speed up the last stages by lopping off the foliage. Lift the bulbs and wash the roots when the tops start to flop and turn yellow. Then hang them up, and allow the tops to die back and dry out gradually. In this time-honoured way, fungal resistance and storage potential are both maximised.

The onion that many gardeners like is the 'perpetual' one that just keeps on duplicating itself, refusing to bolt or flower. This onion does not need to be stored, because it is always available straight from the garden. Its formal name is *Allium fistulosum* (see Table 15), and it came originally from Asia. The common name 'Welsh' onion is a total misunderstanding. The bulb swells very little, and practically the whole plant can be eaten. Left alone, such an onion will form a clump (see Figure 124). The plants can be separated easily and spread about, or harvested, according to need.

GARLIC

One obvious difference between garlic and most onions is that the bulb is subdivided into many smaller units (cloves), each of which is capable of forming a new plant. Another is that garlics have narrow, strappy leaves, whereas onions (and chives) have hollow, cylindrical leaves that taper to a point. We might well ignore Gerard's opinion that garlic 'destroys the magnetic power of the loadstone'.

White-sheathed or purple-sheathed garlics are the two most common forms. In the United States, more than 50 heirloom varieties showing great diversity of flavour and culinary potential are available (Weaver, 1997). Louis van Deven (1992) lists a number of sources, including the Garlic Seed Foundation. According to David Stern, Director of the Garlic Seed Foundation, the consumption of garlic per head of population in the United States has doubled during the 1990s.

LEEKS

The only leek of note in the Yates' 1930 listing was the Musselburgh, named for a town near Edinburgh in Scotland about a century before. However, the first leek brought to Australia as seed was the Large Flag or London Flag, a darker green, and not as cold-hardy as the Musselburgh. In fact, both the London Flag and the Musselburgh trace their descent from the earlier French variety, Gros-Court (Weaver,

TABLE 15. ONIONS AND RELATED CULTIVATED SPECIES

Allium ampeloprasum	great-headed garlic
A. cepa	onion, shallot[1]
A. christophii	flowering onion
A. fistulosum	spring onion (Chinese/Japanese onion)
A. porrum	leek
A. sativum	garlic
A. schoenoprasum	chives
A. tuberosum	Chinese chives
Tulbaghia violacea	garlic chives[2]

1. *Allium acalonicum* is an old name for shallot, indicating its origin, but this is now included in *A. cepa*.

2. A form of *A. schoenoprasum* from Asia is also known as garlic chives.

1997). Autumn Giant is another variety available from Greenpatch Organic Seeds (see Useful Addresses). Seedlings can be transplanted at any stage, and should be spaced 10 centimetres apart. Fortunately, leeks do not need fertiliser as often as Yates recommend.

Leeks have traditionally been blanched by progressively covering them with soil. This also reduces the flavour, and is scarcely worth the trouble, since leeks are mild anyway. Leeks may be planted from spring through to autumn, but leeks grown from seed in autumn may need two years to reach full size.

GARLIC CHIVES

The plant that has taken over this common name is *Tulbaghia violacea* (see Table 15). The flower structure is unusual in this family, with the ovary concealed in an inferior position.

The brightly coloured flowers (see Figure 3) are just as strongly flavoured as the leaves, and can also be used for garnishing.

Celery and rhubarb

Celery (*Apium graveolens*) belongs to the Umbelliferae family (see Chapter 9). The part of the plant that is generally eaten is the leaf stalk (petiole). The leafy parts can be eaten in soups, and the seeds can be used for flavouring.

As with the celery plant, it is the leaf stalk of rhubarb (*Rheum rhaponticum*) that is eaten — but not the leaf lamina. Because of the oxalate content, these are poisonous to us, although not to the denizens of the compost heap (see Figures 25 and 26). The plants grow from crowns, and they need as much full sun as can be given. When cutting the leafstalks, take only about half the number of leaves showing, and work from the outside inwards. Never let any leaves lie on the ground, or they will develop diseases such as chocolate spot (*Ascochyta* species).

Discourage plants from flowering by cutting off inflorescences as they appear. Plants can be grown from seed, but they will not all breed true, reflecting the cultivated rhubarb's hybrid origin. The plant will easily reproduce itself vegetatively, and crowns are usually passed from one gardener to another. There are supposed to be several named varieties, but these have not been clearly defined.

Asparagus

Many Australians first met asparagus (*Asparagus officinalis*) out of an Edgell's can. Fresh, steamed asparagus tastes much better. The plants can look a bit raggy from time to time (see Figure 127), but respond to trimming. Feed them often. Patience will be rewarded with delicious spears, which represent the reproductive stems. Note that male flowers and female flowers are produced on different plants, and both kinds will be needed to produce more seed. Norman de Vaus (1976) recommended selecting male plants for an increased yield of spears, also suggesting 20 years as the lifetime of the plants. Parsley is supposed to be their companion, but it is better to avoid umbellifers altogether, and choose from various plants with shallower root systems.

13.
Fruits as vegetables

'By their fruits ye shall know them.'

St Matthew 7:20

Terminology

All the plants discussed in this chapter are regarded as vegetables, even though the edible part of the plant is strictly a fruit. In the first examples the fruit is a berry: a fleshy fruit containing two or more seeds, derived from one or more ovaries. For tomato, capsicum and eggplant (Solanaceae), the number of fused ovaries is two, and the ovules show central or axile connection. For the cucurbits, the number of fused ovaries is three, and the ovules are connected around the periphery. These differences are obvious if a sliced cucumber is placed side by side with a transversely cut tomato, or a capsicum cut long-ways.

Maize (Indian corn) produces cobs from female inflorescences where each of the many kernels represents a fruit. The thin fruit walls and the seed coats are fused together, and this fruit is termed a caryopsis. Functionally, the kernel is a seed, but one that will not be removed from the cob without human intervention.

The fruit of a legume is also called a legume, and is a pod derived from a single ovary, containing a row of seeds that are attached alternately to the fused upper (adaxial) margins. The immature pods can be eaten whole, or seeds can be shelled at more advanced stages. In wild species, this pod usually splits open along both seams when it is fully mature and dry, but in cultivated legumes the pod remains closed. Instead of being scattered, the mature seeds are easily gathered.

Tomatoes

The English name tomato comes from the Mexican *tomatl*, but the scientific name has caused many problems. By special resolution of the International Botanical Congress held in Berlin in 1987, the binomial for tomato was determined to be *Lycopersicon esculentum*, rather than *L. lycopersicum*. So the second name, devised by Philip Miller in 1754, was upheld over the first, from Linnaeus in 1753. What finally weighed against the name that had priority was the fact that the epithet (the second or specific part of the binomial) added no new information beyond that already conveyed in the generic name, and so was considered redundant.

The name that was judged the better one was happily also the one preferred in common usage. This is one taxonomic decision that can be applauded. Getting rid of all lazy epithets would be a logical move based on this precedent, but this has yet to happen.

A second question about the name was raised more recently. A detailed study of *Solanum*, the genus to which potato and eggplant belong, has identifed the section of *Solanum* from which the first *Lycopersicon* species evolved (Spooner, Anderson and Jansen, 1993). Should all *Lycopersicon* species be relegated to *Solanum*? The name-changing would be horrific, even though tomato was known as *Solanum lycopersicum* in the United States for a long time (Burr, 1865). Fortunately, given the extent of evolution that has continued to occur in both potatoes and tomatoes under cultivation, there is very strong justification for keeping *Lycopersicon* distinct. The scientists who carried out this study realised that the name would not change for 'practical' reasons. Binomials are social constructs as well as indicators of identity and relationship, and they should not be interfered with lightly. The special ruling from 1987 is also a strong consideration.

Now to the plant. In the sixteenth century, when first brought from the New World, tomatoes were adopted with gusto in Italy by 1554, then in France, other parts of Europe, and finally in England by 1583. But they were not universally liked. Tomatoes were still regarded as poisonous, and not eaten much in the United States until early in the nineteenth century. Fearing Burr (1865) estimated that their consumption there had increased fourfold in the 20 years preceding publication of his book. Even as late as 1865 in Australia they were still a novelty, and one gardener in Sydney recommended them as a dessert in the proceedings of the Horticultural Society for that year. By the end of the nineteenth century, however, there were dozens of cultivars, with a splendid range of colours shown by the ripe fruit: white, yellow, orange, red, purple and sometimes striped, a form prized in Southern Mexico from the time of the Zapotec (Gould, 1983; McLeod, 1994b). Eighty-four cultivars grown in the United States between 1868 and 1937 were listed by Gould (1983).

For many years the tomato has been the most popular and abundant home garden vegetable crop. One key factor reinforcing the popularity of tomatoes has been that the development of flavour is superior in the home garden, especially when compared to the tasteless but tough varieties grown for the fresh vegetable market, such as the dreadful Floradade. Another factor is that common soil-borne diseases can be overcome by purchasing superior-tasting varieties grafted onto disease-resistant rootstocks.

Many gardeners attempt to grow too many tomato plants, and spend their lives staking, tying, pinching out buds, pruning and spraying. Most of this activity is unnecessary and ill-advised. Pruning to increase the size of the fruit occasions a reduction in overall yield, as Norman de Vaus (1976) correctly pointed out. And a tomato monoculture, like any other, should be avoided. Place a few carefully chosen plants among companions (see Chapters 2 and 10), keep them fed and watered, and remain vigilant for pests. Give any surplus seedlings away. Spread out the production over a longer time by starting early, and germinate seeds inside the house if need be (see Chapter 6). Waiting for soil temperatures of 20°C or more, as sometimes recommended by 'experts', wastes many months of fly-free production.

Small fruits need no support, but it is wise to support larger fruits. These are more attractive to fruit fly than small fruits, and when a fruit is stung, the loss is much greater than with a small fruit. For this reason, I try to get my large-fruited plants finished by Christmas, with a succession of small-fruited types following. Green loopers eat fruits as well as leaves, so remove each tomato from the plant as it 'breaks' (shows first orange colour) as a further precaution against loss. Never put tomatoes in the refrigerator — keep them in a bowl at room temperature until they have ripened sufficiently.

The following profiles are of tomatoes that can be fully recommended for organic cultivation. Many more are available through the Seed Savers' Network (about 200), Diggers' Seed Club (see Useful Addresses) and nurseries.

CUATOMATE

From 10 varieties trialled in the 1997–98 summer season, one stood out as superior for flavour, productivity and disease-resistance, which appears to cover most problems except powdery mildew. This local champion is the cherry tomato Cuatomate. A typical plant is 1.5 metres tall and suitable for a large pot. Clusters of about eight fruits occur on axillary shoots (see Figure 128). Each is small, about 2.5 centimetres in diameter all round, and sweetly flavoured, even when orange. The plant is cold-tolerant. Not only can late-summer plantings be relied upon to produce during autumn, but in suitable areas, autumn seedlings can be grown through the winter to give very early spring crops.

GROSSE LISSE

This is the famous Tomate Rouge Grosse Lisse of Vilmorin-Andrieux (1885). *Lisse* means smooth or polished, and *grosse* means large or plump. Grosse Lisse is the same as Trophy, which was bred by Dr Hand of Baltimore, Maryland, and released in 1870. He crossed the small, smooth and juicy Love Apple with a much more convoluted or lobed variety, then selected for large, smooth fruit from the unstable F1 hybrid and subsequent progeny. As Weaver (1997) points out, a woodcut published by the *American Agriculturist*

indicates that the variety was not yet uniform at the time of its release. Nevertheless, it proved to be very good fresh or canned, and was extremely popular.

Today Grosse Lisse is a tall plant (see Figure 176), with large fruits, smooth to slightly ribbed, and flattened top and bottom, so that the diameter (9 centimetres) is greater than the thickness (6 centimetres). Grosse Lisse is always highly regarded in taste tests, and is the benchmark by which others are judged. Grow from as early in the season as practicable. In September it can often be found in nurseries as a grafted seedling, where the rootstock has superior resistance to fungal diseases. An Australian version, grown in Camberwell in Victoria since the 1930s, is available through the Seed Savers' Network.

LEMON BOY

Full marks to Julie Firth (1996) in Western Australia for selecting this tomato from the progeny of an unstable F1 hybrid. The fruit is medium-sized, globose, lemon yellow and well flavoured. The plant is vigorous, and resistant to soil fungi and nematodes. Available from the Seed Savers' Network.

PURPLE CALABASH

A large, strongly lobed tomato, about 10 centimetres in diameter, with a purple skin. This one is for cooking. Do not even think about eating it fresh. Available from the Seed Savers' Network and the Diggers' Seed Club (see Useful Adresses).

TOM CAT

The tomato 'with nine lives', reflecting its resistance to nine major diseases, including tomato spotted wilt virus. The yield of fruits is abundant. These are red, firm, high in acid and absolutely delicious. At first they are clearly lobed or ribbed, up to 8 centimetres in diameter and 6 centimetres deep. Later fruits develop an 'ox-heart' shape, and may be smaller. Such irregular fruit is unpopular for commercial production, but this variability scarcely matters in the home garden.

YELLOW CHERRY

This small, round, yellow tomato is currently available through the Seed Savers' Network. It differs from Gold Nugget (United States) by not being seedless. Its pedigree is uncertain, but it could have developed directly from a red cherry tomato, or by reversion of fruit size from a larger yellow form. The general virtue of yellow tomatoes is their lower acidity, and this suits many palates, especially those of children.

Sweet peppers

The naming of capsicum or chilli peppers has caused enormous confusion, due in part to the great abundance of cultivated forms developed by the inhabitants of South and Central America before the arrival of Europeans. The distinguished ethnobotanist Charles B. Heiser and his colleagues resolved most of these problems, beginning in the 1950s (Simmonds, 1979). Common, annual or sweet peppers (*Capsicum annuum*) were first domesticated in Mexico, long before the Aztecs became dominant. The earliest preserved seeds from Tehuacan date from before 5000 BC. Of the other species of chilli peppers, *C. frutescens* had a wide distribution in lowland tropical America, and *C. chinense* was the most common type in the Amazon basin (in Brazil). Heiser considers these two are really the one species, *C. frutescens*. Two more species are quite distinct: *C. pubescens* is a highland species, widely grown in the Andes, and *C. baccatum* has a more southerly, overlapping distribution, centred on Bolivia. The allocation of varieties to species is discussed by Michael Bailes (1999). He prefers to keep the Habaneros chillies distinct because of their

pronounced fragrance, and supports the name *C. chero* instead of the geographically 'dopey' name *C. chinense*. Botanical discourses are never over.

Although many sweet peppers (*Capsicum annuum*) may once have been almost as pungent as the 'hottest' representatives of other species, there was strong selection in Europe for mildness of flavour. Soon after their introduction by the Spanish in the sixteenth century, sweet peppers became especially popular in Hungary, where new styles of cooking were developed to accommodate paprika (dried, powdered capsicum fruit wall). The heart or bell pepper was once distinguished as another species (*C. grossum*), but differences in the size of the fruit are no longer considered significant, and these peppers are included in *C. annuum*.

The ripe fruits of *C. annuum* are rectangular, tapered or narrow, to a large degree hollow, and usually red or orange. They represent the most concentrated readily available source of vitamin C, as values around 300 milligrams of vitamin C per 100 grams edible weight of pepper are common. Even unripe green peppers attain 50 milligrams of vitamin C per 100 grams fruit weight, and so have double the content of fully ripened tomatoes.

The plants are erect, sturdy and shorter than tomatoes, with single white flowers held in the axils. The last fruits may senesce as the earlier ones develop fully, and because ripening takes several months, planting should be commenced as early in the spring as possible. Despite the epithet '*annuum*', many varieties of this species belie their Eurocentric name and last more than one year. However, the fruits from the second summer are likely to be smaller. The yield will be higher when peppers are grown as an annual.

Give peppers plenty of full sun. Treating them as if they were tomatoes pays dividends. They should not be over-fertilised at the outset, but can be given extra compost and

Dynamic Lifter after flowering has
commenced, and plenty of water. The root
system is very adaptable. Many varieties are
now available through the seed-saving
networks and specialist nurseries, such as
Chilli Seeds Australia (see Useful Addresses).
A nematode-resistant variety, Charleston Belle,
was released by Southern Exposure Seed
Exchange in 1998.

Eggplant

The eggplant or aubergine (*Solanum melongena*)
originated in Asia. Its ancestor must have been
carried away from Gondwanaland on the
Indian plate, since at least 20 species of
Solanum are indigenous to India. The
aubergine was cultivated in China from the
fifth century BC, and came to Africa with
Persian and Arabian travellers, before arriving
in Europe in the fifteenth century.

Its cultivation is similar to that of tomato
and capsicum, and seeds should be planted as
early as possible in the spring. The plants are
generally no more than 1 metre tall, and the
flowers are larger than those of potato (see
Figure 125). Precautions should be taken to
prevent crossing if growing two or more
varieties at the same time (see Figure 44). A
productive plant should yield at least eight
fruits.

The colour of the fruit is generally a glossy
purple, white or green, and there is one called
Turkish Orange. The size and shape of the fruit
vary also. White Egg (SSN 1247) does
approach an egg shape (see Figure 126), but
most are more pendulous, wider towards the
base than near the stalk. White Egg was
regarded as purely ornamental by the French,
but it is just as edible as the rest. Be careful
handling the prickly calyx, and pick young
rather than old. About 20 varieties are listed
by the Seed Savers' Network.

Squashes, pumpkins and potkins

Cucurbita pepo is one of six cultivated species
of cucurbit emanating from Central or South
America. This species includes the old-
fashioned green vegetable marrows and the
scalloped white squashes that were still
popular 50 years ago. These had just about
departed from Australian kitchens when
zucchinis were 'discovered'. Squashes, too,
have made a comeback, as the very small,
bright yellow form, cooked whole. Zucchinis
and 'summer' squashes (see Figure 133) are
meant to be eaten immature. As Weaver
(1997) explains, 'squash' comes from the
Algonquian word askulasquash, referring to
this immature, unripe condition. Prompt
removal from the vine keeps the supply
coming.

In Australia we also have Table Queen (deep
green, see Figure 134), and Sweet Dumpling
(variegated green and white, Figure 134).
Table Queen is a dwarf form of Ebony Acorn,
which came from the Arikara Indians in North
Dakota following the Lewis-Clark expedition
of 1804–06. Sweet Dumpling corresponds to
the Mandan Yellow Squash, where 'yellow'
refers to the flesh, not the skin. The colour
intensifies on cooking. Although these are also
Cucurbita pepo, they are really 'winter' squashes
and are meant to be eaten fairly mature (see
Figure 137).

It is often difficult to define a pumpkin,
which could belong to any one of the
cultivated *Cucurbita* species, or an interspecies
cross. A 'potkin' was simply a small cucurbit
(weighing about 1 kilogram), cooked in the
pot, skin on, after slicing into halves or
quarters. There are quite a few 'potkins' still to
be found, such as Delucia (green and round).
These look like the American buttercup or
kabocha squashes, which belong to *C. maxima*.
Many pumpkins have persisted in Australian
gardens only because they were easy to grow,

despite the truly awful flavour of some. The advent of the butternut has revived interest in pumpkins generally.

BABY BLUE

Despite the name, which aptly reflects its appearance (see Figure 134), this is a variety of *Cucurbita maxima*. The small fruit (about 1 kilogram) is fairly round both in height and diameter (typically 15 centimetres), and the skin is a variable mixture of grey-green and vegetable green. The flesh occupies about 2 centimetres all round, and the flavour is fair. The seeds are large, 2 centimetres by 1 centimetre, with about 200 per fruit. This variety may have originated in Tenterfield, New South Wales.

BUTTERNUT

The original butternut pumpkin is a distinct species, *Cucurbita moschata*. What we call butternut today has resulted from a complex series of crosses between *C. moschata* and *C. pepo*. It has the benefit of resistance to zucchini yellow mosaic virus, derived from *C. moschata*. Other 'bridging' *Cucurbita* genotypes have also been produced, to assist the transfer of resistance to cucumber mosaic virus, and powdery mildew (Kyle, 1993). One person credited with improving the butternut pumpkin introduced to Australia more than 20 years ago is Dr Gordon Edwards of the Waite Institute, in Adelaide, South Australia.

Butternut has an economic fruit shape, with less space devoted to the seed compartment, and lots of uninterrupted orange flesh at the end nearer the stalk. The fruit can be narrower at the neck than at the base, or fairly uniform in width. Butternut is one of the tastiest kinds of pumpkin, steamed or baked, but it does not keep very long. This is because the protein that inhibits fungal protein-digesting enzymes is present only in low concentration in the rind (see Murray, 1989). Nevertheless, storage for about three months is feasible. A very long

storage life simply cannot redeem those inferior kinds of pumpkin that are pallid, distasteful or gritty.

GOURMET

After butternut, this is the best-tasting pumpkin I am aware of, yet its origin is hard to pin down. Apparently from Western Australia, it is squat, about 20 centimetres in diameter, only half that height (10 centimetres), light green, and with about 200 large seeds of a type suggesting *C. maxima*. The orange flesh occupies a narrow band, up to 3 centimetres around, so the large seed cavity suits this fruit very well for stuffing and baking.

IRONBARK

The largest pumpkins like Ironbark belong to *C. maxima*. Both names tell us something important, but some people actually like pumpkins that are enormous and difficult to cut. This one is Cinderella's coach material. Cleavers and mallets were traditionally used to open them (Fanton and Fanton, 1993).

JARRAHDALE

A medium-sized pumpkin (*C. maxima*) with a round outline shape, grey-green at first, but turning yellow as it matures. From Western Australia, and recently made available in the United States via Johnny's Selected Seeds.

QUEENSLAND BLUE

Probably related to Ironbark. Some versions of Queensland Blue are more ribbed than others. The flavour is formidable.

Cucumber

The cucumber (*Cucumis sativus*) comes from India. The name was 'cowcumber' before the committees got to it. The Romans went to great trouble to keep it warm, and it is one of the classic greenhouse plants that responds well to extra carbon dioxide. There are limits though. Some varieties fail to produce female flowers with 'double' CO_2.

The cucumber is picked immature, and generally sliced and eaten raw, or pickled. The Seed Savers' Network's first accession was an heirloom pickling cucumber of German origin, from the Barossa Valley in South Australia (Fanton and Fanton, 1993). Most available varieties have either green or white skin. Among the white forms, Crystal Apple (see Figure 135) has an unusual rounder shape, and has been highly regarded for more than 70 years.

Maize

According to a display in the Kempsey Museum, 853 379 tons of maize was produced in New South Wales in 1888. Most of this was from areas along the coastal rivers, such as the Manning and the Macleay. The main varieties grown were Early Leaming, Golden Superb, Big Yellow, Yellow Hogan, Yellow Dent, Golden Palm, Red Butcher and three with white kernels: Hickory King, Silver Mine and Macleay White. Early Leaming is derived from the Leaming, a variety that took more than 30 years to develop, selected by Mr J.S. Leaming, starting in about 1850. Some real detective work would be needed to relate all of these kinds back to their American precursors.

The nature of maize requires that small clusters of plants be grown, rather than a single long row. This is because pollen is shed from the male flowers in the tops of the plants (see Figure 136), to be received by the silks of the female flowers arranged around the cobs, held lower down on each plant. Synchrony in flowering is vitally important. Too many stragglers among the female inflorescences will mean their missing out on pollen, hence many infertile cobs. Uniform seed size helps to ensure that most plants develop evenly, and when kernels are saved for sowing, those from the tip and the base are discarded.

Growth temperatures are also important with maize, as different varieties have exacting requirements for fertilization and kernel development. The use of 'acclimatised' ears for seed gives best results, even when these are of shorter length than might be standard for the variety (Wenholz, 1917). These characteristics of maize have been well known for many years, reflecting its cultivation by American Indians in every conceivable climate. At Prospect, in Princeton, Colonel George Morgan assembled a vast collection of maize varieties. The Reverend Manasseh Cutler, visiting in July 1787, recorded that he had corn growing 'from different kinds of seed, collected from the different latitudes on this continent, as far north as the most northern parts of Canada, and south as far as the West Indies'.

SWEET CORN

For the home garden, standard maize varieties can be picked immature to provide sweet corn, or special kinds can be grown. Yates in 1930 recommended Golden Bantam and Golden Sunshine, the latter being shorter, slightly earlier, and with twelve rows to the cob, rather than eight. More recently, hybrids such as Golden Cross Bantam, Miracle and Rosella have been offered. These may have higher yields than the open pollinated Golden Bantam, but cannot be recommended because they are F1 hybrids (see Chapter 17). Similar objections apply to the 'supersweet' varieties, such as Snogold and Honeysweet Improved. A grower would have to purchase fresh seed repeatedly in order to have these varieties every year, whereas saving seed from the open-pollinated varieties is more efficient: it saves money, and helps to acclimatise and perpetuate the cultivars concerned.

POPCORN

Several dwarf varieties (about 1 metre tall) suitable for popcorn are available in the Seed Savers' Network, including Strawberry, and Surprise (SSN 1324). Strawberry is an ancient Indian variety, named for the shape of the cob and the colour of the kernels (see Figure 138). Some of the attractive multicoloured Indian corns can also be popped.

Legumes

As noted already throughout this book, legumes are vitally important to the organic garden. Peas (*Pisum sativum*) and broad beans (*Vicia faba*) should be planted in the autumn and winter, or if this is not possible because the winter is too severe, plant broad beans in the autumn, then dwarf peas in the spring. Dwarf beans should be planted as soon as possible in spring, and climbers in late spring when the weather has settled down. Cooler climates suit runner beans (*Phaseolus coccineus*), whereas common beans (*P. vulgaris*) and lima beans (*P. lunatus*) are suited generally. Snake beans are best grown under tropical conditions, extending to the north of New South Wales.

PEAS

Peas come from the Old World. The wild progenitors of pea, from the Mediterranean, are *Pisum elatius* and *P. humile*. All garden cultivars belong to a single species, *Pisum sativum*. Snow peas with flattened, fleshy pods do not represent a distinct subspecies, and differences in seed shape or pigmentation do not warrant such distinction either. Many of these differences result from simple genetic alterations (alleles), as discovered by Gregor Mendel in the mid-nineteenth century (Murray, 1999, 2003). The differences between garden peas and field peas are also trifling. The latter tend to have coloured flowers (see Figure 140), round seeds and yellow embryos, whereas garden peas usually have white flowers, wrinkled seeds and green embryos. However, these characteristics do not belong exclusively to either kind of pea. Snow peas especially show a mixture. All kinds can be made to interbreed (see Figure 141), and all belong to the one species.

The first peas brought to Australia were a dwarf marrow and a field pea. By 1803 there is no mention of the field pea, but four kinds were recorded in a letter from Governor King to Lord Hobart (Davidson and Davidson, 1993). I believe the 'tall marrowfat' in this communication refers to one of Thomas Andrew Knight's peas given to Governor King by Sir Joseph Banks before he returned to Australia in 1800. The other two new ones were the Charlton, an old English variety, and a blue boiler known as 'Blue Spanish'. The nearest we have to the Charlton today is an 1842 release called Prince Albert.

To grow peas, it is fundamentally important to know how tall they will get, in order to support them appropriately. There are basically three kinds: tall (1.3 to 2.5 metres or more), semi-dwarf (between 0.9 and 1.3 metres tall), and dwarf (less than 90 centimetres). It is important to judge the height of the support correctly. Stakes with mesh or strings are needed for taller peas in the garden, but in pots I use cylinders of mesh with a central stake. These height differences result primarily from differences in the length of the internode (the piece of stem between two nodes), and from the number of internodes produced.

The pea plant supports itself with tendrils. These are modified leaflets that coil around adjacent objects. Each pea leaf, which is technically 'pinnate', consists of some paired leaflets, and some tendrils, unless the plant is a 'semi-leafless' variety, when the leaf consists entirely of tendrils (see Figure 142). In this case, photosynthesis is conducted mainly by the stipules that flank each node.

Peas are self-fertile. By the time a flower first fully opens, fertilization has already occurred. The pod extends first, and then the seeds enlarge. The best stage for picking garden peas is at full size, before there are signs of shrivelling or yellowing in the pod wall. Snow peas, however, are picked as flat, green pods while the seeds are still very small, and eaten whole. Many peas take about 100 days between planting and flowering. Those that flower in shorter times were traditionally divided into 'first early' and 'second early' types, examples being Melbourne Market and Greenfeast, respectively. It is important not to plant 'first early' peas too early, because they will flower too soon (see Table 16), and the yield will be very much reduced. The same thing happens if they are planted too late; that is, in September.

BROAD BEANS

Broad beans (*Vicia faba*) are also 'Old World' legumes. The identity of the wild progenitor is not certain, and it may be extinct. The large-seeded varieties we are familiar with appeared in about AD 800, in Spain and Portugal. In 1803 there were four kinds in New South Wales: Windsor, Long Pod, White Blossom and Mazagan (Davidson and Davidson, 1993). We still have the Large or Green Windsor and the Long Pod, now Early Long Pod or Leviathan. Within the Seed Savers' Network there are about 20 more varieties, including Aquadulce Claudia from Seville, and several that have purple seedcoats (see Useful Addresses).

The plants are upright and very sturdy, with square, hollow stems (see Figure 143). They usually do not need support, and they will cope with more clay in the soil than peas will. The flowers are usually black and white (see Figure 144), and are self-fertile. The earliest flowers usually do not set pods, but pods will come as the weather warms up. The pods do not hang like those of peas and common

TABLE 16. TIME TAKEN FROM PLANTING TO FIRST FLOWERING FOR A RANGE OF GARDEN PEAS

VARIETY	DATE PLANTED	TIME (DAYS)
Earlicrop Massey (dwarf)	10 March 1996	35
	27 May 1994	64
	7 June 2004	73
Melbourne Market (dwarf)	23 March 1996	37
	2 June 1995	77
	21 July 1994	62
Eureka (dwarf)	24 March 1996	38
	31 May 1995	62
	8 July 1997	53
Greenfeast (dwarf)	24 March 1996	62
	10 June 1995	81
	22 July 1994	71
Medusa (semi-dwarf)	29 April 2004	63
	18 June 1999	79
	7 August 2000	65
Mayfair (semi-dwarf)	28 April 1996	106
	29 May 2003	110
	28 June 1994	85
Quite Content (tall)	28 April 1996	106
	7 June 2003	110
	20 July 1994	80

beans, but jut out. The shape of the seed is peculiar. If orientated like a pea seed with the hilum (separation scar) at the bottom, they are taller than broad, rounded at the ends, but undulating in width. They should be eaten while they are young and tender, because they become bitter as they get older. If saving seeds for replanting, do not be concerned if the pod blackens as it dries out. This is normal.

COMMON BEANS

The most common bean is the common bean — *Phaseolus vulgaris*. Like other species of

TABLE 17. PRODUCTION PARAMETERS FOR BEANS MOSTLY GROWN IN 30 CM POTS IN WOLLONGONG, NSW (2002–03 OR 2003–04 SUMMER SEASONS)

VARIETY	PODS/PLANT	SEEDS/POD	SEEDS/PLANT	PLANTS/POT	TOTAL SEEDS
DWARF KINDS					
Boston Beauty	4.0	4.0	16	3	48
Boston Beauty	4.0	3.6	15	4	60
Soldier (SSN 886)	5.3	3.8	20.3	3	61
Soldier (SSN 886)	8.0	3.5	29	1	29
Penguin	6.2	4.9	30	5	151
Penguin	13	3.8	50	1	50
CLIMBERS					
Calabrian Snowcap	5.75	2.8	16.3	3	49
Calabrian Snowcap	4.5	2.4	10.75	4	43
Cousin Jack (Zebra)	5.25	5.9	30.75	4	123
Krassner (type 1)	5.67	5.4	30.67	3	92
Krassner (type 1)	5.5	3.9	21.5	4	86
Muffet	5.67	5.7	32	3	96
Frost Bean (Fig. 51)	10.67	4.0	42.3	3	127
Purple King	7.67	7.4	57	N/A – garden (6)[1]	342
CLIMBING LIMA BEANS					
Christmas lima	16	1.7	27	1	27
Christmas lima	5.67	2.2	12.3	3	37
Civil War lima	16.67	2.4	39.67	3	119

1. The 'number of plants per pot' does not apply as these plants were not grown in a pot.

Phaseolus, it came from the New World. Beans flourished throughout Europe from the sixteeth century onwards, and then they were taken back to the United States with immigrants. So it is sometimes hard to distinguish between beans cultivated traditionally by the Native Americans and beans reintroduced from Europe. There are at least 1000 kinds of common bean, as well as lima beans (*P. lunatus*) and runner beans (*P. coccineus*). In 1803 there were six kinds of dwarf common bean in New South Wales, plus one scarlet runner (Davidson and Davidson, 1993).

As with peas, it is important to know how tall beans will get. There are climbers, up to 2 metres or more, then there are semi-viners that don't get much above 60 centimetres, and then dwarf or bush beans do not need support at all (see Figure 145). The bean leaf, in contrast to that of the pea plant, consists of three leaflets and no tendrils. This kind of leaf is called 'trifoliolate'. A tall bean climbs as the stem twines in an anti-clockwise manner. Canes can be placed singly or overlapping to form a tripod or 'tepee' (see Figure 14). Semi-vining beans start off as though they were going to be climbers, but stall at an early stage. They need short stakes, such as a piece of bamboo about 60 centimetres above ground.

The flowers of beans (see Figures 145, 146 and 147) are self-fertile, as with peas and broad beans. Climbing beans are often held to be superior to dwarf or semi-dwarf beans, but in terms of absolute yield, dwarf beans can be grown twice over in the same time that it takes climbers to get around to flowering and fruiting once. Dwarf beans at the height of summer require only 32 days between planting and flowering. Tall beans often take at least 70 days between planting and flowering, and some take at least three months. Occasionally, a climber is found that takes only 45 days (Calabrian Express). Nevertheless, the most productive bean I have ever grown was a climber, Purple King, planted in November (see Table 17).

These results are for the yield of mature seeds. This is not quite the same as growing beans primarily for eating as immature pods. So long as flowering continues, the removal of some pods for eating should not affect the final seed yield significantly. Some interesting features emerge. The number of seeds produced per plant can exceed 50 for both climbers and dwarf plants. Also, for a given cultivar, the number of seeds per plant is affected by the number of plants per pot. I like to plant three or four seeds per pot, against the likelihood that one or two plants might be lost as casualties before maturity. But three or four plants surviving in the one pot will result in a suboptimal seed yield per plant, especially for climbers (see Table 17). The yield per plant is highest with only one or two plants per pot, but planting so few seeds per pot is a much riskier strategy, and is not recommended, as it could easily result in no yield at all.

LIMA BEANS AND RUNNER BEANS

It pays to diversify your beans. The leaves of lima beans and runner beans are thicker and tougher than those of common beans, so they are more resistant to white fly and two-spotted mite. This does not mean that they escape absolutely, simply that these beans in company with common beans are the least preferred option. Lima beans are supposed to emit volatile chemical signals attractive to predatory mites whenever they are colonised by the two-spotted mite. Having grown lima beans as well as common beans over more than 10 years, I can vouch for the fact that this does happen. Volunteer predatory mites have appeared in late summer to early autumn, without my having to import them from a supply company (see Table 1 on page 8). In conjunction with cooler night temperatures, this stops the appearance of two-spotted mite on my autumn-growing dwarf beans.

Runner beans die back to tubers, which reshoot in the next spring. But keeping lima bean plants over winter into a second summer season can afford two-spotted mites an opportunity for early expansion. It is better to break their tenure, either by eliminating all beans over winter, or else finding a secluded corner for the lima beans. I have such a position on my eastern boundary, behind my workshop and garden shed.

SNAKE BEAN

Snake bean (*Vigna unguiculata* subs. *sesquipedalis*) has a long slender pod, but it is never really 6 feet long, as its botanical name implies. Best grown in the tropics, it will prosper as far south as northern New South Wales. The Seed Savers' Network has at least nine varieties available (see Useful Addresses). The pods should be sliced and cooked like green beans.

ASPARAGUS PEA

The asparagus pea (*Lotus tetragonolobus*) is not a pea, and does not taste like asparagus. This short plant has striking crimson/crimson lake flowers (see Figure 150). The pods have four crinkly flaps, running lengthwise, hence the species name. Plant the seeds, which are like miniature beans, in late winter or early spring for picking in summer, unless you live as far north as Byron Bay, where they can be planted in the autumn. Whole pods should be picked young, no more than 5 centimetres long, and steamed or stir fried, exactly like snow peas. They provide texture rather than flavour.

14.
Fruit and nut trees

'I do not envy any man living. I have never heard
of any work or occupation or vocation that seems to me to rival
that of the scientist, especially of the scientist who is equally a
humanist and whose research and study and experiments and
discoveries are all directed to the end that man may find this old
sphere a better and more beautiful place in which to live.'

Luther Burbank, *The Harvest of the Years* (1927, page 108)

General advice

With only limited space in which to plant trees, it is important to be selective. Find out what does well locally. Trees that require little or no maintenance allow you to spend time doing the things you would rather do. Any tree that fails to prosper has occupied space that another could have utilised to better effect. Avoid those with complicated pollination groups and requirements, like cherries. Leave them in the 'too hard' basket, unless you can find a self-pollinating variety like Stella, or would like to try out a multiple graft on a dwarfing rootstock. Avoid fly-prone types of low nutritional value too, like the loquat. Grow what grows best.

Always clear fallen fruit and leaves from the ground beneath a tree. This is fundamental to controlling fruit fly and some other pests, especially fungal diseases. Infested fruit can be boiled, or drowned and buried. Do not take the risk of feeding infested fruit to birds or animals that might not consume it totally. When leaves fall from deciduous species, rake them away and compost them. Remove any diseased, mummified fruits from the canopy that have not fallen of their own accord. Interrupt the life cycles of pests that overwinter in leaf litter under the trees, or in their bark, by painting trunks with gummy barriers in autumn (North, 1999). Kaolin-containing barriers (Philbrick and Gregg, 1966) serve the same function. Kaolin can also be sprayed on fruit to block access to fruit fly.

If there is going to be serious competition between fruit-eating birds (see Figures 152 and 157) or flying foxes and fruit-growers, install appropriate nets and meshes. Protected cropping is sometimes the only humane solution. On the north coast of New South Wales, flying foxes have had to develop a taste for coffee, so little unprotected fruit is now left to them.

Pomefruit

Apples (*Malus* species) and pears (*Pyrus* species) in the family Rosaceae have a fruit called a pome, named for Pomona, the Roman goddess of fruits and harvests. In addition to the ovary, such a fruit includes fleshy tissue derived from other parts of the flower, the receptacle and hypanthium, which completely surround the stiff, cartilaginous ovary walls. Apples and pears have been cultivated for thousands of years. Cultivated apples (*M. domestica*) are usually distinguished by name from the wild crab apple (*M. sylvestris*, see Figure 151). A useful guide to cultivars is that published by Roger Yepsen (1994). Most improvements came from chance seedlings (just like our Australian Granny Smith), until the advent of deliberate hybridisation, a procedure exploited brilliantly by Thomas Andrew Knight.

In contrast to some of his contemporaries, Knight was very clear about his crossing and selection criteria. What also made his technique so powerful was his reliance on grafting. He put new seedlings onto established rootstocks, which accelerated the ability of these scions to flower, and in turn, bear more fruit and seeds. He saved countless years in this process, and generated many more useful combinations than would normally have been seen in a dozen lifetimes. In 1806 Knight published his book *Treatise on the Culture of the Apple and Pear and on the Manufacture of Cider and Perry*. This became widely read in the United States, reinforced by extracts published in journals and magazines.

His modus operandi inspired later American breeders, such as Charles M. Hovey and Luther Burbank, as well as Thomas Rivers in Britain.

Several hundred varieties of apples and pears are still to be found in Australia. Accessible collections were made by several members of Heritage Seed Curators Australia (HSCA) including David Aumann (Yarram), Alan Broughton (Bairnsdale), Stephen Murphy (Tree Holme Nursery, Teesdale) and Keith Robertson (Apples of Bygone Years, Creswick), all in Victoria, plus Jonathon and Robyn Banks, (Pialligo Apples, near Canberra). Bob Magnus in Woodbridge, Tasmania (see Useful Addresses) is particularly adept at grafting rare apple scions onto dwarfing rootstocks. These people are all helping to make interesting varieties much more widely available.

With limited space, a multiple-grafted tree might appeal. Several of these have been developed by Treemendous Trees & Shrubs. For example, an apple tree with scions of both Granny Smith and Golden Delicious is currently available. Alternatively, the same company's Ballerina series, including Maypole and Polka, can be guaranteed not to become overly large.

Stonefruit

Plums, nectarines, peaches and apricots are all fruits in which a central seed is enclosed by the innermost, woody layer of the fruit, the endocarp (see Figure 154). Technically, they are drupes: fleshy fruits containing a single seed. The proportion of the fruit occupied by the tasty, fleshy mesocarp has increased during domestication and cultivation over thousands of years.

The European plum (*Prunus domestica*) has been grown throughout the world, and there are many distinct forms, including the greengages and the French Mirabelles

(McLeod, 1994b). Some of the most significant improvements in the plum, however, occurred as a result of hybridisation between the Japanese plum (*P. salicina*) and the American plum (*P. americana*). These crosses were conducted by Luther Burbank at Santa Rosa in California. Two of the best new plums were called the Burbank ('very large, conical, heart-shaped, red with white bloom'), and the Satsuma ('red flesh, very juicy, firm, delicious in flavour and delightful in aroma') after the province in Japan where Burbank's seedlings of *P. salicina* had been obtained (Burbank and Hall, 1927). In 20 new plums produced between 1889 and 1901, Burbank improved the rate of fruit growth, earliness to bear, and the flesh to stone ratio, and in some he increased the sugar content, important for those that were to be dried as prunes.

The Burbank and other American plums came to Australia very soon after release. They were acquired directly from Luther Burbank by Thomas Henry Miller, and grown at his orchard Poplar Gardens in Tenterfield, New South Wales. Thomas Miller produced the first commercial crop of cherries in Tenterfield, and also established the apple-growing industry there. He was interested in the improvement of a wide range of fruit trees, rather like George Morgan in the United States a century before. The progeny of his own crosses and selections were spread to other growers, further ensuring that today's varieties continue to show the benefits of Luther Burbank's creative endeavours.

Peaches and nectarines (both *P. persica*) are very similar except for the skin: fuzzy on peaches (see Figure 153), but smooth on nectarines (see Figure 155). The peach originated in western China. The apricot (*P. armeniaca*) also came from western China, and like the peach, is self-fertile. As noted in Chapter 8, it took a long time for the apricot to reach England. By then, considerable selection for lateness of flowering had occurred, in order to reduce fruit loss due to frosts. English peaches were further modified in the United States, some of the most notable varieties coming from William Crawford and John Smock of Middletown, New Jersey, in about 1840.

Stonefruit need a cold winter, but recent selection to modify this requirement and shorten the low-temperature exposure has led to what are now termed 'low chill' fruit trees. Their advantage is that they can be grown in warmer climates. Graeme Richards, at the Hawkesbury Campus of the University of Western Sydney, is interested in the development of 'low chill' varieties. Young trees currently on offer in nurseries will be labelled to indicate whether they are 'low chill' or not. Alan Broughton maintains heritage varieties of plums and peaches, in addition to his apples, pears and grapes. Again, for those with limited space, Treemendous Trees & Shrubs have released a dwarf peach (Pixzee), a dwarf nectarine (Nectazee), and a two-way grafted nectarine, the scions being Goldmine and May Grand. Others may follow.

Citrus

Even the smallest garden has room for one or two citrus trees. Despite shedding most of the flowers that form, they are surprisingly productive, with colourful fruits. Many citrus diseases are avoided by grafting productive scions onto disease-resistant stocks. Seven stocks are commonly employed, and the combination should be clearly indicated on the label. Always remove any new growth that comes from below the junction of the scion with the stock (the 'graft union').

The lemon (*Citrus limon*) is not suited to the tropics. The wild or 'rough' lemon, with thorns, is still widely grown, and also used as a stock. Among named varieties, Eureka is adaptable, with fewer thorns (see Figure 158).

Meyer is better suited to cooler conditions. There is generally a seasonal gap at Christmas, lasting well into summer, so any tree producing at this time is extremely valuable. Seedling lemons can be grown readily from seeds, but give them good drainage, as they are on their own root systems.

In contrast, the lime (*C. aurantifolia*) is tropical. The one most frequently encountered in Australia is the seedless Tahitian lime, which grows at least as far south as the Illawarra, and bears small fruit between autumn and spring. Lemon and lime trees are usually about 3 metres in height, and slightly more in circumference.

Mandarines (*C. reticulata*) are excellent fruits because they peel so easily compared to oranges. Popular varieties are Imperial (early season), Clementine and Emperor (both mid-season). A recent dwarf form, Chinoti, has compact foliage and small fruits. The tangelo came from a cross between a mandarine and a grapefruit. The grapefruit itself (*Citrus* x *paradisi*) came from the West Indies. The fruit is typically very large. Apart from the usual type with lemon-yellow segments, such as Marsh, some with purplish flesh have also been bred; for example, Ruby and Star Ruby.

Kumquats (or cumquats; *Fortunella* species) are small trees, with very small fruits, sometimes variegated. With their strong and characteristic taste, they are good for jams or flavouring brandy.

Avocado

Persea americana originated in Mesoamerica. There are three races, which hybridise readily, and all commercially important cultivars came from chance seedlings. Despite standard advice about not bothering to grow seedlings from avocado seeds, some excellent backyard trees are to be found. They generally yield masses of fruit with minimal effort. The avocado fruit is a simple drupe: a fleshy fruit containing a single seed. The common forms have either a deep purple skin, or remain green at maturity. Play safe and plant a named variety such as Fuerte or Hass, unless you have room to experiment.

Babaco

Although the tropical pawpaw (*Carica papaya*) can be grown under subtropical conditions, babaco (*C. pentagona*) is better adapted to cold climates, coming from higher altitudes in Ecuador. The fruit is smaller and narrower than a pawpaw (see Figure 159). As there is considerable variation in texture and flavour, Mick Brew, in the Adelaide Hills, South Australia, is breeding more predictable varieties.

Banana

The species name is incomplete (*Musa* sp.) because the edible, seedless banana is an infertile hybrid, perpetuated vegetatively by division, or in tissue culture. Provided they get enough full sun, bananas can be grown satisfactorily further south than Wollongong (see Figure 160). It may still be necessary to get a permit from NSW Agriculture to move plants around the countryside. Many Sydney plants came from Coffs Harbour in the 1960s. Bananas can be very productive, and they are surprisingly drought-resistant. One- to two-year-old Williams plants can withstand water stress for up to 50 days (Kallarackal and colleagues, 1990).

Mango

The mango (*Mangifera indica*) comes from India. In terms of the volume produced, it is one of the most important tropical fruits. The cultivar most prevalent in Australia is Kensington Pride, but there are more than 30 varieties known to the Seed Savers' Network, some with superior anthracnose-resistance. The best way to maintain a good variety is by grafting buds onto suitable stocks. The mango is usually a medium-sized tree, but it can reach more than 30 metres under ideal conditions. If protected from frost in its young stages, it can grow well south into New South Wales (see Figure 156), but will not normally attain its maximum size. In many gardens, that is an advantage. The yield can be drastically reduced if rain occurs at the time of flowering.

Olives

The olive (*Olea europea*) has been cultivated in its countries of origin around the Mediterranean for at least 6000 years (Zwingle, 1999). Individual trees can live for hundreds of years. In the preface to his report *The Olive and Olive Oil* (1887), Joseph H. Maiden expressed the view that 'in the whole of NSW, between the Dividing Range and the coast, this most useful tree will flourish'. More than a century later, we are still waiting for this to happen. Import replacement is a distant prospect. For experience with the olive, we look to South Australia, where trees from various sources have been grown since the 1840s, and to Western Australia, where the monks at New Norcia introduced their own varieties after 1860.

The invasive nature of the tree was made abundantly clear, Maiden noting that 'the trees grow freely in South Australia, springing up like young gum trees'. With this warning, there is no reason why an olive tree might not be grown more than occasionally in the back garden. Olives may be pressed for oil, or preserved. Verdale and Manzanillo, suitable for both purposes, are propagated by Alan Broughton. There appear to be more than 20 varieties in Australia, coming directly from Italy, France, Spain and Portugal.

Sapote

White sapote or sapodilla (*Manilkara zapota*) comes from southern Mexico to Venezuela. Latex drawn from the bark of the tree is the traditional source of gum (chicle) for the manufacture of chewing gum. Far more worthwhile is the fruit, which has pale flesh, a delicate flavour and silky texture. White sapote can be grown well away from the tropics in Australia, even in Mediterranean climates.

Tree tomato

Tree tomato or tamarillo (*Cyphomandra betacea*) is another member of the Solanaceae family that comes from Peru. Yates in 1930 described it as 'subtropical', but it can certainly grow in Melbourne. The tree is very short, about 2 metres tall. Elongated orange fruits follow attractive flowers (see Figures 161 and 162).

Nut trees

Strictly, a nut is a whole fruit with a hard coat, like a hazelnut, but in general usage 'nut' is applied to a hard seed contained in a dry pod or follicle, like a macadamia, or a seed surrounded by a stony endocarp, like the almond (*Prunus amygdalus*). The seeds of these 'nuts' consist mainly of a large embryo, adapted for the storage of oil, protein and minerals.

The extremely hard shell is a drawback to growing macadamia nuts, but they are native (*Macadamia integrifolia* and *M. tetraphylla* and their hybrid off-spring, Proteaceae). The shells can be composted eventually, or used as fuel for the processing plant. It may be 10 years before the tree flowers and fruits for the first time. The flowers are surprisingly small, and there are hundreds of them. Very few actually produce a fruit, but once a tree becomes established, the yield increases. The fruits are shed and easily collected from the ground. When dry and brown, peel off the outer layer, and use a hammer or 'maca cracker' to open the nuts. Do not store them very long. Fresh is best.

The pecan (*Carya illinoensis*) is a cousin of the walnut, and was originally brought to Australia to provide for the northern hemisphere's off-season by Deane Stahmann, who planted 70 000 trees over 700 hectares at Trawalla, near Moree, in 1971. Stahmann Farms Inc. (see Useful Addresses) now produces 3000 tonnes of nuts per annum from these trees. For more than 15 years this property has been pesticide free. Native wasps and fungi have been employed to control borers and stem-girdling beetles (ABC Television, *Landline*, 10 July 2005).

Surprisingly, some pecan plantations are having trouble with the green vegetable bug (see Figure 170), and a new predator, the feather-legged fly, is currently being trialled. However, many unattended street trees in Richmond, New South Wales, yield bountiful nut supplies in springtime with no maintenance whatsoever. They are not even pruned, because they are not under powerlines. These deciduous trees cope with frosts in winter, and 42°C maxima in summer. With easily broken shells, and a more delicate flavour than the walnut, you could not imagine a better nut — if you have the space for at least two trees of compatible mating types.

15.
Fruiting vines and strawberries

'Berries, many of which are members of the Rose
family, are just as ornamental as flowering shrubs, as
attractive in flower, delicious in fruit and delightful
in their autumn suits of vivid foliage.'

Louise Riotte (1974)

Passionfruit

The familiar purple passionfruit (*Passiflora edulis*) came from Brazil. Worldwide there are about 370 species of *Passiflora*, many originating in Central and South America. More than a dozen species are present in Australia, most being introductions (Satterthwait, 1982). Two species are endemic (*P. cinnabarina* and *P. herbertiana*) and another is indigenous, shared with other countries of the South-west Pacific (*P. aurantia*). So there are quite a few alternatives to choose from.

The flower of the passionfruit is an extraordinary and beautiful structure, replete with its own mythology. This grew from the efforts of Franciscan missionaries, who went to the New World in the wake of the Spanish conquests. The passion flower was used as a teaching aid to represent the Passion of the crucified Christ, as outlined below. In 1753 Linnaeus took the systematic name for the genus directly from the common name, and also the family name, Passifloraceae.

The first trap for the unwary is that the outermost parts of the flower are not the calyx, but three green leafy bracts. Then there are five sepals, which are distinguished from the petals by their position (they enclose the rest of the flower), their width, their exterior colour and ornamentation. For instance, in *P. edulis* (see Figure 163), this colour is green, and along each spine a flange projects, culminating in a soft point. The petals are narrower and more uniform in colour. They may be the same colour as that displayed by the sepals, or different. The petals alternate with the sepals, and are clearly distinct from them. However, for the convenience of maintaining a good story, the sepals (calyx) and petals (corolla) are often classed together as 10 perianth segments.

Next comes an unusual structure, the corona, located inside the petals and surrounding a circular trough, which contains the nectary. The main corona of the passion-fruit is frilled, finely divided radially, and often multicoloured. Inside this corona there may be two or three more concentric coronas, very much reduced in size. Another familiar flower with a corona is the daffodil, where the tube is the corona. Opinions differ as to whether a corona represents an array of infertile stamens, or an extra petal-like layer. It certainly serves an attractive function, like the petals, and is far removed physically from the stamens.

From a stalk or pedestal in the centre of the flower there project five fertile stamens with large anthers, longer than they are wide. These are aligned like the five sides of a pentagon, but they can pivot on their filaments, and shake out pollen if disturbed. At their base, halfway up the pedestal, the stamens surround three fused ovaries, which sit like an orb beneath separate styles leading to three knobbly stigmas. For effective pollination, nectar-seekers must touch the overhanging anthers and stigma lobes on their way to and from the circular nectary. Mature anthers are very likely to be bumped by flying insects, or birds. A bicoloured display of brilliant red flowers with yellow anthers and stigmas, as in *P. coccinea*, is attractive to birds (see Figure 164). The main corona is also much reduced in this species.

To return to the Passion symbolism, there are various stories that need to be sifted to eliminate the unlikely. The following is the kernel that is left. The green bracts represent the crown of glory; the 10 perianth segments represent the ten Apostles who attended the crucifixion; the corona represents the crown of thorns; the anthers represent the five wounds; and the threefold ovary represents the three persons of the Trinity.

EDIBLE PASSIONFRUITS

The fruit of the passionfruit vine is a berry. There are no central partitions, and the ovules that become seeds are attached in three regions around the perimeter, as in a cucumber. The green fruits take more than three months to mature, during which time the seeds become enclosed in a sweet, juicy pulp. This has the rich flavour we have come to associate with fresh fruit salads, or topping with ice-cream, flummery or pavlova. The final skin colour change can take place in just one or two weeks. Be alert to fruits dropping of their own accord: look on the ground, as well as on the vine. A single vine should produce at least 60 to 80 fruits over about six weeks of summer in its most productive years.

Surplus fruits store well in the freezer. According to Thomas and Corden (1970), passionfruit pulp is a good source of vitamin C: at 24 milligrams per 100 grams, it is the equal of shelled green peas or a fresh sun-ripened tomato. Passionfruit is also an excellent source of fruit sugar, potassium and other minerals.

Apart from the very popular *P. edulis* and its hybrids, other species with edible fruits include the Australian native *P. cinnabarina* (crimson passion flower) from New South Wales and Victoria. Over the past 10 years the banana passionfruits have become popular again: *P. antioquiensis* (originating in Colombia) and *P. mollissima*, from the Andes (see Figure 165). Banana passionfruits are so-called because of the shape and yellow colour of the fruit, and not because they taste like banana.

ORNAMENTAL PASSIONFRUITS

Trellises, wires and weldmesh panels are ideal supports for passionfruits and can disguise boundaries by producing 'living' fences. All species produce handsome foliage, some with unusual leaf shapes. The large leaves of *P. coccinea* and *P. laurifolia* are simple and ovate (see Figure 166), unlike the more typical maple-leaf shape.

Passiflora coccinea produces bright red flowers over a lengthy period, throughout and beyond the winter, when colour is welcome in the garden. This provides good contrast to spring-flowering types like *P. edulis*, which continues to flower for at least four months. Other species, such as *P. caerulea* (blue crown passionflower) from Brazil, flower from late spring to autumn. In this species, the main corona is violet, cream and purple, and everything above the stamens is purple. It is thus possible to build up a series of passionfruits to flower year round. Although these flowers have splendid visual appeal, they are not strongly fragrant. Of the species common in Australia, only *P. laurifolia* (see Figure 166) has fragrant flowers.

GROWING PASSIONFRUITS FROM SEED

Vines of *Passiflora edulis* last from three to six years, and are most productive after their first summer, so it is important to plan for their eventual replacement. Because passionfruits are largely tropical and do not usually cope well with drought or frosts, there is a prevailing view that their seeds do not keep, and they must be washed and planted at once. Although this inability to be stored is typical of the seeds of many rainforest trees, such 'recalcitrance' is not a problem with *P. edulis*.

The seeds possess a tough, black, embroidered coat. They are streamlined, and clearly adapted to surviving passage through the alimentary canal of a bird or a mammal. Where mature fruits have been shed, dried out, and then broken into the ground, seeds germinate throughout the first year afterwards (at least). These volunteer seedlings can be moved directly to better positions, or potted up first. My current 'no name' passionfruit is superior to Nellie Kelly, which tends to die early. Some of the smaller seed companies

stock alternative passionfruits; for example, Greenpatch Organic Seeds (see Useful Addresses). The Australian Plants Society often has *P. cinnabarina* seeds available to members.

Chokos

The choko vine is rarely seen nowadays, but was very popular in the first half of the twentieth century. It is just as easy to grow as a passionfruit, and useful for covering blank walls. The flowers are undistinguished, and the pear-shaped green fruits remain green as they mature (see Figure 167). This makes it difficult to tell for certain that chokos picked for eating are sufficiently young and tender. The test is that the seed is still milky. There is nothing worse than a tough choko, and this is the real reason their popularity has waned. For the generations in a hurry, it is too much trouble to get the picking right.

Grapes

Grapes deserve a whole chapter, but space limitations forbid. A single vine trained over a pergola provides summer shade, winter sun, grape leaves for wrapping food and grapes, for eating or for making wine. The critical factor for success in avoiding mildews is adequate circulation of air around the leaves. This means sufficient height for the foliage above ground, and this should not be too dense (see Figure 168). Whatever variety is chosen, grafting onto *Phylloxera*-resistant stock is mandatory.

Melons

Melons, like squashes, belong to the Cucurbitaceae family. Most familiar are cantaloupe or netted musk melon (*Cucumis melo*), and watermelon (*Citrullus lanatus*) from South Africa. There is also a 'jam' melon from Asia, which is harvested young for stir fries, or included in jam when mature. Chilacayote (*Cucurbita ficifolia*) comes from the highland tropics of Central to South America. The fruit looks a lot like a watermelon, but it has white flesh. It can be eaten young, like a squash.

Strawberries

The strawberry is not a fruit, but a false fruit: an enlarged receptacle studded with tiny pips, each one a seed surrounded by dry fruit coats. These are the true fruits, termed achenes. The name 'strawberry' has got nothing to do with straw mulches either. It comes from old English 'streabariye', meaning 'the runner that strays' (Farndale, 1994). Strawberries are perennials that reproduce by runners (stolons) as well as seeds. Like violets, the individual plants have very short stems, with a radiating cluster of leaves on long stalks. Each leaf, however, is divided into three leaflets.

Until the eighteenth century, strawberries were simply picked from plants of the English and European wild strawberry (*Fragaria vesca*). The strawberries we know today are descended from the progeny of a natural cross of two American species that occurred in France in 1790. These parents were the geographically disparate *F. chiloensis* and *F. virginiana*, brought together on another continent. Our strawberry is called *F. x ananassa*, the 'x' indicating the hybrid origin.

The famous English plant breeder, Thomas Andrew Knight, released the Downton strawberry in 1817, then the Elton in 1828.

These were of moderate size and excellent flavour. By comparison, all those larger-than-life strawberries with good colour and little flavour, so beloved of commercial producers, seem to have come from Keens Imperial, released by Michael Keens in 1806, or Keens Seedling, released in 1821. In the United States, Hovey's Seedling became one of the most important varieties midway through the nineteenth century. According to Darrow (1966), Charles Hovey used Keen's Seedling as a parent in many of his crosses. By 1865, the Elton, Keen's Seedling, Princess Alice Maud, Nimrod, British Queen, Ketley's Goliath, Myatt's Eliza and Eleanor, Sir Harry, and Old Carolina were all being grown in New South Wales.

Strawberries that acquired viruses became less productive, and were inevitably replaced with the next 'creation' of the plant breeders. More than 100 named varieties from the late nineteenth century have now vanished. We still have Royal Sovereign (from Thomas Laxton, 1892) and Jubilee (1897), which was still being grown in palace gardens in 1951 (Shewell-Cooper, 1952). More recently, the Cambridge series has been popular in England (Akeroyd, 2005), and Riotte (1974) has described cultivars available in the United States.

Since the 1970s, virus-free strawberry plants have been recovered from virus-affected material by the process of tissue culture and regeneration of new plants. It is possible to take rediscovered varieties through this process when necessary. Many gardeners (myself included) have no idea what the cultivar name of their strawberry might be. Mine has been in the family for at least 60 years, and is still vigorous.

16.
Handling pests and diseases

'It is still common to find a man who is going at
spraying with enthusiasm, but who cannot explain
a single definite object in view. He merely knows, on general
principles, that spraying is useful. To such a man, spraying is
spraying, whether he uses arsenicals, or bordeaux, or both ...
and his results are about equal to his knowledge.'

Liberty H. Bailey (1920)

Avoidance of pests by timing

Timing can be all-important. Growing plants earlier or later than their main seasons can be extremely productive. Consider autumn, a neglected season, reserved by some for maintenance tasks like repairing the lawn-mower, pruning, weeding and applying manure. But we can grow more plants as well. Let's track the daylight through autumn. Near Sydney and Adelaide, which have approximately the same latitude, there is more than 12 hours of daylight until the end of March. By the end of April, daylight is still 10 hours and 45 minutes. But by the end of May, we are approaching the winter solstice, and daylength has reduced to about 10 hours and 10 minutes. At the winter solstice, 21 June, daylength is just short of 10 hours. Therefore, much can be made of growth opportunities in the first two months of autumn. Day temperatures are commonly about 25°C maximum, even though night temperatures are on the way down, and are generally between 10°C and 15°C. In New South Wales, April 2005 was the warmest April since 1996, with an average maximum of 26.9°C.

It is still possible to grow lettuce, rocket, beans and tomatoes, according to variety. A good bean to plant in February is Romano, a dwarf variety with long pods, in which the seeds do not develop rapidly. This is not a problem, as there is no intention in this season of saving seeds. Eat all the pods produced, which should total 70 grams per plant over March and April. Another good autumn bean is Staley's Surprise. Late summer plantings of small tomatoes yield abundantly in April and May (see Cuatomate, on page 109). A larger red tomato described as 'Siberian' makes excellent growth during autumn, yielding well in June. The only pests about should be green loopers, snails and slugs. Do not carry tomato production too far into winter, however, because the fruits will lack flavour.

Avoidance of pests by rotation

In the eighteenth and nineteenth centuries, agriculture in many places became repetitive. The combination of monoculture and monotony guarantees pest problems. Crop rotation was 'rediscovered' by Thomas William Coke (1752–1840), and applied to his estate in Norfolk after 1776 (MacDonald, 1913). Instead of planting cereal after cereal (usually rye), followed occasionally by turnips, he devised a sequence of two years cereal, followed by two years pasture for sheep. He manured heavily, and used rape-cake as a top dressing. As a consequence, the fertility of his sandy soil improved enormously, and he was able to grow wheat instead of rye.

In the fertile Nepean-Hawkesbury flood-plain regions of western Sydney in the colony of New South Wales, crop rotation was practised by some of the early landholders (including some of my own antecedents). One such system was described by James Atkinson in 1826 (reprinted in 1975, see Davidson and Davidson, 1993). His was a five-crop rotation over four years, commencing with wheat sown in autumn, followed by turnips sown in early summer, then by barley in early spring the next year,

then by grass to be cut for hay, followed eventually by peas sown in August of the fourth year, and harvested in December.

This field sowing of late peas is unusual in two respects: first, not many grew peas as a field crop, and second, David Mann (1811) had recommended that a field crop of peas be sown much earlier, in May. Eventually, Australian rotations included pasture legumes such as sub clover or lucerne (alfalfa) instead of peas or beans.

Since the rust problems of early wheat varieties had not yet been solved (Wrigley and Rathjen, 1981), most early landholders grew maize as well as wheat, or instead of it. Although few included legumes as a field crop, even fewer grew oats (Davidson and Davidson, 1993). Most peas at this time would have been home garden peas, not recorded in market figures. However rotation was managed, those who did not return sufficient organic material to the soil ran into trouble, and often sold out, James Ruse included. Those who did manage their soil correctly ate nutritious food that they had produced themselves, and barring accidents, lived long and healthy lives.

Crop rotation has been adapted from mainstream agriculture for the home gardener, its intention being 'to ensure that a member of one particular vegetable family is not continually grown in the same soil' (*Yates Garden Guide*, 27th edition, about 1957). There is a dual purpose in this: to prevent the excessive removal of any particular mineral nutrient, and to starve out pests or diseases that depend on specific plants. The second effect is far more important than the first, which can always be remedied by continuing to add compost and manures.

Yates suggested a planting sequence beginning with legumes, followed by green or leaf crops (chiefly brassicas) or tomatoes, followed then by root crops (carrots, turnips, beetroots, onions or potatoes). Cucurbits could also be included in this last group, as fruit-set is particularly dependent on there not being too much nitrogen in the soil.

Beatrice Hunter (1977) recommended a similar scheme, with the significant qualification that on soils deficient in organic matter, legumes should take the place of root crops, and follow the 'heavy feeders' belonging to Yates' second group. She also advised against planting tomatoes after peas or beans.

Refinements were also suggested by Norman de Vaus (1976), who warned that 'not only do some root crops belong to the same family as certain leaf crops, but some non-related vegetables can be affected by similar diseases'. As examples, he suggested that cauliflower or cabbage plants should not be followed by turnips, as all were susceptible to clubroot and blackleg. Nor should brassicas be followed by beets. Similarly, potatoes and tomatoes are both susceptible to wilts (*Fusarium* and *Verticillium*), as well as root-knot nematodes, and should not follow one another.

Consideration of all these suggestions brings us to the three 'rules' of rotation:

- **1ST RULE:** Do not put an annual in the same places where it has previously been grown without an intervening crop of something different.
- **2ND RULE:** Do not follow an annual with another member of the same family.
- **3RD RULE:** Do not follow an annual with plants that are likely to share some of the same pests and diseases.

Having established these rules, it is important to know when to follow them, and when to break them. Readers of my earlier book *Growing Peas & Beans* (Murray, 1999, page 32) will be aware that I have consistently broken the second rule by following peas with common beans, both in the open garden and in pots. I have done this for more than 30 years without ill-effect. The persistence of

suitable strains of *Rhizobium* in their off-seasons, when they depend on organic matter in the soil, attests to the quality of my compost. Where lima beans are concerned, however, it should be recalled that their strain of *Rhizobium* is 'slower' than those that are specific for peas and common beans, and in competition with the others, it disappears (*Horticulture* 1934, reprinted 1994, Vol. LXXII, No. 6, page 65). So lima beans should be grown separately from peas and common beans, and if necessary, inoculated.

I can also confirm that bean pests do not live on peas, and vice versa, despite the views of some authors that these common garden legumes share their pests and diseases. This is rarely true, and in my experience involves only the occasional cool season green looper on peas. With suitable choice of cultivars, the growing sequence can be deliberately extended to peas, beans, and then beans again, all in the space of 12 months. A deliberate demonstration of this possibility involved one of the bean cultivars mentioned in the previous section, which was planted after peas and another bean in the same pots, as follows:

- **1ST PLANTING:** Semi-leafless pea, Elektra, 15 April to 24 August 2004. Flowered after 59 days, and mature pods harvested for seed.
- **2ND PLANTING:** Cold-tolerant dwarf bean, Staley's Surprise, 1 September to 28 January. Seed saved during December; later pods eaten.
- **3RD PLANTING:** Dwarf beans, Romano, 1 February to mid-April 2005. Pods eaten entirely (see Figure 169).

Semi-leafless peas grow steadily and do not flower too soon like some normal garden peas would if planted this early (see Table 16 on page 115). To condense the growth of three annual legumes to fit 12 months exactly,

TABLE 18. POWDERY MILDEW-RESISTANT SNOW PEAS RESULTING FROM A CROSS OF HUNGARIAN SNOW PEA (SSN 266, MILDEW-SENSITIVE) WITH DWARF OREGON (RESISTANT)[1]

EMBRYO COLOUR, POD TEXTURE	FLOWERS WHITE	FLOWERS COLOURED
TALL PLANTS (>1.5 m)		
yellow embryos, smooth pods	Candida	Delta Procilla
yellow embryos, rough pods	Super Nova	Delta Galina
green embryos, smooth pods	Cygna Claudia	Delta Augusta
green embryos, rough pods	Arcadia	Delta Matilda
SEMI-DWARF PLANTS (1–1.3 m)		
yellow embryos, smooth pods	Genevieve	Delta Despina
yellow embryos, rough pods	Stella Nova	Delta Moravia[3]
yellow embryos, rough pods		Delta Louisa[4]
green embryos, smooth pods	Sonja	
green embryos, rough pods	Oregami[2]	
DWARF PLANTS (40–90 cm)		
yellow embryos, rough pods	Ada Australia	Delta Joanna[5]
green embryos, rough pods	Hildegard	

1. As this was my fourth cross in 1995, 'Delta' is used to indicate all those with coloured flowers

2. Closest to the resistant parent, Dwarf Oregon   3. Selected for paired flowers in 2002

4. The inside of wing petals is variegated (calico)   5. Small flowers

turnaround times for the pots were abbreviated. For the first and second crops, 30-centimetre pots were supplemented with compost (4 trowels-full) and Dynamic Lifter (about 300 grams, three-quarters of a bean-can full). Ash slurry was applied once, in August, as the pea pods matured. Between the two bean crops, compost only was applied.

Rotation is important for members of the 'heavy feeding' group (Yates' second group), but strict rotation is not always necessary when mixed plantings help to control pests and diseases; for example, planting *Bidens pilosa* or *Tagetes* species to counteract root-knot nematodes, or planting zonal pelargoniums with beans to deter white-fly, or planting marvel-of-Peru with tomato. The use of properly prepared compost and the avoidance of sawdust and peat can suppress a variety of nematodes, as well as the pathogenic fungi mentioned earlier (see Chapter 3).

For some conditions, letting soil lie fallow may seem to be the simplest solution. This is an ancient tradition. In Leviticus, fallowing is stipulated every Sabbath or seventh year. However, the idea of letting the soil 'rest' is quaint. The living soil never rests. To let gardens lie fallow for the whole summer or a whole year as Norman de Vaus (1976) recommended is really wasting an opportunity. A mixed herb garden would certainly be better than nothing.

Choosing disease-resistant varieties

Another way of avoiding problems is by planting varieties with known resistances to viral, bacterial or fungal diseases. *Fusarium* resistance is now the usual condition in peas, just as late blight resistance is normal in potatoes. A new blight-resistant potato, Sarpo Mira, was released in Britain in 2004 (*The Garden*, 129(11), page 834). Powdery mildew-resistant peas, rust-resistant beans, and wilt-resistant tomatoes can all be chosen. Wouldn't it be good to have blemish-free snow peas without the usual burden of fungicide residues? To address this problem, I have bred 17 new powdery mildew-resistant snow peas of all conceivable heights (see Table 18). In addition, I have bred two mildew-resistant semi-leafless garden peas (Elektra and Medusa). All of these varieties are available through the Seed Savers' Network. Delta Moravia will also be available from Greenpatch Organic Seeds (see Useful Addresses).

Beans can be found that are resistant to such diseases as common bean mosaic virus (Contender), 'summer death' (Canyon), anthracnose (Wellington Wonder and Windsor Longpod), as well as rust (Gourmet's Delight and Westralia). Having a wider range of varieties with complementary resistances means that any particular disease should never

cause a total loss. The use of disease-resistant rootstocks with grafted scions is strongly recommended for tomatoes, and is essential for the cultivation of fruit trees and vines (Alexander, 1990; Chapters 14 and 15).

Ants

Ants are great scavengers. They function as the undertakers of the biosphere, dismantling and removing the bodies of insects, other arthropods, worms, birds and animals. Size is no object.

Ants running up and down your plants can indicate the presence of aphids, even when they are hidden, as in the leaf folds of tall bearded iris. Some ants farm aphids (see Figure 187), feeding on their 'dew', and moving them from place to place to improve their exudation. This can encourage other plant diseases, such as sooty moulds, and the transmission of viruses. Ants are also responsible for moving root mealy bugs (*Rhizoecus falcifer*). Yes, they do make nests in pots, but only when the soil is dry enough. Adequate watering will keep them moving to more acceptable locations. They can be kept out of tree canopies with barrier glues, painted around the trunk of each tree. There is no need to treat ants with borax. This poison is not selective. If mixed with sugar, as some thoughtless individuals advocate, the borax is likely to become attractive to pets and children as well. There is no need to kill ants at all.

Sap-suckers

So far as these pests are concerned, 'every year is different' (Daisy Burton, personal communication, 1999). I know exactly what she means. I find that white fly and passionvine leaf-hoppers (see page 135) show enormous fluctuations in abundance from year to year. When we had bushfire smoke and a rain of ash at Christmas 2002 there were no whitefly to be seen afterwards. But vigilance is paramount.

There are many kinds of aphid; for instance, green on roses, peas, or eggplant; yellow on fennel; grey on tall-bearded irises, and black on lemon trees or asparagus peas. Each punctures the sugar-rich phloem cells with its stylet and draws off the sap. Excessive numbers can be reduced simply with jets of water. However, it is important to consider aphids as a food source for predators. This is the corollary of opting for 'natural' methods of control. Providing nectar for the adults is straightforward (see Chapter 2), but to conserve any predator, a food supply should be allowed at all stages. So do not eliminate aphids unless this is absolutely necessary (for example, in the autumn, if growing peas). In spring, aphids can safely be left as a food supply for the new larvae of hoverflies and lady beetles. In late summer to autumn, the orange lady beetle with black spots, *Hippodamia variegata*, can be seen amongst the aphids on fennel flowers and fruits (see Figure 188). If a young, green praying mantis (see Figure 7) takes up residence in the top of an eggplant in midsummer, it will farm the aphids, eating the largest, and keeping the visible numbers around the 20 mark. You will never have a large praying mantis if you do not look after the small ones.

Predators should be encouraged to deal with mealy bugs too, but if a major concentration is discovered, perhaps in leaf sheaths, then try a white-oil spray. This is the conventional remedy for scale insects, especially on citrus. It is a physical method, and works by suffocating the coated insect. Do not use white oil if the foliage is not sturdy enough, or if a biological control agent (see Table 1 on page 8) has already been released.

Shield or 'bronze orange' bugs (*Musgraveia sulciventris*) are pests of citrus trees. They begin life green, changing colour to drab green, copper, bronze and vivid orange, then finally mature to winged, purple adults (see Figures 173 and 174). They enlarge at the expense of young fruit, preferring to suck sap from the stalks. Not only will fruits grow more slowly than they should, but many will end up dry, diseased or dead. The simplest way to get rid of these bugs is to pick them off by hand into a container, tip them onto a path, and squash them quickly underfoot. Use rubber gloves to handle them, otherwise their strong-smelling exudate will stain your skin a dark orange colour that takes days to wear off. If you have to look upwards into the foliage while doing this, then wear protective goggles as well. Look out for eggs, laid in batches on the undersurface of leaves (see Figure 174). It is easier to remove a few leaves and squash all the eggs than to find the young after emergence.

Very similar to this species is the green vegetable bug (*Nezara viridula*), which used to infest beans, tomatoes (see Figure 170) and many other plants. Successful IPM programs (see Chapter 1) have largely controlled this pest in most parts of Australia. However, *Riptortus serripes*, a pest of the tropics, is now causing some concern in northern coastal New South Wales, as it attacks bean pods. This native bug is much more slender than *Nezara*, about 2 centimetres in length, chocolate brown with a cream edge. It has long antennae, two short spines projecting from the upper thorax, and strong rear legs. Some bugs of various shapes and colours are predatory, and useful, so do not kill any bugs until you have seen what they eat, or made an attempt to identify them (for example, see Zborowski and Storey, 2003).

The passionvine leaf-hopper (*Scolypopa australis*) can be found on many kinds of plant, not just passionfruit vines (see Figure

172). They are about 1 centimetre long, almost black, with lacy, largely transparent wings. Spiders catch some of them, but they are easily killed by cupping hands around them and clapping as they spring into the air. Apart from diverting plant resources to their own growth and reproduction, they can transmit virus diseases; for instance, to late potatoes and to beans. Affected leaves may be stunted, bronzed and wilted. They will keep coming back if you encourage them by having mulberry trees, or carob (*Ceratonia siliqua*), where they will flourish on the developing green pods as well as on young shoots.

White fly are not flies at all. They belong to the order Hemiptera, like all the other bugs and hoppers described here, and there are now about 20 species in Australia. They progress through nymphal stages on the underside of a leaf, abrading the surface, and coating it with debris (see Figure 171). Their presence increases the possibility that viruses, bacteria or fungi might gain entry. Deterrent plants have been indicated (see Chapter 2), but no deterrent is absolute. These plants work best in conjunction with spiders, with webs in the actual plants under attack. This combination works extremely well. Biological controls for white fly are also available (see Table 1 on page 8).

Leaf- and stem-chewing pests

A hand lens, magnifying about tenfold, is useful for checking that mites are actually still present on suspicious patches on the undersurface of leaves. Mites can be controlled with sulfur powder as a first resort, or with specific predators (see Chapter 1, and Table 1 on page 8). For other pests, such as caterpillars, guidelines differ among the various groups of organic growers and, paradoxically, some organic treatments are out

of favour. For example, the National Association for Sustainable Agriculture Australia (NASAA) bans the use of derris dust (containing the respiratory poison rotenone), because it has adverse effects outside the range of target organisms, especially for fish. But most gardeners do not have fish in locations where they would need to worry about this. Derris dust is a renewable plant product, and the best alternative would be a preparation containing Bt proteins, such as Dipel.

There is no more certain method of attracting cabbage white butterflies (*Pieris rapae*) and their stumpy green caterpillars than by planting cabbages, cauliflowers or the leafy green tatsoi (see Figure 177). Although some trust in mint to keep these caterpillars off cabbages (Reid, 1992), this is mere wishful thinking. White butterflies mock this presumption, and sip nectar from mint-family flowers. The green caterpillars hide in the crevices among the rosette leaves by day, and come out to feed at night. If the application of derris dust is kept entirely to these locations on these plants, then beneficial larvae on other plants and honey bees are easily spared. The responsible organic gardener is certainly capable of exercising appropriate care in the precise application of derris dust, and also in observing a short withholding period just before harvest (minimum three days). Without some measure like this there would be no brassica harvest for the gardener. Don't forget that this caterpillar can also support itself by eating nasturtium leaves, aligning itself along the vein, which provides perfect camouflage (see Figure 178).

The green looper (*Chrysodeixis eriosoma*, see Figures 179 and 181) has the ability to feed on a wide range of plants (see Chapter 2). When small holes begin to appear in otherwise sound green leaves, look under the leaf and remove the culprits by hand. Some help will be provided by various general predators, including paper wasps and small lizards, which will climb a stem, snatch the occasional green grub, and run away with it.

Odd caterpillars observed as individual specimens should usually be left alone. Every butterfly that sips nectar and helps to pollinate flowers was once a caterpillar that ate something. One summer recently I noticed rows of holes appearing along some young bean pods, the culprit being a fat green caterpillar, about 1 centimetre long at maturity. I put some in a container to pupate, and out came the grass blue butterfly (*Zizula hylax*), a native species that I normally encourage in my front garden. This infestation has not been a recurring problem, and I don't kill them unless they are superabundant. The orchard butterfly (*Papilio aegeus*, see Figure 184) has peculiarly marked green caterpillars that can easily be seen on citrus leaves (see Figure 183). Any citrus tree can support a few with no discernible impact on yield. Without cocoons, the pupae are easily seen, too. Children can be encouraged to watch the intriguing process of metamorphosis. This native species is well worth supporting, in preference to shield bugs. Even the last green loopers of the season should be left alone, because they will probably have been parasitised directly by wasps (see Figure 180). Save the predator.

Now, to a pest I have never seen. Yes, it's in the good pest books, but to date it has not infested my beans. I am indebted to Mary Bennett (Queensland) for the following description: 'There is a hideous insect of some kind tunneling into my late beans (April). They seem to prefer the area where the leaf joins the main stem, where there is normally a single hole, as if it's been pierced. These areas then darken to brown, and when they are broken open, there are small white maggots. There are also what look like pupae, mid-brown in colour. Because I never have any problems with beans, these have invaded without my noticing them. I have never heard of fruit-fly in beans, but the maggots look just like them.'

This is an excellent description of bean fly (*Ophiomyia phaseoli*). The adult is a small black fly, 2 to 3 millimetres long, and eggs are generally laid in the leaves (McMaugh, 1991). The larvae tunnel into the stems, rendering the plant fragile, and prone to breakage. Yields are adversely affected. The cure is first to clean up an existing infestation by gathering affected plants and burning them. Then in the next season, anticipate the problem, and treat bean plants routinely with derris dust or Dipel. This fly is more prevalent in summer and autumn than spring, and it prefers coastal areas.

Slugs and snails

Trapping, or interception with torchlight patrols, are the main methods available to organic gardeners if synthetic chemicals are to be avoided. Deterrence, by using bands of dry sand, lime, ash or rice hulls is also useful when young seedlings are vulnerable, but there is a problem in keeping these boundaries dry. Taking the trouble to do this, however, may give seedlings the start they need to keep ahead of the munchers. Looking in places where they are liable to 'roost', such as in trees, vines and senescing tomato plants, is a good strategy for rounding them up. Check under pot rims and in handle spaces, especially if leaf damage is beginning to occur. Patrols on wet mornings are profitable, too. During rainy weather, put all spare bin lids on the ground, next to gardens and pots. As the weather fines up again, gather up all the lids, and remove the slugs and snails that found shelter. Drowning is another option. Small glass jars, placed in depressions in the ground, and filled with beer or suspended yeast lees, act as a suitable lure.

Lizards such as the blue-tongue like eating snails. Encourage lizards by providing reptile habitat near the gardens. Natural mulching materials, such as bark and leaves, a few rocks, and old bits of pipe with a wide-enough diameter for the passage of the lizards, are all that is needed.

There are numerous stories about what you can do to deter snails and slugs from reaching and chewing your plants. Some stories are true, but many are not. Rubbing lanolin around the rim or wall of a plastic pot does not work. And the recent suggestion that coffee or coffee grounds can be used to deter snails has no foundation either.

There is no substitute for regular examination of the places snails and slugs are likely to occupy, such as between the bricks placed under pots, or under lids placed on pots before seedlings emerge. The torchlight patrol is most effective, as they are largely nocturnal in their movements. If snails are numerous, patrols two or three times a night can be rewarding. If you do find new damage to seedlings, look immediately nearby. Come back to these locations the very next night, because snails and slugs are creatures of habit, and they do return to the sites of their last meal. You can ensure that it is their last meal.

Aren't there any organic baits for snails? Not really. The traditional bait for snails and slugs, metaldehyde, releases formaldehyde. This compound is not specific for molluscs. It can poison dogs and children directly, and lizards, if they eat poisoned snails. No organic code would countenance the use of metaldehyde. Multiguard is a cereal preparation containing iron chelate, which is much less toxic to dogs. Although the content of iron-EDTA has been reduced from 90 to 60 grams per kilogram, this is still too high a concentration of iron for regular use in the garden. Iron is a micronutrient (see Table 4 on page 28 and Table 6 on page 35) and scattering too much iron about will unbalance mineral nutrient supplies. Moreover, in my experience, this material simply does not work. The snails and slugs that frequent my garden prefer real plants as food.

Fruit-eating larvae

There are many kinds of fly with fruit-eating larvae (which are maggots, since they lack legs). Characteristically, they develop inside fruit once eggs are deposited under the skin. A fruit that has been 'stung' in this way may develop a discolored, flat patch around the point of entry. Get rid of obviously infested fruit by boiling or deep burial, to stop newly emerging adults from reinfesting later fruit. If you are losing more than the occasional fruit, try protecting them with 'jackets' made of nylon stocking (see Figure 176), individual bags or traps.

Seed-eating pests

The pea weevil is another pest I have never personally encountered, although it is officially present in New South Wales. James (1998) describes them as 'brown with gray, black, and white markings and are $1/5$ inch (0.5 centimetre) long'. The supposed occurrence of pea weevil in New South Wales is the reason given for peas having to go through quarantine to Tasmania. A precautionary treatment is two days in the freezer after thorough drying, as noted in Chapter 6. This is far preferable to drenching the ground with Diazinon before planting, then spraying with Malathion at flowering, as recommended by James (1998).

There are other weevils to worry about, including a bean weevil. I have occasionally seen this one, in packets of seeds left open and unprotected. Seeds to be stored safely must be enclosed (see Chapter 6).

My cats have in the past kept rats and mice from becoming serious garden pests. But now that my one cat does not frequent the back garden at night, I have had to resort to the old-fashioned traps, set well above dog level in the workshop. I had no idea how well off I had been in the past until maturing pea pods were being totally ransacked one season (in 2004). The rats responsible were so fastidious they were shelling the embryos out of their seedcoats, and for some time I believed the culprit might be a ringtail possum. Eventually they were all killed, either trapped or caught by the dogs. Don't underestimate the destructive power of rats and mice in the garden. Get rid of them safely, without using baits that might be taken by some other animal.

Fungal diseases

Soil-borne pathogenic fungi have been mentioned frequently. These include 'damping off' fungi such as *Pythium* and *Fusarium*. Far more serious are diseases caused by *Phytophthora* (see Chapter 11), and by *Sclerotinia* or *Sclerotium*. Persistent sclerotia (hard, black bodies) left in the soil allow the latter to survive for a long time, so if you notice sclerotia, treat the soil with copious amounts of *Triochoderma*-containing compost (see Chapter 3), and do not grow susceptible plants again for several years.

A vast array of fungal diseases can affect the leaves of plants, and later, the fruits. Rusts usually develop orange-brown spots in the infected patches, although there is a white rust of crucifers (see Figure 189). If rust appears on the leaves of a bean, a gladiolus, a rocket or a rose, I do nothing. If it happens to my tall bearded iris, I cut off all affected areas, and spray with an extract of casuarina needles (see Figure 190):

In a 4 litre saucepan place about 2 litres of needles. Cover with water, and boil for one hour. Allow to cool before spraying. Use a spray pack with an open tube, and rinse it out with water afterwards. Do not store this extract for more than a few days.

Ascochyta and anthracnose often cause brown spots on fruits, or on leaves and stems. For a mango, the effect is only skin deep at first, allowing enough time to eat the fruit. Other rots like *Botrytis cinerea* will demolish a whole fruit, such as a strawberry, very quickly. Powdery and downy mildews appear as white patches or tufts (see Figures 182 and 186). Sulfur powder is the only treatment I apply, and this is adequate for peas.

Many fungal diseases can be discouraged by keeping plants adequately watered and the leaves dry. A period of water stress followed by high humidity often facilitates infection, so avoiding these circumstances tends to keep plants healthy. Some leaves with powdery mildew, especially older ones, can be left alone, in order to provide food for adult yellow and black lady beetles (*Illeis galbula*) and their young (see Figures 185 and 186). Even when powdery mildew occurs, it is best managed and not eliminated completely.

Bacterial diseases

There are six common genera of pathogenic soil-borne bacteria, but they do not normally infect plants unless some entry point is provided by physical disruption, such as the impact of raindrops or hailstones, or tears caused by wind. Irregular patches of dead tissue in leaves can indicate rain damage, followed by bacterial invasion. Often such damage is limited and the plant survives. Keep affected areas as dry as possible. Dusting with sulfur powder is often beneficial, even though it is not supposed to be. Sometimes, however, the whole plant will die. As plant bacterial infections are not transmitted simply by contact, it is perfectly all right to put the remains of such plants into the compost.

Diseases caused by viruses

There is usually some obvious deformity when viruses have proliferated (see Figure 191). Leaves may be twisted, with mosaic patterns due to selective loss of chlorophyll. The peach leaf-curl virus generates a bubbly effect. The plant may often continue to function, but no cure is possible. If the affected region is a small part of a larger plant, such as the top of a pea plant, trim it off, dry it well and burn it completely. Some viruses can be carried into the seeds, so be careful not to keep seeds from virus-affected plants unless there is information that it is safe to do so. For instance, bean common mosaic virus causes distortion but no mottling, and is transmitted in the seeds, but bean yellow mosaic virus is not carried in the embryo.

17.
Plants old and new

'... as is still the case today, a few unscrupulous
seed dealers were putting their names on plant
material that others had developed.'

Kent Whealy, Preface to reprint (1988) of Fearing Burr Jr (1865),
Field and Garden Vegetables of America

The rise and fall of plant breeding

Examples of improved varieties of cultivated plants have been described throughout this book. Sometimes the improvements were the results of natural crosses, recognised as superior in some way, and maintained accordingly. So we have brussels sprouts, swede turnips, strawberries, cabernet sauvignon and pinot chardonnay grapes, all the progeny of natural crossing performed by insects and reinforced by subsequent selection.

Deliberate attempts to breed new varieties of food plants began in earnest in the late eighteenth century, with Thomas Andrew Knight (see Chapters 14 and 15). In the nineteenth century there was a magnificent flurry of breeding activity, but the revolution is over. Most of the varieties generated in the nineteenth century have been lost, and for diverse reasons. Many were superseded, and disappeared as superior alternatives took their place. Some were lost through changing fashions. Many were lost accidentally, because gardeners took for granted the role of the seed supply houses. When these small family companies were taken over increasingly in the 1970s and 1980s, their offerings were rationalised to an extreme degree.

Finding heritage fruits and vegetables

For many years scientists have been warning of pending losses, not only of cultivated plants, but also of closely related wild species. These are often able to provide characteristics worth transferring, such as cold tolerance or disease resistance. Kent Whealy set out to preserve varieties of cultivated plants by forming the Seed Savers' Exchange (SSE) in the United States in 1975. This became a major volunteer network of gardeners, prepared to share the seeds of what they could find and grow. By

1984, the SSE had established its headquarters at Heritage Farm, Decorah, Iowa (Weaver, 1997).

The concept soon spread. The Seed Savers' Network (SSN) in Australia was formed in 1986 by Jude and Michel Fanton, who began by following up Michel's desire to obtain authentic ingredients for French cuisine. The response to Michel's advertisements was overwhelming, leading to a successful network and publishing a book on the subject (Fanton and Fanton, 1993). The SSN provides a general forum for gardeners becoming interested in saving and exchanging seeds. Heritage Seed Curators Australia (HSCA) followed in 1992, founded by Bill Hankin. The HSCA accommodated gardeners prepared to take on curator responsibility for a distinct group or groups of plants, and included fruit tree and potato enthusiasts. My role was as curator for peas. Alas, the HSCA has been disbanded, as there were not enough volunteers in the one locality to occupy all the committee positions.

Whatever the plant, the number of varieties available through the SSN is very much greater than can be found in retail outlets. Offers are made through the newsletters, published twice a year. All that is necessary to gain access to these collections is to belong (see Useful Addresses).

How much have we lost? For many vegetables, the losses exceed 90 per cent of cultivars previously recognised. These estimates result from comparing cultivars known in the United States in 1903 with the holdings of their national collection in 1983 (Fowler and Mooney, 1990). The great popularity of tomato (see Chapter 13) has kept at least 200 cultivars going. The loss of cultivars for tomato in the United States was only 81 per cent, but this is still a staggering number in absolute terms.

Some varieties are styled 'heirlooms', because they have been handed down from generation to generation, often travelling with immigrants to new countries. Many heirlooms have never been sold to the public through seed companies, and have come to light following the formation of the seed-saving networks. Among legumes, we have two examples that have been in the care of a single custodian for a long time: Yorkshire Hero garden pea, and Kitchen King climbing bean.

In the latter part of the nineteenth century, Yorkshire Hero became very popular in Australia, displacing Champion of England. The plant was about 1 metre tall, producing peas of medium size. In local horticultural shows there was a special category just for Yorkshire Hero peas. This cultivar was still dominant in Victoria in 1937, according to the 24th edition of Brunning's *Australian Gardener*, and it was sold by Yates until about 1971. Then it was thought to have been lost. In 2001, Mary Bennett located a person who had been growing Yorkshire Hero for 44 years — Hector Scholl, from Toowoomba, Queensland. In a similar fashion, she had earlier (in 1995) introduced seeds of Kitchen King climbing bean to the seed-saving networks, having obtained some from Ron Jones, the son of Gordon Jones, who had maintained this bean for 76 years at the Saumarez Station in Armidale, New South Wales.

Other heirlooms have been handed down in families for generations, sometimes for periods of between 100 and 150 years. The runner bean Bullabun (see Figure 146) came from Lviv in western Ukraine with Ukrainian immigrants, and was transmitted to HSCA by Sonia Panasewich (nee Goodman). Revived heirlooms offset some of the official losses. So, too, do releases from strategically important public collections, such as the Australian Temperate Field Crops Collection at Horsham in Victoria, and the Tropical Crops Genetic Resources Centre at Biloela in Queensland.

The safest place for rare varieties is in the hands of gardeners. By actively growing and perpetuating thousands of varieties in many places, accidental losses and local disasters can be circumvented. But in Britain and Europe, it is now illegal to grow or sell seed of varieties that are no longer registered, a process that costs considerable amounts of money each year. Some recent losses in Britain have come from the inability of gardeners to afford to pay for registration. A correspondent in *The Garden* pointed out that a broad bean (*Vicia faba*) called the Sutton had lost its registration in the very year it had been given an Award of Gardening Merit (Larkcom, 1999). This thoroughly regressive and inequitable facet of loss adds to that from historical attrition. The only way such varieties can be maintained is through voluntary networks of gardeners.

Breeding new varieties today

Professional plant breeders today have unprecedented access to collections of plants from around the world, under the auspices of the Consultative Group on International Agricultural Research (CGIAR), and the United Nations Food and Agriculture Organization (FAO). But producing new varieties that become popular among growers can have an unintended adverse impact on the land races and wild forms that provide gene pools for breeders. Fowler and Mooney (1990) relate the story of how Dr Carlos Ochoa from the International Potato Center (CIP) in Lima, Peru, witnessed the total disappearance of 45 traditional primitive forms, in favour of an improved variety he himself had bred — Renacimiento, meaning rebirth. It is a great pity when such plants become extinct in their natural setting. It means that reference plants cannot be collected ever again. The material held in these collections becomes all the more vulnerable to total loss.

Determining whether a variety is new or not presents another problem. The quotation from Kent Whealy at the beginning of this chapter is extraordinarily apt. The theft of intellectual property involving plant varieties is a modern corollary of legislation that was intended to promote plant breeding by rewarding the breeder: first the *Plant Varieties Rights Act 1987*, then the *Plant Breeders' Act 1994*.

Taking unwarranted commercial credit for growing out a few plants once and saving their seeds, or registering a plant found in someone else's garden, became growth industries in Australia. This is because the Plant Breeders' Rights (PBR) office has not consistently followed the requirements of the Act when assessing applications. A survey in the late 1990s found more than 100 instances where PBR should not have been awarded (Hankin, 1998, 1999). First and foremost, varieties 'of common knowledge' are supposed to be ineligible for the award of PBR in Australia. This has not prevented the PBR office actually making such awards, even after investigation periods of up to three years.

Second, in many cases, no evidence of any breeding program taking place was ever provided, either in published proceedings or in response to written enquiries. Even if bona fide crosses had been performed, the progenitors were seldom clearly identified, and so they were not included in trials that were supposed to demonstrate how distinctive or novel the 'new' variety was. Sometimes 'new' varieties were simply compared with one another, but not with their immediate progenitors, identified or not. In terms of scientific method, these comparisons were fundamentally flawed. Without comparisons with the progenitors, no scientific evidence of novelty has been advanced at all. PBRs awarded in the absence of such published evidence are ipso facto invalid.

Third, the stability of any claimed new variety is also a requirement of the Act. No one can assess stability without a 'snapshot' on at least two occasions, separated by an appropriate time interval. In New Zealand, trials are held in two consecutive years, and conducted by the awarding authority. This is a much better system, but still not ideal. Five years is a more appropriate test interval, assuming one generation has been grown each year. A procedure like this would follow what is done by the Royal Horticultural Society, which conducts trials, and publishes the results. Five years later it repeats trials of the same varieties, and the results are published again. Those varieties that perform as they did previously are endorsed. Those that fail to perform consistently are listed accordingly (for example, capsicum peppers, England, 1999).

A consequence of this legal requirement for stability is that all F1 hybrids are at once disqualified from being considered for PBR, except when such hybrids can be propagated asexually, as in the case of the new *Achillea* hybrids perpetuated by runners and division (see Chapter 9). F1 hybrids reproducing sexually, whether by self-pollination or outcrossing, will segregate immediately. This instability is nothing new. It has been well documented since the rediscovery of Gregor Mendel's observations in 1900 (Murray, 1999, 2003). What it means, logically and scientifically, is that most F1 hybrids are not qualified even to receive cultivar names, let alone PBR.

The networks of gardeners who have already rescued many popular varieties from extinction are now vigorously documenting and sharing descriptions of varieties 'of common knowledge', to reinforce attempts to prevent their restrictive acquisition by those seeking reward without effort. Alienation of our common genetic heritage must not be allowed to continue unchallenged. Every gardener who perpetuates plants can help to ensure that varieties belonging in the public domain actually remain there. Meanwhile,

procedures for awarding PBR for Australian native plants have improved. All such applications are referred first to the Australian Cultivar Registration Authority (ACRA), and claims for novelty checked against the ACRA database.

Genetic engineering: back to the drawing board

It is ironic that genetically engineered plants are the ones being shunned for ethical reasons, rather than F1 hybrids, and plants unfairly covered by illegitimate PBR. The production of F1 hybrids ties up considerable resources of arable land, personnel and facilities. It is inefficient, but profitable, because it is a way of getting growers to buy fresh seed every year. Varieties that reproduce reliably from seed cannot create the same dependency between grower and supplier. So why should we gardeners reward such massive inefficiency? Non-hybrid plants have a superior ability to be propagated, and to become acclimatised to local growing conditions.

However, for gardeners to automatically prohibit the cultivation of genetically modified plants other than those engineered for herbicide-resistance would, in the future, be ill-advised. All proposed new releases should be examined individually on their merits. Herbicide-resistant food plants are undesirable because their cultivation has already led to an increased burden of herbicide residues in processed grain products (Murray, 1999, 2003). But plants with a greater range of inherent resistances to pests and diseases will need less cosseting with pesticides, and one way of producing these plants is by integrating the new 'molecular' techniques with conventional methods of plant breeding (Murray, 1991; Kyle, 1993). These methodologies are not mutually exclusive, despite Monsanto's (1995) proclamation: 'As a cart is to a car, plant breeding is to bio-technology'. To borrow a different metaphor, the score is on the board for plant breeding, while biotechnology is still padding up.

Another valuable genetic modification would be to inhibit ethylene production by the plant itself, prolonging fruit or vegetable storage time without adversely affecting quality. Blocking ethylene production by genetic methods is much safer than treating produce with nitric oxide (NO), a toxic substance, a contributor to photochemical smog, and a greenhouse gas, all in one. This retrograde technology is starting to gain an airing in the media (*The Land* No. 3966, 15 April 1999), and needs to be stopped firmly in its tracks.

The potential benefits of specific genetic modification have been evident, but unrealised, for many years. A lettuce that has been modified to be resistant to lettuce necrotic yellows virus is being trialled at Gatton, in Queensland. Such a plant should be welcomed, provided it is shown to be safe to eat. A cabbage modified to produce Bt proteins in its leaves, thereby poisoning any white butterfly caterpillars that started to feed on it, would also have a definite following among home gardeners. Because they have other priorities, vertically integrated multinational agrichemical companies are often reluctant to develop plants with minor markets. Smaller players have intellectual property impediments to overcome before the obvious development becomes remotely possible.

Transgenic cotton and maize plants able to produce a single Bt protein in their leaves were released under patent by Monsanto. But the transformed cotton plants, styled 'INGARD', were a disappointment to farmers in Australia. Trials are continuing, and cotton plants transformed to express two Bt proteins rather than one have performed so well that most cotton growers are adopting transformed cotton plants.

The usefulness of a Bt-transformed plant will last only as long as it takes pest organisms to respond by developing resistance. The more Bt proteins expressed in the transformed variety the better, as the chances of resistance developing are minimised. I have suggested six distinct Bt proteins as a reasonable goal, expressed in specific tissues, and tailor-made to be safe for human consumption (Murray, 2003).

Unintended expression of Bt protein in pollen occurred in the initial releases, including StarLink maize, and this means death to insects collecting and eating the pollen. This is just as undesirable as spraying non-selective insecticides, and such plants should not have been released. So with appropriate precautions, Bt-transformed crucifers would be worth trying out. We cannot afford to neglect any avenue of plant improvement that will lessen the need for pesticides: whether by conserving and resurrecting plants that used to be widely grown, or devising new genotypes for already cultivated plants, using all the intelligent means at our disposal.

18.
Eating home garden produce

'... equally bad is the raising of new varieties lacking in good flavour, and abolishing old kinds, from supposed deficiencies in size. It generally means that the new ones are coarse; it sometimes means that they are useless.'

William Robinson, Preface to *Vilmorin-Andrieux* (1885)

The need for fruits and vegetables

We are all fundamentally vegetarians. By that I mean that it is possible to gain all our nutritional requirements from an essentially vegetarian diet, provided that a source of vitamin B_{12} is included (for example, eggs, or mushrooms grown on real manure). This proviso is necessary because plants do not make vitamin B_{12} (cobalamin), although they do contain trace amounts of cobalt (see Table 4 on page 28). Plant foods are absolutely essential to our health and longevity. The converse is not true. A diet based on animal products alone is the way to an early grave.

This primary dependence on plant foods has come about because our hominid ancestors two to four million years ago were omnivorous, and included a fairly high proportion of fruits in their diet. Plant storage organs featured as well: tubers and rhizomes that could be dug up easily with sticks. Their

non-plant foods were probably eggs, worms and insects at first, then seafoods in habitats close to the coast.

The main reason human brains have evolved to the extent that they have is related to the need to remember both spatial and temporal patterns of food availability. 'Natural selection strongly favours traits that enhance the efficiency of foraging', concluded Katharine Milton (1993), who supported this rationale for brain development during evolution with studies of two related species of monkeys: howler monkeys (*Alouatta palliata*) and spider monkeys (*Ateles geoffroyi*).

Leaves constitute 48 per cent of the diet of howler monkeys, with fruits 42 per cent. But for spider monkeys, these proportions shift away from leaves (22 per cent) in favour of fruits (72 per cent). At more than 900 metres, the daily range of spider monkeys is twice as great as that of howler monkeys. With a typical adult weight of 6 to 8 kilograms in each case, the brain size of the spider monkey

(107 grams) is double that of the howler monkey (50 grams) in both absolute and relative terms. The digestive tract of each monkey is also adapted to the diet: the spider monkey has a shorter colon and faster throughput of food, whereas the howler monkey has a longer colon and slower passage of food, as befits a true herbivore.

We humans are omnivores, rather like the spider monkey. We were gatherers before we became hunters and gatherers, and later still, gardeners. So we should be very good at remembering where our 'ripe' foods are, and at what times of the year. A mixed gardening pattern should not be such a great challenge after all. We are already well adapted to profiting from a complex food supply.

Nutritional virtues of plant foods

Plant foods are indispensible sources of complex polysaccharides that provide bulk. These insoluble polymers come from plant cell walls, and include cellulose, a polymer of glucose, and pectin, especially abundant in citrus fruits, and which enables a jam to set. While in transit in the alimentary canal, these various sugar polymers hydrate to form gels, and in this state they can be partly digested by our intestinal bacteria. By stimulating regular bowel movements, plant polysaccharides protect against bowel cancer. Many also promote a general lowering of cholesterol concentration in the bloodstream.

Starch, sugars and oils provide our major carbon and energy sources. All three are present in developing or mature seeds, the proportions varying with plant species, and stage of development. For example, developing bean seeds have more sugar but less starch than mature seeds. In contrast to cellulose, starch is a polymer of glucose that is readily hydrolysed by our digestive enzymes. The branched-chain form, amylopectin, is not degraded totally, and the branch-points remain as food for bacteria that produce butyrate. This apparently protects against bowel cancer.

Starchy seeds may sometimes have significant oil content, but oil seeds tend to have no starch. The macadamia nut (see Chapter 14) has one of the highest recorded oil contents, at about 75 per cent of edible dry matter. In composition, its oil is reasonably close to olive oil, dominated by mono-unsaturated fatty acids. The other common fruit with significant oil content is the avocado, with about 10 to 15 per cent by weight.

The sugars abundant in naturally sweet plant foods include sucrose, glucose and fructose. Sucrose comprises one glucose and one fructose, joined together, but is readily hydrolysed to release its two components. Both glucose and fructose are hexose sugars (containing six carbons each), but fructose differs slightly from glucose, and its name actually means 'fruit sugar'. All can be oxidised via respiration, or used to synthesise a wide variety of cell constituents.

The minerals that plants take up, transport and accumulate (see Table 4 on page 28) can provide our essential requirements, too. Claims that plant foods are inadequate as sources of specific mineral cations, such as calcium or iron, are not correct. The CSIRO has promoted beef as the best source of iron, especially for women, but this is merely propaganda on behalf of beef producers. Too much meat is still eaten in Australia, but the per capita figures are trending downwards over recent years, indicating general acceptance of messages about balanced diets and healthy eating.

To maximise mineral uptake, it is important to avoid oxalates in green leaves, such as silverbeet, and all those trendy plants like rainbow chard and warrigal greens. Oxalate robs the diet of minerals by binding them permanently. A high concentration is immediately toxic, as with the leaves of rhubarb. The best greens are snow peas, snap peas, shelled peas, green beans and broccoli. These provide abundant free organic acids and amino acids that chelate mineral cations reversibly, and so assist their uptake.

Plant foods are essential sources of vitamins. Vitamin C contents have been mentioned throughout earlier chapters, as many fruits are excellent sources, including capsicums, citrus fruits, and developing pea and bean pods. Tomatoes, potatoes and onions are also significant sources, since large quantities of these vegetables are eaten. As vitamin C content decreases with storage time, it is important to eat potatoes and onions when they are still reasonably fresh, in order to gain their full benefits. Vitamin E is a lipid-soluble anti-oxidant vitamin, which cooperates with water-soluble vitamin C to maintain cell components that are sensitive to damage from free radicals. Vitamin E is a normal component of chloroplasts, and so is present in all green plant tissues. It also accumulates in oil-rich plant foods, such as the embryo of maize kernels, avocado fruits and in a wide variety of oil seeds.

The B-group vitamins, and folate, are all synthesised by plants. Even after cooking, shelled peas and beans have higher vitamin B_1 (thiamin) contents than cooked meats. Pumpkin seeds are rich in vitamin B_3 (niacin), while peanuts are exceptionally rich in both riboflavin (vitamin B_2) and niacin. Plant foods also supply various forms of vitamin B_6 and vitamin K.

Apart from vitamin B_{12}, mentioned at the beginning of this chapter, there is another vitamin we need to ingest that plants do not manufacture. This is vitamin A (retinol, or retinyl esters), necessary for the synthesis of the pigment-protein complex rhodopsin, involved in rod (black and white) vision. There is no vitamin A in plants whatsoever.

But the orange pigment beta-carotene (or β-carotene) is a precursor of vitamin A, and is abundant in certain orange fruits and vegetables, including peaches, nectarines, apricots, oranges, mandarins, mangoes, some bananas, pumpkins, carrots and some sweet potatoes.

Colour is not an infallible guide to beta-carotene content, and most orange-yellow carotenoid pigments in plants cannot function as sources of vitamin A. For example, the lycopenes in tomatoes and capsicums cannot be modified to produce any vitamin A because they lack ring structures at either end of the molecule. Lycopenes, however, do function as anti-oxidants in their own right. Clearly, green or white tomatoes are useless as sources of any of these anti-oxidants.

Fruits have a very low protein content compared to leaves and seeds. But most published values for protein content in tables of food composition are incorrect. The reason is simple. The calculation is based on nitrogen (N) content, multiplied by an arbitrary factor, with the underlying assumption that all the N belongs to protein. This arithmetic procedure neglects the well-known fact that nucleic acids (DNA and RNA) also contain nitrogenous bases. These ought to be estimated separately, so that their contribution to total nitrogen can be subtracted. But this does not happen. Protein content is routinely over-estimated, by a factor approaching double.

The seeds of cultivated legumes are nevertheless well endowed with protein, with contents often ranging between 20 and 30 per cent of dry matter. There are major differences according to species, and also among varieties within a species. Plant sources of protein are often disparaged, and said to be incomplete. This archaic attitude is based on information that has not been brought up to date. Older analyses were not corrected for the breakdown of some of the essential amino acids that takes place during acid hydrolysis of the sample.

When this is done, or improved analytical methods are applied, legume seeds, whole pods and seedlings (sprouts) are seen to be capable of providing a balanced supply of all of the essential amino acids (Murray, 1999).

To cover all nutritional requirements, known and unknown, it is wise to eat from a broad spectrum of different foods. But if you want to eat staple vegetables like peas, carrots and potatoes every single day, there is no health reason why you should not. There is enough flexibility in the human diet to compensate for any single items or food groups that sometimes need to be avoided, such as wheat protein, cucurbits, peanuts, soybeans, or fruits with high salicylate contents.

Advantages of organic food

The chief health advantage of organic food is its freedom from pesticide residues. An additional benefit of growing your own plant foods is freshness. Produce from your own garden can be harvested immediately before cooking and eating it, and will have optimal flavour accordingly. But is plant food that is grown organically richer in nutrient content because of the way it was grown? And are modern cultivars lacking in certain nutrients compared to heirloom and heritage varieties? These are topical questions, but they have never been adequately addressed by research.

In a survey by Food Standards Australia New Zealand (FSANZ) published in 2004, potassium, sodium, magnesium, calcium, iron and zinc contents were compared for 44 fruits and vegetables sampled in the early 1980s, and in 2000–01. Heaton (2004) concluded that 'the comparisons are next to useless'. As a plant scientist I would go further. Averaging the mineral contents of 44 disparate items purchased in different locations around

Australia and in different seasons is a meaningless and unscientific exercise. Such averages conceal inequalities. No conclusion can be drawn, and the results certainly cannot be used to support the view that nothing has changed.

Conversely, there are retrospective studies that suggest that there have been reductions in nutrient content. An item in the *Sun Herald* (21 March 2004, page 42) referred to a UK study by 'mineralogist' David Thomas, who claimed that many vegetables and fruits as currently grown were deficient in nutrients compared to such produce grown in the 1940s. Losses claimed were 'half the sodium and calcium, 76% of copper and 25% of iron'. Before we can logically blame current farming practices, however, there are two basic problems of scientific methodology that must be accommodated.

First, in order to draw any firm conclusions from such a retrospective comparison, it is important to be sure that the earlier procedures for analysis were as sensitive and accurate as modern procedures. This is not always the case, as I found when searching for information on the mineral contents of pea seeds. For instance, zinc was significantly underestimated in earlier procedures, whereas manganese and iron were both overestimated by a factor of 10 (Balfour, 1975, page 332). Obviously, such massive errors will skew any retrospective comparison.

Second, it is vital to compare like with like. There are simple genetic differences amongst the cultivars of a single species that can result in substantial differences in nutrient contents. Analyses of some of my own pea seed samples, conducted by the Waite Analytical Service in 2002, revealed a threefold variation in the seed content of calcium (see Table 19). Accordingly, an apparent loss of half the calcium content for peas grown 60 years apart could readily be explained by a difference in cultivar. These new results also confirm that cadmium has not

TABLE 19. MINERAL NUTRIENT CONTENTS OF MATURE PEA SEEDS (AS PARTS PER MILLION OF SEED MASS)[1]

Cultivar	Year	K	P	S	Mg	Ca	Zn	Fe	Mn	Na	B	Cu
Delta Galina[2]	2000	12000	6000	2100	1340	940	66	55	11	25	13	6.7
Delta Procilla[2]	2000	13800	5800	2300	1340	620	80	57	10	46	13	5.8
Cygna Claudia[2]	2000	12100	5700	2100	1240	420	69	53	9	26	16	6.8
Quite Content	1996	15200	6600	2300	1360	740	79	59	15	20	17	5.8
Eureka	1997	13000	6700	2200	1500	1190	83	57	17	59	14	5.4
Pea (dry)[3]	pre-1978	9900	3000	1300	1160	610	35	47	–	380[4]	–	4.9

1. In addition, several elements were at or below their limits for detection: cobalt (<0.9 ppm), nickel (<1 ppm), aluminium (<6 ppm) and cadmium (<0.4 ppm). Molybdenum was also at the limit of detection in four out of five samples.

2. New cultivar, post 1995, see Table 18.

3. Results for a commercial split field pea reported in *The Composition of Foods* (A.A. Paul and D.A.T. Southgate, 1978).

4. The disparity is an order of magnitude, and this value is unlikely to be accurate.

been transmitted from soil treated continually with Dynamic Lifter (see Table 7 on page 44). The ability of developing seeds to exclude cadmium, even when grown on soils contaminated with heavy metals, was discovered by Professor John Lott and his colleagues (Lott, 1984).

In many respects my organically grown peas are superior to the commercial sample from about 20 years before. This is true of both new and old cultivars. But the only way to be sure of the influence of cultural practices on food composition is for some institution to set up a comparison of the same cultivars under a range of different fertiliser regimens. Then, and only then, could some scientifically valid conclusions be drawn about the influence of cultivation practices and genotype on food composition. Meanwhile, I am satisfied that a soil enriched in organic matter is the prerequisite to a balanced acquisition of nutrients by food plants (see Chapter 4).

Storage and preservation

Home-grown vegetables and fruits are the freshest possible. They do not have the opportunity to dehydrate and lose condition by having to travel from markets and shops. To make the most of this advantage, there are a few simple steps that should be taken immediately after harvesting.

Vegetables should be trimmed as necessary, and washed outside the house, then brought to the kitchen free of soil. The first key to quality is temperature. A brief sojourn in the crisper will maintain the quality of freshly picked peas, beans, salad leaves, capsicums, carrots, parsnips, sweet corn and stem vegetables. Bring them out just before they are to be cooked, and delay the shelling of peas or beans as long as possible. This will minimise the loss of sugar through conversion to starch.

Relative humidity is the critical factor for keeping potatoes and onions. These should be kept as dry as possible, and cool, but not cold. A dark, well-ventilated cupboard, as far from the stove as possible, is ideal for potatoes, which should be shielded from light. This is less important for onions, and as noted earlier, growing the right onion (see Figure 124) means there is no need for storage. Tomatoes should not be chilled at all. Avocados may be chilled after they have softened at normal temperatures, but if chilled too soon, they will never soften.

For medium-term storage, many vegetables can be frozen after dicing and blanching. This is a brief heat treatment that will inactivate enzymes whose continued action would lead to deterioration in quality. Bring the water to the boil first. Steam for two minutes, then drain and transfer vegetables to freezer bags, then immediately to the freezer. Aim to use frozen vegetables within three months.

Many fruits can be dried without substantial losses of vitamins and minerals. Using the sun is the most satisfactory method, but a low oven or special incubators are useful for occasional gluts. Preserving fruit with a Fowler's Vacola kit is also recommended. The glass containers provide a more visually rewarding array than a stack of cans in the cupboard. Another way of utilising excess fruits is to make jams and chutneys (see pages 151–3).

It is simplest to pick fresh herbs in season. Drying some is an option, but do not be tempted to dry more than really necessary. Many people hoard dried herbs in a corner of their kitchen, and there they sit, unused and unattractive. Preparing a range of herb vinegars (see Figure 192) also allows flavours to be preserved and used very effectively.

Some useful recipes

The following recipes have been chosen because they show off the main ingredients at their best. For solids, 1 cup is taken as 200 g (7 oz). For liquids, 1 cup is 220 mL (8 fl oz).

A good measuring jug will show the alternatives. Note that the English pint is 20 fl oz, but the American pint is 16 fl oz.

BEETROOT WITH HERBS AND SPICES
Beetroot is marvellous with complementary flavours. Vary these combinations until you find the ones that appeal.
beetroots (at least 3 or 4)
vinegar
sugar
1 teaspoon black peppercorns
1 teaspoon mustard seed
1 teaspoon coriander seed
1 teaspoon salt
The number of beetroots is not vital. Choose a number that will fit conveniently into a saucepan, and do not trim off their stalks or damage the skin until after cooking. Just cover the beetroots with water, and bring to the boil. Simmer until tender when pierced with a fork. Wait until they are cool enough to handle, then peel, top and tail, and cut into even slices. Stack these into jars pre-rinsed with boiling water. Add bay leaves and cinnamon bark or sprigs of a herb such as rosemary, oregano or thyme.

Separately prepare preserving vinegar, in the ratio 1 cup of vinegar, 1 cup of water, ½ cup of white or brown sugar, 1 teaspoon each of black peppercorns, mustard seed, coriander seed and salt. Combine in a small saucepan, and bring to the boil for 5 minutes. Fill the jars by pouring in the vinegar mixture, and seal. Keep refrigerated after opening.

BORSCH
500 g (1 lb) fully ripe red tomatoes
1 or 2 cloves of garlic
beetroots (at least 4)
1 lemon or lime
2 cups red wine
salt, pepper and herbs to garnish
1 small carton of sour cream
Skin the tomatoes by covering them with boiling water for about 1 minute, moving them into cold water, and then peeling. Slice them roughly into

quarters. Crush the garlic, trim the beetroots, and dice them before cooking. Combine the beetroot and tomato pieces, garlic, the juice of the lemon or lime, and add the wine. Bring to the boil, and simmer until the beetroot is tender. Add salt and freshly ground black pepper. Cool before eating. Serve in individual bowls, adding swirls of sour cream, garnished with any favourite herb.

DILL PICKLES

salt

small to medium size cucumbers

dill leaves

vinegar (see instructions for preserving vinegar in beetroot recipe)

Dissolve a dessertspoon of salt in a saucepan of water, and soak cucumbers overnight. Rinse jars with boiling water, and pack the cucumbers with some dill leaves. Pour in vinegar to cover, and seal. Wait three weeks before using.

EGGPLANT AND CHICKPEA CASSEROLE

2 cups boiled chickpeas

3 small eggplants about 250 g (½ lb) each

1 bulb onion (or 3 perpetual onions)

olive or macadamia oil for frying

500 g (1 lb) tomatoes

sprigs of rosemary

2 cups white wine

Soak the chickpeas in water overnight, with several changes. Boil them in water for about 1 hour, let stand, and drain. Slice the eggplants and the onion, then fry in oil. Remove when the eggplant is just browning. Pack a casserole with the eggplant, onion, chickpeas and tomatoes. Position rosemary leaves throughout. Pour in the wine. Cover with lid, and bake at 180°C for 1 hour.

GUACAMOLE

2 ripe avocados

1 lemon or lime

1 clove of garlic

chopped coriander leaves

chopped serrano chilli (optional)

Cut the avocados lengthwise and remove the seed. Spoon out the flesh into a bowl. Juice the lemon or lime, and crush the garlic. Blend these with the avocado until a uniform paste is obtained. Sprinkle with the coriander leaves and serve as a dip. Include the chilli if you prefer this salsa hot.

HERB VINEGAR

Various members of the mint family (see Chapter 9) make excellent herb vinegars. Simply cut clean sprigs of a length to suit the bottle, put them in position, and fill the bottle with wine vinegar or cider vinegar (see Figure 192). Seal, invert a few times to get bubbles to the top, and stand for an indefinite period. Nasturtium flowers can also be used. Adding a hot chilli pepper is another option, according to taste. Use herb vinegars for salad dressings, or just add a dash to pasta or rice before serving.

JAMS — CITRUS

Simply follow the ratio of 1 kg (2 lb) fruit to 1 L (2 pts, American) of water to 1 kg (2 1b) of sugar. Jams can be prepared from any single citrus fruit, or from combinations, such as lemon and lime. Grapefruit and ginger go well together.

GRAPEFRUIT AND GINGER JAM

3 grapefruit (1 kg or 2 lb)

water (1 L or 2 pts, American)

100 g (3½ oz) ginger

sugar (any kind, 1 kg or 2 lb)

Wash the grapefruit and peel off the skins. Slice these finely and place the pieces in a broad saucepan, of capacity about 4 litres (8 pints), together with the water. Trim off the white pith, chop, and place in a bag made from the foot of a nylon stocking. Slice the fruit segments into small pieces, putting any seeds into the bag with the pith. Add the fruit to the saucepan. Peel the ginger, slice into small discs, and add to the saucepan. Tie off the bag, and submerge it near the handle, so that the top can be clamped by the lid.

Bring to the boil, then simmer for 1¼ hours. Allow to cool. Squeeze out the bag. Resume heating with the lid off. Measure out the sugar and add this slowly, with stirring, until all has dissolved. Increase the heat sufficiently to reduce the contents to the point of setting. When the jam sets, dribbling off the stirrer, turn off the heat. Sterilise jars and their lids by standing boiling water in them for a few minutes. Drain the jars, then ladle in the jam. Put on lids when the jam is cool enough not to create condensate in the lids.

JAMS—STONEFRUIT

The key to making jams from stonefruit is to use very little water, and to always add a lemon to provide pectin. The ratio becomes 1 kg (2 lb) fruit to 200 mL (7 fl oz) water to 1 kg (2 lb) sugar. The fruit should be firm and under-ripe. Plums and nectarines are faster to handle than peaches, because the skin does not have to be removed.

1 kg (2 lb) stonefruit
1 lemon
water (200 mL or 6 fl oz)
sugar (any kind, 1 kg or 2 lb)

Wash the fruit and peel off the skin of the lemon. Slice this finely and place the pieces in a broad saucepan, of capacity about 4 litres, together with the water. Trim off the white pith, chop, and place in a bag made from the foot of a nylon stocking. Slice the lemon into small pieces and add to the saucepan. Cut open the stonefruit to remove the stones, putting these into the bag with the lemon pith. Slice the fruit into small pieces and add these to the saucepan. Tie off the bag, and submerge it near the handle, so that the top can be clamped by the lid.

Bring to the boil and then simmer for 1 hour. Allow to cool. Squeeze out the bag. Resume heating with the lid off. Measure out the sugar and add this slowly, with stirring, until all has dissolved. Increase the heat sufficiently to reduce the contents to the point of setting. When the jam sets, dribbling off the stirrer, turn off the heat. Sterilise jars and their lids by standing boiling water in them for a few minutes.

Drain the jars, then ladle in the jam and close the jars when the jam is cool enough not to create condensate in the lids.

MANGO CHUTNEY

1.5 kg (3 lb) mangoes (about 5)
1 bulb onion or 5 perpetual onions
2 cloves of garlic, crushed or sliced
250 g (9 oz) top-quality sultanas
500 mL (16 fl oz) vinegar of choice
2 teaspoons salt
1 tablespoon grated ginger
325 g (12 oz) caster sugar
1 teaspoon ground cinnamon

Peel the mangoes and slice the flesh away from the fibrous stone. Chop, and add to a large bowl. Chop the onion and garlic, and add these. Measure out the sultanas, vinegar, salt and ginger. Add all of these to the bowl, mix, and cover. Stand overnight. Transfer to a broad saucepan and stir in the sugar over a low heat, until dissolved. Add the ground cinnamon and bring to the boil, then simmer uncovered for 1¼ hours. Ladle into hot, sterilised jars, as above. If you prefer hot chutney, include one small chilli pepper, finely chopped, with the ingredients that stand overnight.

RATATOUILLE

3 cloves of garlic
2 bulb onions (or 6 perpetual onions)
olive or macadamia oil for frying
3 or 4 eggplants, about 250 g (½ lb) each
4 zucchinis
500 g (1 lb) tomatoes
2 large capsicums, of contrasting colours
1 or 2 cups white wine
basil leaves

Slice the garlic and onion, and add to a large frying pan with oil. Fry for 5 minutes. Chop the remaining vegetables into slices and chunks. Add the eggplant and zucchini to the pan, and fry until browning begins. Add the tomato, capsicums, a generous handful of basil leaves, and the wine. Mix together, cover the pan, and simmer for about 40 minutes. Add more wine as necessary to keep from drying out.

TOMATO RELISH

2 kg (4 lb) fully ripe red tomatoes
1 lemon
3 medium-sized apples
3 cloves of garlic
2 bulb onions (or 6 perpetual onions)
2 tablespoons freshly grated ginger
1 cup honey
1 cup wine or herb vinegar
1 tablespoon mustard seeds
2 teaspoons salt

Skin the tomatoes by covering them with boiling water for about 1 minute, transferring them to cold water, and then peeling. Slice the lemon into fine pieces. Peel and core the apples, then slice them into pieces. In a large saucepan, combine the tomatoes, apple and lemon pieces. Crush the garlic and slice the onions, and combine all remaining ingredients in the saucepan. Bring to the boil, and then simmer on low heat for at least 2 hours, until tender, and reduced. Pour into sterilised jars and seal. Keep in the cupboard until required, and refrigerate after opening.

Useful addresses

ARTHUR YATES & CO. LTD
21A Richmond Road, Homebush NSW 2140
phone: (02) 9763 9200
fax: (02) 9763 9300

ACRA
Australian Cultivar Registration Authority
Australian National Botanic Gardens
GPO Box 1777, Canberra ACT 2601
e-mail: Frank.Zich@deh.gov.au
web: www.anbg.gov.au/acra/index.html

AUSTRALIAN PLANTS SOCIETY
PO Box 744, Blacktown NSW 2148
phone: (02) 9621 3437
fax: (02) 9676 7603
e-mail: secretary@austplants-nsw.org.au

AUSTRALIA'S CO-OPERATIVE CENTRE FOR WEED MANAGEMENT
web: www.weeds.crc.org.au

BASIX
Building Sustainability Index, NSW
web: www.basix.nsw.gov.au

BAY SEED GARDEN
PO Box 1164, Busselton WA 6280
Penny Coulson
phone: (08) 9752 2513

BENEFICIAL BUG COMPANY
Locked Bag 21, Richmond NSW 2753
phone: (02) 4570 1331
fax: (02) 4578 3979
e-mail: info@beneficialbugs.com.au
web: www.beneficialbugs.com.au

BFA
Biological Farmers of Australia
PO Box 530, Chermside Qld 4032
phone: (07) 3350 5706
web: www.bfa.com.au

BIOLOGICAL SERVICES
PO Box 501, Loxton SA 5333
phone: (08) 8584 6977
fax: (08) 8584 5057
e-mail: info@biologicalservices.com.au
web: www.biologicalservices.com.au

BIO-PROTECTION
PO Box 35, Warwick Qld 4370
phone: (07) 4666 1592
fax: (07) 4666 1639

BIORESOURCES PTY LTD
Samford Qld
phone: (07) 3289 4919
fax: (07) 3289 4918
e-mail: richard@bioresources.com.au
web: www.bioresources.com.au

BOTOBOLAR VINEYARD
Kevin and Trina Karstrom
PO Box 212, Mudgee NSW 2850
phone: (02) 6373 3840
fax: (02) 6373 3789
e-mail: botobolar@winsoft.net.au
web: www.botobolar.com

BUGS FOR BUGS
28 Orton Street, Mundubbera Qld 4626
phone: (07) 4165 4663
fax: (07) 4165 4626
e-mail: Info@bugsforbugs.com.au
web: www.bugsforbugs.com.au

CHILLI SEEDS AUSTRALIA
The Fragrant Garden
25 Portsmouth Road, Erina NSW 2250
phone: (02) 4367 7322
web: www.fragrantgarden.com.au

COMMUNITY AID ABROAD
PO Box 184, Kilkenny SA 5009
phone: 1800 088 455
fax: (08) 8341 2958
e-mail: mailord@caatrading.org.au

DIGGERS' SEED CLUB
PO Box 300, Dromana Vic 3936
phone: (03) 5987 1877
e-mail: orders@diggers.com.au
web: www.diggers.com.au

EDEN SEEDS AND SELECT ORGANIC
MS 905, Lower Beechmont Qld 4211
Alf Finch, phone: 1800 188 199
fax: (07) 5533 1107
web: www.edenseeds.com.au

FAIRBANKS SEEDS
Melbourne Markets Box 35
542 Footscray Road, Footscray Vic 3011
Stuart Bales
phone: (03) 9689 4500

GOODMAN'S SEEDS
PO Box 91, Bairnsdale Vic 3875
John Goodman
phone: (03) 5152 4024

GOURMET GARDENS
PO Box 1892, Esperance WA 6450
phone: (08) 9071 6512

GREEN HARVEST
52/65 Kilcoy Lane via Maleny Qld 4552
phone: (07) 5494 4676
fax: (07) 5494 4674
e-mail: inquiries@greenharvest.com.au
web: www.greenharvest.com.au

GREENPATCH ORGANIC SEEDS
PO Box 1285, Taree NSW 2430
Neville and Sophia Donovan
phone/fax: (02) 6551 4240
e-mail: enquiries@greenpatchseeds.com.au
web: www.greenpatchseeds.com.au

HONEYSUCKLE COTTAGE NURSERY
Lot 35 Bowen Mountain Road,
Bowen Mountain NSW 2753
Judyth and Keith McLeod
phone/fax: (02) 4572 1345
e-mail: kamcleod@zeta.org.au

BOB MAGNUS
Cygnet Road, Woodbridge Tas 7162
phone: (03) 6267 4430

MR FOTHERGILL'S SEEDS PTY LTD
22 Prime Drive, Seven Hills NSW 2147

NASAA
The National Association for Sustainable
Agriculture Australia Ltd
PO Box 768, Stirling SA 5152
phone: (08) 8370 8455
fax: (08) 8370 8381
e-mail: nasaa@dove.mtx.net.au
web: www.nasaa.com.au

THE NATIONAL ASTHMA CAMPAIGN
615 St Kilda Road, Melbourne Vic 3004
phone: 1800 032 495
fax: (03) 9214 1414

NEW GIPPSLAND SEEDS & BULBS PTY LTD
PO Box 1, Silvan Vic 3795
phone: 1800 887 732
fax: (03) 9737 9292
e-mail: newgipps@bigpond.com
web: www.possumpage.com.au/newgipps

OLD MOLE TOOLS
Richard G. Bird
e-mail: oldmoletools@bigpond.com

ORGANIC GROWERS OF AUSTRALIA
PO Box 6171, South Lismore NSW 2480
phone: (02) 6622 0100
web: www.organicgrowers.org.au

OVAA
Organic Vignerons' Association of Australia
PO Box 503, Nurioopta SA 5355
phone: (08) 8562 2122
fax: (08) 8562 3034

PHOENIX SEEDS
PO Box 207, Snug Tas 7054
Michael Self
phone: (03) 6267 9663
fax: (03) 6267 9592
e-mail: phnxseed@ozemail.com.au

POTAGER SEEDS
Catherine Page
PO Box 5089, Alphington Vic 3078

RELN PLASTICS PTY LTD
phone: (02) 9605 9999
fax: (02) 9605 9222
web: www.reln.com.au

ROSNAY ORGANIC WINES
Rivers Road, Canowindra NSW 2804
web: www.rosnaywines.com.au

SAVANNNAH ENVIRONMENTAL PTY LTD
PO Box 150, Bulimba Qld 4171
phone: (07) 3395 6800
fax: (07) 3395 5322

SSN—THE SEED SAVERS' NETWORK
PO Box 975, Byron Bay NSW 2481
phone/fax: (02) 6685 6624
e-mail: info@seedsavers.net
web: www.seedsavers.net

SHIPPARDS NURSERY
PO Box 66, Nambour Qld 4560
Isabel Shippard
phone: (07) 5441 1101

STAHMANN FARMS INC.
Locked Bag 9007, Toowoomba Qld 4350
phone: 1800 773 343
fax: 1800 330 499
web: www.stahmannfarms.com.au

STANDARDS AUSTRALIA
Customer Service Centre
PO Box 1055, Strathfield NSW 2135
phone: 1300 654 646
fax: 1300 654 949
e-mail: sales@standards.com.au
web: www.standards.com.au

TRADE WINDS TEA AND COFFEE PTY LTD
PO Box 63, Revesby North NSW 2212
phone: (02) 9792 1094
fax: (02) 9792 1086
web: www.tradewinds.org.au

YILGARN TRADERS
333 David Road, Waggrakine WA 6530
phone: (08) 9938 1628
fax: (08) 9938 3868
e-mail: yilgarn@midwest.com.au

Glossary and biographical notes

ACETYLCHOLINE A neurotransmitter, and the first word in the index of Rachel Carson's book *Silent Spring* (1962) (see acetylcholinesterase).

ACETYLCHOLINESTERASE The neurotransmitter acetylcholine is released from small vesicles at a synapse, or nerve cell junction. This furthers the nerve impulse in the receiving nerve cell. Once this task has been fulfilled its concentration is reduced again through breakdown by this enzyme — it hydrolyses the ester bonds of acetyl groups, releasing these as acetate, and converting acetylcholine back to choline. If this enzyme is inhibited, it cannot help to remove acetylcholine, and so the original stimulation cannot be stopped. Often the inhibition is fatal. Many pesticides, both organophosphorus and organochlorine, inhibit acetylcholinesterase. They are not 'anti-cholinesterase compounds' as currently mislabelled, because choline itself is not broken down by this enzyme.

ACTINOMORPHIC As applied to flowers, literally star-shaped or regular, with several axes of symmetry.

AEROBIC Requiring oxygen, which allows a more efficient form of metabolism. Glucose is completely broken down to carbon dioxide and water.

ANAEROBIC Without oxygen; sugar breakdown that occurs in the absence of oxygen is called fermentation (see fermentation).

ANION A negatively charged ion that may consist of a single element (e.g chloride, Cl^{-1}) or a combination, often with oxygen (e.g. sulfate, $SO_4{}^{2-}$).

ANNUAL A plant that completes its life cycle inside one year.

ANTHOCYANINS Water-soluble plant pigments with colours in the range violet-blue-lilac-pink-mauve-magenta-purple.

AXIL The junction of a leaf stalk with a stem.

AXILLARY BUD A bud in an axil. These may grow to produce flowers, or shoots which later bear flowers.

AXIS The root-stem-shoot system of a plant embryo, and during later growth, an imaginary line parallel to and through the stem — hence adaxial (facing towards the axis) and abaxial (facing away from the axis).

BINOMIAL The two-part systematic or scientific name of a species; the first name is the genus, the second the 'epithet'. A Latin form is used, even if the words have Greek or other derivation, and by convention, the binomial is italicised or underlined. Gaspard Bauhin (1560–1624) devised this system on a small scale, then Carl von Linne applied binomials in such a way that they became the norm (see Linnaeus).

BORDEAUX MIXTURE A combination of lime, water and bluestone (copper sulfate), developed by Dr Pierre Millardet in 1885 for use against downy mildew of grape. Try 20 g each of bluestone and lime, dissolved separately, then combined and made to a total of 10 L. A corresponding recipe with imperial measures would be 1 oz, 1 oz, and 1.5 gallons. Add the lime solution to the copper sulfate solution with stirring, not vice versa. Keep suspended and use immediately.

BULB A storage organ composed of swollen, fleshy leaf bases. It retains a central shoot, axillary buds and root initials. Bulbils are smaller bulbs produced vegetatively around the original bulb.

BURBANK, LUTHER (1849–1926) The Russet Burbank potato was just the beginning. Burbank emulated practical plant breeders like Knight. Constructing novel hybrids, then crossing the progeny of such hybrids repeatedly with one of the original parents, was his forte. He had little time for geneticists, as he attempted to 'guide the life forces into the desired habits or channels'.

CARSON, RACHEL (1907–64) An American biologist and author who spent much of her career at the Woods Hole Oceanographic Research Institute. Her first three books reflect this interest, but she will always be remembered for *Silent Spring* — an eloquent title.

CELLULOSE A polymer of glucose with the oxygen bridges that link glucose units forming (β bonds, rather than α bonds, as in the amylose fraction of starch. A major building material of plant cell walls, and perhaps the most abundant single compound in the biosphere.

CHROMOSOME The visible manifestation of a portion of DNA with accompanying proteins, containing genetic and operational information. An egg or sperm cell contains the haploid number of chromosomes (n) and a normal body cell contains the diploid number (2n), unless a species is polyploid (usually 3n, 4n or 6n).

CLAY A layer or deposit of finely divided aluminosilicate minerals, with a great many possible minority components; plastic when hydrated, and an impediment to the free movement of water. Particle diameters are less than 0.074 mm in some definitions, but less than 0.005 mm in others.

COKE, THOMAS WILLIAM, LORD LEICESTER (1752–1840) A long-serving member of parliament, but better known for his agricultural endeavours at his property Holkham, in Norfolk, where he rediscovered the benefits of crop rotation. His famous annual gatherings were called 'Coke's Clippings', as they began with shearing, then grew to encompass demonstrations of all kinds of newly invented agricultural implements. Coke presented numerous prizes for these, and for articles on agricultural topics. MacDonald (1913) records that he was the first commoner raised to the peerage by Queen Victoria, as he had declined this honour on several previous occasions.

CORM A condensed stem, with buds, storage materials and the capacity for regrowth.

DE JUSSIEU, ANTOINE LAURENT (1748–1836) At the age of 15 he began work with his uncle, Bernard, and this culminated in the publication of a new natural classification system for plants, *Genera plantae* (1789). Many of his 100 'orders' survive as families in current systems.

DE JUSSIEU, BERNARD (1699–1776) The son of an apothecary, a student of Pierre Magnol, and a contemporary of Linnaeus. He removed corals from the plant kingdom, although Linnaeus had classified them as his 65th plant order. In 1759 he rearranged the plantings in the garden of La Trianon, Versailles, according to a natural system, developed further and published by his nephew Antoine Laurent.

DICHLORO DIPHENYL TRICHLOROETHANE (DDT) Used widely as an insecticide after 1939, now banned. Fat-soluble (hydrophobic), accumulating in adipose tissues, DDT causes a thinning of the eggshell in birds, usually fatal to the enclosed chick.

DOLOMITE The double carbonate salt of magnesium and calcium. Commercial preparations labelled dolomite are mixtures of limestone and dolomite, with variable proportions of magnesium carbonate.

DRING, LADY DEBORAH (BORN 1899) Daughter of Major General G. Cree, she spent much of her life in India until 1947. Interviewed by Charles Allen in 1974 for his BBC program.

ENDOSPERM A distinct tissue inside the seed formed following the second fertilization event, the fusion of one sperm cell with the two polar nuclei. Endosperm cells are polyploid: triploid (3n) or greater.

ENZYME A catalyst of biological origin, usually a polypeptide, or protein comprising several distinct polypeptides. The active or catalytic site can be formed within a single polypeptide, or by an arrangement of cooperating groups projecting from different polypeptides. Enzymes have the ability to speed up or facilitate metabolic reactions that would not otherwise take place under normal conditions of temperature and pressure.

EVELYN, JOHN (1620–1706) This contemporary of John Ray promoted the growing of trees in England, from oaks to oranges. He kept bees in a hive surrounded by glass panes, so that he could observe them making combs and honey. He was well known ultimately as a diarist, like his friend Samuel Pepys, although his diary was almost thrown out, and not published until 1818.

FEEDING DETERRENTS Compounds that deter insects from eating plants, but which do not necessarily kill them; e.g. the triterpenoid azadirachtin, from the neem tree (*Azadirachta indica*). Many deterrent compounds are stored in the glandular hairs on leaf surfaces.

FERMENTATION Metabolism in the absence of oxygen; in plants, as in yeast, glucose is broken down to carbon dioxide and ethanol (see von Liebig). Methane is a major product of anaerobic metabolism in certain bacteria. In horticultural literature, 'fermentation' is often misapplied to aerobic breakdown.

FERTILIZATION The fusion of egg and sperm cells in the ovule to form an embryo following the delivery of two sperm cells via the pollen tube of a compatible pollen grain; the second sperm cell proceeds to fuse with two 'polar' nuclei, generating the endosperm tissue, which may or may not be present when the seed is mature.

FRUIT The fully developed ovary wall, with or without accessory tissues, and generally enclosing seeds. Fruit development can sometimes occur in the absence of viable seeds.

GENE A discrete unit of inheritance, represented by a length of DNA located in a chromosome.

GENETIC ENGINEERING The modification of an organism's genetic information by methods other than breeding and selection.

GERMINATION Seeds are said to germinate when some part of the embryo, generally the radicle, first emerges. Pollen grains also germinate: a pollen tube emerges, growing through the style to the ovule, allowing passage for two sperm cells to enter the embryo sac.

GREW, NEHEMIAH (1641–1712) A pioneering microscopist and plant anatomist, who studied the production of pollen in anthers, and gave early descriptions of the variety of shapes and sizes among pollen grains, likening some to 'miniature peppercorns, Holland cheeses and fish'.

GYPSUM Calcium sulfate dihydrate, $CaSO_4.2H_2O$, useful for improving the texture of clay-rich soils, and as sources of Ca and S. Commercial preparations with less than 15 per cent S, or significant heavy-metal contamination, should be rejected. 'Lypsum' is acceptable because it is a mixture of 17 per cent limestone and 83 per cent gypsum, essentially free of cadmium.

HYBRID A hybrid plant is derived by crossing two distinct parents, which may be different species of the same genus, or two varieties of the same species. 'First filial' or F1 hybrids are unstable because they are heterozygous at a number of gene loci, and alternative alleles will segregate whenever the second (F2) and subsequent generations are produced by self-fertilization, or further cross-fertilization.

KNIGHT, THOMAS ANDREW (1759–1838) The instigator of deliberate crossing and selection as a stimulus for plant breeding. He gave Sir Joseph Banks some of his new peas, probably leading to their introduction to New South

Wales with Governor Philip Gidley King in 1800. In 1804, he and Banks co-founded what was to become the Royal Horticultural Society.

LAWES, JOHN BENNET (1814–1900) At Rothamsted, he developed a way of treating bones with sulfuric acid, producing the first superphosphate. This was shown to give splendid results with Norfolk turnips (1842). Later, he switched to using rock phosphate as the substrate (see superphosphate). If anyone should take the blame for an overemphasis on NPK fertilisers, it is this man, not Justus von Liebig.

LINDLEY, JOHN (1799–1865) A nit-picking mediocrity, who attributed the potato blight to water uptake and 'dropsy', in the teeth of evidence indicating a pathogen. Borrowing heavily from A.-P. de Candolle, he wrote four versions of a supposedly 'natural' system for classifying plants. He concluded that a system of classification based on close relationships and lines of descent could never exist. His tidy alternatives for Magnol's family names that ended with '-ae' rather than '-aceae' also contradict phylogeny. Rightly ignored for more than a century, these names were dusted off and recycled in the 1980s. While Lindley was fiddling, Charles Darwin was developing insight: 'The Natural System is founded on descent with modification ... the characters which naturalists consider as showing true affinity between any two or more species are those which have been inherited from a common parent, all true classification being genealogical'. This ideal is still the way forward.

LINNAEUS, CAROLUS (CARL VON LINNE) (1707–78) The son of a Swedish Lutheran pastor, but an inveterate tobacco smoker nonetheless, and this contributed to the debilitating illness of his final years. Because of the sheer number of plants he described and named, he is credited with shortening plant names to the binomials we know today, although this was first done by Caspar Bauhin in his *Pinax* of 1623. Earlier writers had adopted the genus, but many species names were long and tedious. They cut the extras to a single word — the epithet. *Species Plantarum* (1753) is a landmark. He was right to pay close attention to floral structure. However, his classification was arbitrary — by the numbers of anthers and ovaries. Reaction against the Linnean classification set in immediately — Michel Adanson (1763) and the de Jussieus (1789) were the first to reject it. While frankly criticising his system, we must praise the man. He was knowledgeable, and a very popular teacher. He was resourceful, too. In 1757 he saved the life of his youngest daughter, Sophia, by applying artificial respiration when she appeared to be dead at birth. His extensive collections were purchased by Sir James Smith in 1783, leading to the foundation of the Linnean Society (London) in 1788.

MAGNOL, PIERRE (1638–1715) One of the great phylogenetic botanists, who recognised some of the most coherent families of flowering plants as Compositae, Gramineae, Leguminosae, Umbelliferae, Labiatae and Cruciferae. He taught both botany and medicine at Montpellier University. His students included the brothers Antoine and Bernard de Jussieu, who together with Antoine Laurent de Jussieu greatly extended botanical classification based on relationships.

MALPIGHI, MARCELLO (1628–94) A pioneering microscopist, who studied a great variety of living cells and tissues. In 1675, 50 years before Stephen Hales, he distinguished the two vascular systems of plants (see xylem, phloem). He described the furrows on the pollen grains of a lily, and was also one of the first to describe nodules on the roots of legumes.

MILLARDET, PIERRE MARIE ALEXIS (1838–1902) In 1882 Dr Millardet noticed the protection afforded grapevines by a concoction of lime and bluestone, splashed on by the vignerons to deter grape thieves. Unpainted vines suffered downy mildew. He experimented, but could not improve on the original recipe, published in 1885 (see Bordeaux mixture).

MILLER, PHILIP (1691–1771) For many years in charge of the Chelsea Physic Garden (the Garden of the Society of Apothecaries), where medicinal herbs and newly arrived exotic plants were grown and described. Known to experiment in the kitchen, he was the first to cook runner bean pods (*Phaseolus coccineus*) as a vegetable.

MORGAN, GEORGE (1742–1810) Born in Philadelphia, he served as a colonel in the Revolutionary Army in the American War of Independence. After this, he developed his property Prospect, now part of Princeton University, with great skill. Like John Bartram, he was a talented organic grower (see Chapter 1). He collected and grew many kinds of Indian corn (see Chapter 13). When he moved to Morganza, Pennsylvania, in 1796, he transferred a marvellous collection of fruit tree seeds and cuttings, and proceeded to introduce many grape varieties (Woodward, 1927).

PHEROMONES Sexual attractants released by female insects. The extreme sensitivity of the male detection system means that pheromones can attract over considerable distances. Synthetic pheromones can be incorporated into specific traps for pest species.

PHLOEM One of the two major vascular systems of plants, localised in veins, and responsible for the transport of sucrose, amino compounds, organic acids, minerals and water in a bi-directional fashion (upwards and downwards). Phloem transport cells are living, unlike mature xylem, and can be destroyed by elevated temperatures. Viruses can be transported in the phloem if injected by an aphid.

PHYTOLITH In a broad sense, a rock formed chiefly from plant remains, such as coal; more specifically, a rock or mineral produced by plants, such as the microscopic opaline silica deposits often produced in leaves, and

sometimes in roots, stems and fruits.

POTTER, HELEN BEATRIX (1866–1943) A talented naturalist, illustrator, artist and author, who is still well known for her series of children's books beginning with *The Tale of Peter Rabbit* (1904). In the 1890s she was hindered from gaining proper recognition for her detailed studies on lichens by W.T. Thiselton-Dyer, the 'professional' botanist she consulted; nevertheless, she did present a paper to the Linnean Society on the germination of fungal spores in April 1897.

PRIMARY PRODUCTION Organisms capable of net assimilation of carbon dioxide into more complex organic molecules are primary producers. This includes some bacteria, Cyanophyceae (blue-green algae), algae, lichens and plants. The energy source that allows primary production to take place is usually light, although certain bacteria are 'chemoautotrophs'.

RHIZOME A thick horizontal stem, partly or totally underground, with buds and roots.

ROBINSON, WILLIAM (1838–1933) An outstanding horticulturist, who moved from Ireland to London in 1861 to begin work at the Royal Botanic Gardens at Regent's Park. A gallant writer, running to many editions, he was a man for all seasons — the criticisms of waste, fashions, seedsmen and taxonomists that he framed so incisively are still applicable today.

SAND A deposit of coarse-grained mineral particles, predominantly of quartz (silica or silicon dioxide), and with limestone fragments from mollusc shells if the deposit is a marine one.

SEED A fully developed ovule, containing a new plant embryo, with or without distinct endosperm.

STOLON A horizontal creeping stem, capable of producing tubers (e.g. the potato) or new plants from buds at nodes (e.g. the strawberry).

SUPERPHOSPHATE There are single, double and triple forms with declining sulfur content: the single is produced by reacting rock phosphate with sulfuric acid and maturing for six weeks; double is obtained by reacting rock phosphate with a mixture of sulfuric and phosphoric acids; triple comes from the reaction of rock phosphate with phosphoric acid alone. Single superphosphate has P, Ca, and S contents of about 9.4 per cent, 20 per cent and 10 per cent, respectively.

SUSTAINABLE AGRICULTURE The cultivation of food plants and other crops in such a way that the soil and its condition are conserved, water is not wasted or polluted, and the product is wholesome, free of xenobiotic pesticide residues. Unwarranted environmental damage must also be avoided. In order to become sustainable, conventional agriculture must shift away from wasteful irrigation practices, and towards renewable sources of energy and fertiliser, rather than continue to depend on fossil fuels and exhaustible mineral deposits. The plants to be grown must also be chosen more wisely.

SUSTAINABLE HORTICULTURE The division between horticulture and agriculture is blurred, but horticulture would include the landscaping industry, and the nursery industry: the propagation of all kinds of plants for sale. Progress towards ecological sustainability in horticulture includes adjusting to the energy, water and pesticide issues listed for sustainable agriculture. In addition, progress involves the appropriate selection of species or provenance, and avoidance of potting mix ingredients like polystyrene, or peat, where mining involves the destruction of scarce wetland habitats, as at Wingecarribee, New South Wales.

SWIFT, JONATHAN (1667–1745) A satirical author, best known for *Gulliver's Travels* (1726). Despite his own early efforts against living in Ireland, he became Dean of St Patrick's Church in Dublin. An articulate opponent of injustice, and whether boycotting English fabrics, or objecting to patents for inferior Irish coinage,

his pamphlets were clear and effective. Many gardening writers have much to learn from Swift.

SYMBIOSIS A relationship between two contrasting organisms showing a degree of interdependence, such as insects taking nectar and pollen from flowers, but bringing about pollination; or cicadas and host trees, where in return for food from the roots, the cicadas improve the roots' access to oxygen by tunnelling to the soil surface.

SYNERGISM An interaction whereby the effect of two substances together is greater than the sum of the effects of the same concentration of either substance alone. A mutually beneficial interaction when applied to companion planting, where species A and species B grow (or taste) better when grown together compared to species A and B grown well apart, or with other (neutral) plants.

TRADESCANT, JOHN, THE ELDER (C. 1570–1638) An avid collector of plants and curiosities, he undertook many overseas excursions, and established his own garden and museum (Tradescant's Ark) at Lambeth. In 1630 he was made 'Keeper of the Gardens, Vines and Silkworms' at Oatlands Palace near Weybridge. He introduced runner beans to Britain, and in 1636 helped to establish the Oxford Physic Garden.

TRADESCANT, JOHN, THE YOUNGER (1608–1662) He succeeded his father as Royal Gardener at Oatlands Palace. Between 1638 and 1653 he made several trips to and from Virginia, introducing more than 200 plants to Britain. Both father and son were honoured by Linnaeus with the genus name *Tradescantia*.

TREW, CHRISTOPH JAKOB (1695–1769) A marvellous career: Count Palatine of the Holy Roman Empire, physician to the court of the Margrave of Brandenburg-Ansbach, and keen botanist. He sponsored the publication of illustrated herbals, including those by Elizabeth Blackwell and Georg Ehret. See Mondadori (1984).

TUBER A storage organ which is often capable of independent growth; tubers may be formed at the ends of stolons, or from roots (tuberous roots), or sometimes from axillary buds.

UREA A waste product of human metabolism, enriched in nitrogen (two NH_2^- groups with a bridging carbonyl group). Friedrich Wohler first demonstrated that a chemically synthesised product was identical with urea from urine in 1828. Urea is readily converted to ammonium ions and carbon dioxide by soil bacteria.

VIABILITY The capacity of a pollen grain to germinate on a receptive stigma surface, or of an embryo inside a seed to remain alive and to germinate.

VIRGIL (70–19 BC) A noted Roman poet whose writings encompassed philosophy, politics and farming practices. From his work we know that the burning of stubble was practised as a measure to counter fungal diseases and to return nutrients to the soil as ash.

VON BINGEN, HILDEGARD (1098–1179) A Benedictine abbess famous for her musical composition, healing, writing and leadership. An exceptional herbalist, she is commemorated on 17 September, the anniversary of her death. See Bobko (1995).

VON LIEBIG, JUSTUS (1803–73) A pioneer of analytical organic chemistry (the chemistry of carbon-containing compounds). Fiery, opinionated, often proved right, but sometimes astoundingly wrong. He could not accept that fermentation was carried out by yeast cells, as discovered by Theodor Schwann. He joined with Friedrich Wohler in 1839 in publishing derisory descriptions of yeast cells which had 'a suctorial snout with which they devoured sugar', then 'a stream of alcohol issued from the anus, at the same time that carbon dioxide bubbled forth from enormous genital organs'. Here is a man who made enemies.

XENOBIOTIC As applied to synthetic chemical compounds, it means compounds that are so alien and novel that living organisms may have no previous exposure to anything like them in the course of their evolution, or if such exposure occurred, it was so long ago that the enzymatic capacity to modify such compounds has been lost. Xenobiotic compounds often successfully challenge and overcome our detoxifying enzyme systems and immunological defences, so causing cancers. Insects manage better than mammals, often unmasking an inherited resistance that predominates in just a few generations.

XYLEM One of the two major vascular systems of plants, localised in veins, and responsible for the transport of water, minerals and amino acids in an upwards direction in response to the transpiration pull arising from the evaporation of water from pores in leaves. Xylem vessels or members are thickened, lignified and dead at maturity, forming strong hollow tubes with capillary dimensions. Water and solutes move by cohesion and adhesion. Solutes are mainly transferred from the xylem to the phloem, and other tissues, at night, when water movement is slowest.

ZYGOMORPHIC As applied to flower shape, there is only one axis of symmetry that could be drawn through the flower. It usually implies that insects or other vectors visit the flower to seek nectar and/or pollen.

Bibliography

Ableman, Michael 1993, *From the Good Earth: Traditional farming methods in a new age*, Thames & Hudson Ltd, London

Akeroyd, Simon 2005, 'The taste of summer on trial', *The Garden*, 130(6), pp. 436–9

Alexander, D.McE. 1990, *Practical Hints for Budding and Grafting Fruit and Nut Trees*, CSIRO, Australia

Allen, Charles (ed.) 1975, *Plain Tales from the Raj*, Andre Deutsch, London

Anley, Gwendolyn 1946, *Irises: Their culture and selection*, W.H. & L. Collingridge Ltd, London

Attwater, Rachel (ed.) 1964, *The Book Concerning Piers Plowman*, by William Langland, translation by D. and R. Attwater, Everyman's Library, J.M. Dent & Sons Ltd, London

Bailes, Michael 1999, *The Fragrant Chilli*, Kangaroo Press, Simon & Schuster Australia, Sydney

Bailey, Liberty H. 1920, *The Principles of Fruit-Growing*, The Macmillan Company, New York

Balfour, E.B. 1975, *The Living Soil and the Haughley Experiment*, Faber & Faber Ltd, London

Beder, Sharon 1989, *Toxic Fish and Sewer Surfing*, Allen & Unwin, Sydney

Beder, Sharon 1993, *The Nature of Sustainable Development*, Scribe Publications, Newham, Australia

Bennett, Peter 1988, *Organic Gardening*, 4th edn, Child & Associates, Frenchs Forest, NSW, Australia

Bidwell, R.G.S. 1974, *Plant Physiology*, Macmillan Publishing Co. Inc., New York

Biggs, Tony 1997, 'Tasmanian pyrethrum', *Good Fruit and Vegetables* 8(1), pp. 10–17

Bingley, William 1831, *Useful Knowledge: Volume II, Vegetables*, 5th edn, Baldwin & Cradock, London

Bobko, Jane (ed.) 1995, *Vision: The life and music of Hildegard von Bingen*, Penguin Books USA Inc., New York

Boddy, Michael and Beckett, Richard, with illustrations by Janet Dawson Boddy 1980, *Surviving in the Eighties*, George Allen & Unwin Australia Pty Ltd, North Sydney

Bradbeer, J.W. 1988, *Seed Dormancy and Germination,* Blackie, Glasgow and London, published in the USA by Chapman and Hall, New York

Briggs, Linton 1985, 'Echium: curse or salvation?' in A. Gibbs and R. Meischke (eds) *Pests and Parasites as Migrants*, Australian Academy of Science, ACT, pp. 152–9

Broadley, Roger and Thomas, Michael 1995, *The Good Bug Book*, Australasian Biological Control Inc., Richmond, NSW

Brown, Amy 1994, *Earthworms Unlimited*, Simon & Schuster Australia, Sydney

Brunning, L.H. 1952, *The Australian Gardener*, 32nd edn, revised by H. Alston, Robertson & Mullens Ltd, Melbourne

Brunning, L.H. 1964, *The Australian Gardener*, 34th edn, reprinted, revised by Ernest E. Lord, Angus & Robertson Ltd, Melbourne

Bubel, Nancy Wilkes 1977, *Vegetables Money Can't Buy: But you can grow*, David R. Godine, Boston

Bulford, Alec 1998, *Caring for Soil*, Kangaroo Press, Simon & Schuster Australia, Sydney

Burbank, Luther and Hall, Wilbur 1927, *The Harvest of the Years*, Houghton Miflin Company, Boston and New York

Burke, Don 1983, *The Lazy Gardener*, Horwitz Grahame, Sydney

Burke, Don 1992, *Burke's Backyard Information Guide*, Vol. 4, Margaret Gee Publishing, Sydney

Burr, F. Jr 1865, *Field and Garden Vegetables of America*, 2nd edn reprint, 1988, The American Botanist Booksellers, Chillicothe, Illinois

Cannon, Grant C. 1963, *Great Men of Modern Agriculture*, The Macmillan Company, New York

Carson, Rachel 1951, *The Sea Around Us*, Staples Press Ltd, UK

Carson, Rachel 1962, *Silent Spring*, Houton Mifflin Company, Boston, Massachusetts

Carter, Mare 1995, 'Relative Utopia', *Australian Country Style*, July issue, pp. 76–81

Child, John 1977, *Australian Spiders*, 3rd edn, Periwinkle Press, Paul Hamlyn, Sydney

Clyne, Densey 1996, *The Garden Jungle*, Kangaroo Press, Kenthurst, NSW

Coley, Hilda M. 1944, *Labour Saving Gardens*, John Gifford Ltd, London

Cooke, Blaise 1998, *Pelargoniums*, Lorenz Books, Anness Publishing Inc., New York

Crawford, Denis 2004, 'Good bugs and where do you get 'em?', *Australian Horticulture*, 102(5), pp. 15–17

Crawford, Denis 2005, 'Jiminy Cricket: more foe than friend', *Australian Horticulture*, 103(5), pp. 12–13

Cribb, A.B. and Cribb, J.W. 1975, *Wild Food in Australia*, William Collins Publishers Pty Ltd, Sydney

Cuffley, Peter 1989, *Cottage Gardens in Australia*, Five Mile Press, Fitzroy, Victoria

Darrow, George M. 1966, *The Strawberry: History, breeding and physiology*, Holt, Rinehart and Winston, New York

Davidson, Bruce R. and Davidson, Hilary F. 1993, *Legumes: The Australian experience*, Research Studies Press, Taunton, UK

Davis, Margaret 1973, *Gardening in Pots: For indoors and outdoors*, Ure Smith, Sydney

Davis, Margaret 1977, *The Small Garden*, Thomas Nelson, Melbourne

Dawson, Imogen 1994, *Food & Feasts in the Middle Ages*, Macmillan Education Australia Pty Ltd, Melbourne

Delamain, Brenda and Kendall, Dawn 1987, *An Introduction to Geraniums in Australia*, Angus & Robertson, Sydney

Descoeudres, Jean-Paul 1994, *Pompeii Revisited*, Meditarch, University of Sydney, NSW

de Vaus, Norman 1976, *Better Vegetable Growing for Australian Gardeners*, reprint of 1973 edn, Lansdowne Press, Melbourne

Douglass, J. 1927, 'Onion trials in New South Wales', *Agricultural Gazette of NSW* XXXVIII, pp. 546–50

Dwyer, Fred 1978, *Georgian People*, B.T. Batsford Ltd, London

Ermert, Suzanne 2001, *Gardener's Companion to Weeds*, 2nd edn, Reed New Holland, Sydney

Evans, Joan 1969, *Life in Medieval France*, 3rd edn, Phaidon Press Ltd, London

Everett, Sue 1999, 'Biodiversity action for the UK's rarest plants', *Plant Talk* 16, pp. 16–17

Fanton, M. and Fanton, J. 1993, *The Seed Savers' Handbook for Australia and New Zealand*, The Seed Savers' Network, Byron Bay, Australia. English edn: 1996, Grover Books

Farndale, Nigel 1994, 'The great strawberry hunt', *Country Life*, 12 May, pp. 58–61

Firth, Julie 1996, *Permaculture Garden Guidelines: Dryland coastal regions*, Yilgarn Traders, Geraldton, WA

Fisher, John 1998, 'Legal issues in harvesting St John's wort', *Agnote* DAI/66, NSW Agriculture, Orange, NSW

Foster, Catharine Osgood 1975, *Organic Flower Gardening*, Rodale Press, Emmaus, PA

Fowler, Cary and Mooney, Pat 1990, *Shattering: Food, politics and the loss of genetic diversity*, University of Arizona Press, Tucson, Arizona

Freeman, Susi 2004, 'Allergy to grevilleas', *Australian Plants*, 22 (No. 181), pp. 355–6

Fretwell, Barry 1995, *Clematis as Companion Plants*, The Green Book Co., Hawthorn, Vic.

Gatehouse, John A. 1991, 'Breeding for resistance to insects', in D.R. Murray (ed.), *Advanced Methods in Plant Breeding and Biotechnology*, C.A.B. International, Wallingford, UK, pp. 250–76

Gill, Malcolm A. and Moore, Peter H.R. 1996, 'Ignitibility of Leaves of Australian Plants', *A Contract Report to the Australian Flora Foundation*, CSIRO Plant Industry. Canberra, ACT

Gordon, Sally, 1981, Australia & New Zealand *Complete Self-Sufficiency Handbook*, Australia & New Zealand Book Co. Pty Ltd, Sydney

Gould, Wilbur A. 1983, *Tomato Production, Processing and Quality Evaluation*, 2nd edn, The AVI Publishing Co. Inc., Westport, Connecticut

Gribbin, John and Gribbin, Mary 1996, 'The greenhouse effect', *New Scientist* 151 (No. 2038), *Inside Science*, No. 52

Grosvenor, Graeme 1984, *Growing Irises*, Kangaroo Press, Kenthurst, NSW

Grosvenor, Graeme 1997, *Iris: Flower of the rainbow*, Kangaroo Press, Kenthurst, NSW

Hadlington, Phillip W. and Johnston, Judith A. 1979, *Australian Trees*, University of NSW Press, Kensington, NSW

Hadlington, Phillip W. and Johnston, Judith A. 1982, *An Introduction to Australian Insects*, University of NSW Press, Kensington, NSW

Hamilton, Geoff 1993, *Pocket Encyclopedia of Organic Gardening*, Readers' Digest Press, Sydney NSW

Hankin, Bill 1998, 'Australia bungles "plant breeders rights"', *The Curator*, No. 10, pp. 4–12

Hankin, Bill 1999, 'Australian biopiracy', 11th Australian Plant Breeding Conference Proceedings, Vol. 2, pp. 4–9

Hankin, Bill and Schmetzer, Debbie 1996, 'An inventory of potato varieties grown in Australia', *The Curator*, No. 8, pp. 8–31

Harborne, J.B. 1982, *Introduction to Ecological Biochemistry*, 2nd edn, Academic Press, London

Heaton, Shane 2004, 'Are minerals in Australian foods declining?' *Australian Organic Journal*, 59, pp. 14–15

Heisey, Rod M. 1996, 'Identification of an allelopathic compound from *Ailanthus allissima* (Simaroubaceae) and characterization of its herbicidal activity', *American Journal of Botany*, 83, pp. 192–200

Hepper, Nigel F., 1994, *Planting a Bible Garden*, HMSO, London

Hoitink, Harry A.J. and Fahy, Peter C. 1986, 'Basis for the control of soilborne plant pathogens with composts', *Annual Review of Phytopathology*, 24, pp. 93–114

Holmgren, David 1997, 'Weeds or wild nature', *Permaculture International Journal*, No. 61, pp. 21–4

Howard, Albert 1943, *An Agricultural Testament*, Oxford University Press, Oxford, UK

Howard, Albert 1945, *Farming and Gardening for Health or Disease*, Faber & Faber Ltd, London

Hozeski, Bruce W. (trans.) 2001, *Hildegard's Healing Plants*, Beacon Press, Boston, Massachusetts

Hunter, Beatrice Trum 1977, *Gardening without Poisons*, 2nd edn, Berkley Publishing Corporation, New York

Hurley, P.J. 1949, *An Encyclopaedia for Australian Gardeners*, 3rd edn, revised, Dymock's Book Arcade Ltd, Sydney

Hurley, P.J. 1956, *An Encyclopaedia for Australian Gardeners*, 8th edn, Dymock's Book Arcade Ltd, Sydney

Hurley, P.J. 1970, *This Week in Your Garden*, 3rd edn, Dymock's Book Arcade Ltd, Sydney

Ingram, Tim 1998, 'Humble umbels', *The Garden*, 123 (11), pp. 802–07

Innes, Miranda and Perry, Clay 1997, *Medieval Flowers*, Kyle Cathie Ltd, London

James, Theodore, Jr, 1998, *Cultivating the Cook's Garden*, Council Oak Books, Tulsa, Oklahoma

Jesiolowski, Jill 1995, 'Put spiders on pest patrol', *Organic Gardening*, July/August, pp. 34–40

Kallarackal, J.; Milburn, J.A.; and Baker, D.A. 1990, 'Water relations of the banana. III. Effects of controlled water stress on water potential, transpiration, photosynthesis and leaf growth', *Australian Journal of Plant Physiology*, 17, pp. 79–90

Kennedy, Ivan R. 1992, *Acid Soil and Acid Rain*, 2nd edn, Research Studies Press, Taunton, UK

Knox, Bruce R. 1979, *Pollen and Allergy*, Edward Arnold, London

Kyle, Molly M. (ed.) 1993, *Resistance to Viral Diseases of Vegetables*, Timber Press Inc., Portland, Oregon

Larkcom, J. 1999, 'Vegetable madness', *The Garden*, 124, p. 922

Leeper, Geoffrey W. 1986, *Introduction to Soil Science*, 4th edn, reprint, Melbourne University Press, Carlton, Victoria

Leeper, Geoffrey W. and Uren, N.C. 1993, *Soil Science: An introduction*, 5th edn, Melbourne University Press, Carlton, Victoria

Leighton, Ann 1970, *Early English Gardens in New England 'For Meate or Medicine'*, Cassell & Co. Ltd, London

Levy, Megan 2005, 'Restrictions get tough from today', *Illawarra Mercury*, 1 June, p. 7

Liddell, Margaret 1994, *Scented Plants: A grower's handbook*, David Bateman Ltd, Auckland, NZ

Llewellyn, Jean; Hudson, Betty; and Morrison, Gordon C. 1981, *Growing Geraniums and Pelargoniums in Australia and New Zealand*, Kangaroo Press, Kenthurst, NSW

Lott, J.N.A. 1984, 'Accumulation of seed reserves of phosphorus and other minerals', in D.R. Murray (ed.), *Seed Physiology*, Volume 1 Development, Academic Press, Sydney, pp. 139–66

McBarron, E.J. 1976, *Medical and Veterinary Aspects of Plant Poisons in NSW*, NSW Department of Agriculture, Sydney

MacDonald, William 1913, *Makers of Modern Agriculture*, MacMillan & Co. Ltd, London

Mackenzie, Toni 1980, *A Small Place in the Country*, Fontana Books, Sydney

McLeod, Judyth 1994a, *Lavender, Sweet Lavender*, 4th edn, Kangaroo Press, Simon & Schuster Australia, Sydney

McLeod, Judyth 1994b, *Heritage Gardening*, Simon & Schuster Australia, Sydney

McLeod, Judyth 2000, *Lavender, Sweet Lavender*, revised edn, Kangaroo Press, Simon & Schuster Australia, Sydney

McMaugh, Judy 1991, *What Garden Pest or Disease is That?* companion edn, Ure Smith Press, Sydney, NSW

Maiden, Joseph H. 1887, *The Olive and Olive Oil; Notes on the culture of the tree and extraction of the oil as carried out in South Australia and the continent of Europe*, Charles Potter, Government Printer, Sydney

Maiden, Joseph H. 1920, *The Weeds of New South Wales*, Part I. W.A. Gullick, Government Printer, Sydney

Makin, R.N. 1918, 'Farmers experiment plots. Potato experiments, 1917–18. Southern Tablelands', *Agricultural Gazette of NSW*, XXIX, pp. 876–8

Mann, D.D. 1811, *The Present Picture of New South Wales: 1811*, John Booth, London, reprinted in 1979 by John Ferguson, Sydney

Marinates, Spyridon 1972, 'Thera-key to the riddle of Minos', *National Geographic*, 141(5), pp. 702–26

Mason, Betsy 2002, 'Mystery of Moon's origins solved', *New Scientist*, 176, No. 2374/5, p. 15

Mayor, Adrienne 1995, 'Mad honey', *Archaeology*, 48, pp. 32–40

Millikan, C.R. 1984, *Symptoms of Nutritional Disorders in Some Common Pasture Legumes*, revision by Rod Clarke, Department of Agriculture Victoria, Melbourne

Milton, Katharine 1993, 'Diet and primate evolution', *Scientific American* 269(2), pp. 70–77

Mithen, Steven J. 1998, 'The Mesolithic Age', in Barry Cunliffe (ed.) *Prehistoric Europe*, Oxford University Press, UK, pp. 79–135

Mondadori, Arnoldo 1984, *L'Erbario del Conte Palatino*, English translation *The Herbal of the Count Palatine by Lucia Woodward* (1985), published by Harrap, London

Monsanto 1995, 'INGARD: Some basic facts and perspectives', pamphlet published by Monsanto Australia Ltd, Melbourne

Moody, Helen 2004, 'Exploring the potential of companion planting', *Australian Horticulture*, 102(12), pp. 30–32

Morgan, Lynette 1999, 'Silica in hydroponics', *Practical Hydroponics & Greenhouses*, 47, pp. 51–66

Morrow, Rosemary 1993, *Earth User's Guide to Permaculture*, Kangaroo Press, Kenthurst, NSW

Muir, Sally; Khoo, C.; McCabe, B.; Fensom, G.; Offord, C.; Brien. J.; and Summerell, B. 1999. 'Some effects of silicon in potting mixes on growth and protection of plants against fungal diseases', Proceedings 12th Biennial Conference, Australian Plant Pathology Society, Canberra, ACT

Murray, David R. 1988, *Nutrition of the Angiosperm Embryo*, Research Studies Press, Taunton, UK

Murray, David R. 1989, *Biology of Food Irradiation*, Research Studies Press, Taunton, UK

Murray, David R. 1991, 'Breeding plants for the 21st century', in D.R. Murray (ed.) *Advanced Methods in Plant Breeding and Biotechnology*, CAB International, Wallingford, UK, pp. 1–22

Murray, David R. 1994, 'Seed longevity and germination', *Australian Garden Journal*, 14(1), pp. 40–2

Murray, David R. 1995, 'Carbon dioxide and plant growth', *Australian Garden Journal*, 14(4), pp. 55–8

Murray, David R. 1996a, 'Seed storage and longevity', *Heritage Seed Program*, 9(1), pp. 15–17

Murray, David R. 1996b, 'Flowers that change colour', *Australian Garden Journal*, 15(4), pp. 37–8

Murray, David R. 1997a, 'Ecological implications of restaurant consumption of bush foods', in *Sustainable Use of Wildlife*, Nature Conservation Council of NSW, Sydney pp. 146–69

Murray, David R. 1997b, *Carbon Dioxide and Plant Responses*, Research Studies Press, Taunton, UK

Murray, David R. 1999, *Growing Peas & Beans*, Kangaroo Press, Simon & Schuster Australia, Sydney

Murray, David R. 2003, *Seeds of Concern: The genetic manipulation of plants*, University of New South Wales Press, Sydney

North, Tim 1999, *Garden Cuttings: Reflections from an Australian gardener*, New Holland Publishers, Frenchs Forest, NSW

Nottle, Trevor 1996, *Gardens of the Sun*, Kangaroo Press, Kenthurst, NSW

Nottle, Trevor 1997, *The New Cottage Garden*, Kangaroo Press, Simon & Schuster Australia, Sydney

Ody, Penelope 1998, *The Herb Society's Complete Medicinal Herbal*, Covent Garden Books, London

Peck, Stan 1974, Stan Peck Answers 600 *Gardening Questions*, Ure Smith, Sydney

Philbrick, Helen and Gregg, Richard 1966, *Companion Plants and How to Use Them*, The Devin-Adair Co., Old Greenwich, Connecticut

Plowman, T.; Ahmad, N.; and Bower, C. 1998, *Monitoring Pesticide and Cadmium Residues in Fresh Fruit and Vegetables 1992–5*, Horticultural Research and Development Corporation and NSW Agriculture, Orange, NSW

Podolinsky, Alex 1985, *Bio-Dynamic Agriculture. Introductory Lectures Vol. 1*, Gavemer Publishing, Sydney

Ragg, Mark 1998, *The Low Allergy Garden*, Hodder & Stoughton, Sydney

Reid, Shirley 1992, *Herbs for the Home and Garden*, Cornstalk Publishing, Angus & Robertson, Sydney

Riotte, Louise 1974, *The Complete Guide to Growing Berries and Grapes*, Garden Way Publishing, Charlotte, Vermont

Robinson, William 1870, *The Wild Garden*, London

Robinson, William 1883, *The English Flower Garden*, reprinted 1996, Bloomsbury Publishing, London

Rodale, Robert (ed.) 1971, *The Basic Book of Organic Gardening*, 13th printing, 1980, Organic Gardening/Ballantine, New York

Rossi, B.V. 1930, *Modern Roses in Australasia*, Mitchell & Casey Pty Ltd, Melbourne, Victoria

Ryan, Moira 1991, *Gardening with the Experts: Organic*, Weldon Publishing, Willoughby, NSW

Ryder, M.H.; Stephens, P.M. (ed.); and Bowen, G.D. (ed.) 1994, *Improving Plant Productivity with Rhizosphere Bacteria*, CSIRO Division of Soils, Glen Osmond, South Australia

Ryland, Andy 1998, 'Biological control of insect pests, now and tomorrow', *Australian Horticulture*, June/July issue, The Nursery Papers, pp. 1–4

Salisbury, Frank B. 1969, '*Xanthium strumarium* L.', in Lloyd T. Evans (ed.) *The Induction of Flowering*, Macmillan, Melbourne, pp. 14–61

Salisbury, Frank B. and Ross, Cleon R. 1978, *Plant Physiology*, 2nd edn, Wadsworth Publishing Co., Belmont, California

Sarton, George 1955, *Appreciation of Ancient and Medieval Science During the Renaissance (1450–1600)*, A.S. Barnes and Co. Inc., New York

Satterthwait, D.R. 1982, 'Passifloraceae', *Flora of Australia*, Vol. 8, Australian Government Publishing Service, Canberra, pp. 149–58

Savell, Bob and Andrews, Stan 1982, *Growing Camellias in Australia and New Zealand*, Kangaroo Press, Sydney

Schlenk, Fritz 1985, 'Early research on fermentation: a story of missed opportunities', *Trends in Biochemical Sciences*, June, pp. 252–4

Seitz, Paul 1996, *The Complete Herb Gardener*, Sterling Publishing Co. Inc., New York

Serventy, Vincent 1966, *A Continent in Danger*, Andre Deutsch, London

Serventy, Vincent 1990, *Your Easy Guide to Green Living*, Child & Associates, Frenchs Forest, NSW

Shewell-Cooper, W.E. 1952, *The Royal Gardeners: King George VI and his Queen*, Cassell & Company Ltd, London

Simmonds, N.W. (ed.) 1979, *Evolution of Crop Plants*, Longmans, London

Simpson, A.G.W. 1985, *Growing Bulbs*, Kangaroo Press, Kenthurst, NSW

Smith, Keith 1995, *Classic Vegetable Catalogue*, T.C. Lothian Pty Ltd, Port Melbourne, Victoria

Spooner, D.M.; Anderson, G.J.; and Jansen R.K. 1993, 'Chloroplast DNA evidence for the interrelationships of tomatoes, potatoes, pepinos and Solanaceae', *American Journal of Botany*, Vol. 80, pp. 676–8

Stockton, B.; Stockton, G.; and Mason, J. 1996, *Growing Pelargoniums and Geraniums*, Hyland House Publishing Pty Ltd, Melbourne

Swain, Roger B. 1981, *Earthly Pleasures: Tales from a biologist's garden*, 4th printing, Charles Scribner's Sons, New York

Swenson, Allan A. 1973, *The Practical Book of Organic Gardening*, Universal Publishing and Distributing Corporation, New York

Thiele, Kevin and Prober, Suzanne 2004, 'Shrinking violets', *Australian Plants*, 22 (No. 179), pp. 259–66

Thomas, S. and Corden, M. 1970, *Tables of Composition of Australian Foods*, Australian Government Publishing Service, Canberra

Thomas, Sian 2005, 'Category with enormous sales POTential', *Australian Horticulture*, 103(3), pp. 51–4

Thornton-Wood, Simon 1999, 'Colour on a plate', *The Garden*, 124(6), pp. 442–7

Tyler-Whittle, Michael 1975, *The Plant Hunters*, Pan Books Ltd, London

United Nations Development Programme 1996, *Urban Agriculture: Food, jobs and sustainable cities*, UNDP Publication Series for Habitat II, Vol. 1, New York

van Deven, Louis 1992, *Onions and Garlic Forever*, L. van Deven, PO Box 72, Carrollton Il. 62016, USA

Vilmorin-Andrieux, Mm. 1885 (originally), *The Vegetable Garden*, English translation with preface by William Robinson, reprint by Ten Speed Press, Berkeley, California

Weaver, William W. 1997, *Heirloom Vegetable Gardening*, Henry Holt and Company Inc., New York

Wenholz, H. 1917, 'Selection of seed maize', *Agricultural Gazette of NSW*, XXVIII, pp. 533–49

Westcott, C. and Nelson, P.K. (eds) 1974, *Handbook on Biological Control of Plant Pests*, 4th printing, Brooklyn Botanic Garden, New York

Whittet, J.N. 1968, *Weeds*, Victor C.N. Blight, Government Printer, Sydney, NSW

Wilkins, V.E. 1927, *Research and the Land*, Ministry of Agriculture and Fisheries, London

Wilson, Paul G. 1998, 'A taxonomic review of the genera *Eriostemon* and *Philotheca* (Rutaceae: Boronieae)', *Nuytsia*, 12(2), pp. 239–65

Wolf, Ray (ed.) 1977, *Organic Farming: Yesterday's and tomorrow's agriculture*, Rodale Press, Emmaus, PA

Woodward, Carl R. 1927, *The Development of Agriculture in New Jersey 1640–1880*, PhD thesis, Cornell University, published by the New Jersey Agricultural Experiment Station, Rutgers University, New Brunswick, NJ

Wrigley, C.W. and Rathjen, A. 1981, 'Wheat breeding in Australia', in D.J. and S.G.M. Carr (eds) *Plants and Man in Australia*, Academic Press, Sydney, pp. 96–135

Yates Garden Guide 1952, and various other years, Arthur Yates and Co., Sydney

Yepsen, Roger 1994, *Apples*, W.W. Norton and Company, New York, London

Zborowski, Paul and Storey, Ross 2003, *A Field Guide to Insects in Australia*, 2nd edn, Reed New Holland, Sydney

Zwingle, Erla 1999, 'Olive oil: elixir of the gods', *National Geographic*, 196(3), pp. 66–81

Index